For Nancy,

Enjoy!

2015

# I DIDN'T BARGAIN
## *for This!*

### MITZI PERDUE

R.J. Myers Publishing Company
Washington, D.C.
Second Edition, Published March 2011

Published December 2010
ISBN -13: 978-1-884108-02-0
ISBN -10: 1-884108-02-4


R.J. Myers Publishing and Consulting Company
Book Design: InitialDesign
Cover Photo: Helene Delilo, Photographer

# Acknowledgement

There are a number of people who played a role in the existence of this book. Number one is my dear sister, Victoria Osborne. A couple of years ago, she wrote her autobiography and then challenged her four siblings to do likewise. We're a somewhat competitive family and each of us, in our own way, responded to Victoria's challenge to write a book. Brother Ernest has published a genealogy that is many hundreds of pages long. Brother Barclay wrote a full length inspirational autobiography, and sister Augusta wrote a book about the family summer home that counts, as far as I'm concerned, as autobiography. Probably it's in our blood, since our father also wrote his autobiography, the World of Mr. Sheraton.

Many thanks to Dr. Stephanie Myers my editor and publisher's representative. Stephanie makes me think of a funny story by a famous columnist, mainly because she is the exact opposite of the story. Mr. Famous Columnist once said that he'd always believed the death penalty really was a deterrent, and he knew this firsthand because he had never murdered an editor. My feelings for Stephanie, in contrast, include admiration, respect, a certain amount of awe, and a growing affection. And, my thanks to R. J. Myers Publishing Company.

# *Dedication*

This book is dedicated to Dr. Robert Cancro, Dr. Sandlin Lowe, Rita Cosby, Lorraine Cancro, Chip Fisher, Michele Squitieri and all the others who labor on behalf of ICAMI, the International Committee Against Mental Illness. The amount of good they do to help people who suffer with Post Traumatic Stress Disorders, especially our veterans, can never be calculated—only admired and applauded.

# Table of Contents

Prologue: September 1967 ........................................................................................ i

**Chapter One: 1941–1952, Lincoln, Massachusetts** .........................................1
How To Horrify A Mother.............................................................................9
Growing Up In A Hotel Family.....................................................................11
Why Sheraton Is Called Sheraton................................................................11
A Rockefeller And How, Most Unfortunately, He Broke His Budget ...........12
Nursery School And Gaming The System ....................................................12
Asthma—Horrible Asthma...........................................................................15
The Functional Equivalent Of A Ghost Story ..............................................17
The Largest Antique Buyer In The World .................................................... 20

**Chapter Two: 1952–1959, Boston**............................................................ 23
Recognition That Humanity Is Paper Thin .................................................. 24
Visual Problems, Music, And The Great Faces And Dancing Agony ........... 26
Why Mother Was Afraid I Would Never Marry ............................................ 27
Ah, My Wonderful Sunday School Teaching Scam ...................................... 28
The Perils Of Not Knowing Musical Conventions........................................ 30
Lights, Camera, Action—And An Unpromising Start To My Media Career... 32
"My Little Friends, The Credit Cards," And Why I Learned To Hate Them ... 34
How The Founder Of Sheraton Did It .......................................................... 35
Family Dynamics ......................................................................................... 45
My Continuing Career As A Scam Artist ..................................................... 51
Richard Wade, First Kiss ............................................................................. 52
An Event That Formed My Character........................................................... 52
Depression And Then My Debutante Year................................................... 53

**Chapter Three: 1959–1965, Cambridge, Massachusetts & Washington, DC** .............. 56
The Archetypal Worst Nightmare ............................................................... 56
It Had An A+ On It ...................................................................................... 57
Life At Radcliffe.......................................................................................... 58
Arthur Houghton, World's Best Guy—For Someone Else ........................... 60
I Sing At Carnegie Hall ............................................................................... 62
I Invent The Internet ................................................................................... 66

**Chapter Four: 1965–1968, New York** ...................................................... 67
In All Modesty, This Is The World's Best Practical Joke............................... 68
1968–1971, New York City, Marriage To Francisco Ayala ........................... 76
Father Ayala Leaves The Church ................................................................. 76
How The CIA Paid For My Being Courted By A Spanish Priest..................... 77
Marriage To Francisco Jose Ayala................................................................ 78
I Break The Law And Risk Jail Time............................................................. 79

**Chapter Five: 1971–1988, Davis, California** ...................................................... **83**

Prodigies ............................................................................................................ 84

1983–1988, Single In Davis ..............................................................................108

What You Won't Read In This Autobiography ................................................109

Well, Yes, I Really Was A Rice Farmer .............................................................110

Fran Dubois, My Anti-Role Model ...................................................................112

Rice Farming, Or Wouldn't It Be Fun To Transform World Food Production ....114

The Business And Professional Women's Club Changes My Life ..................116

The Beginnings Of My Career As A TV Hostess And Producer ....................118

My Near-Death Experience On Camera (And I'm Not Kidding!) ...................122

Attention-Getting Shows .................................................................................124

The Show That Never Aired .............................................................................125

How I Got To Be Assemblyman Greene's Mother—And What Happened Next ....127

Maureen Reagan, President's Daughter And New BF ...................................129

The Show Grows ...............................................................................................130

Becoming A Syndicated Newspaper Columnist ...........................................131

Becoming A Syndicated Radio Hostess..........................................................132

TV Syndication? Not With That Icky Lisp! .......................................................132

TV Syndication? Only If You Can Sell It! ..........................................................134

The Farmer's Cookbook Series .........................................................................137

American Agri-Women......................................................................................138

President Reagan, An Untold Story .................................................................138

The United Nations Decade On Women, And Courage Lessons From The Israelis ....140

How A Bottle Of Coke Became Almost The Most Beautiful Thing I've Ever Seen....141

Augusta's Dream From Age Twenty Comes True, Along With A Nightmare ....143

Presidency Of American Agri-Women.............................................................145


**Chapter Six: 1988–2005, Salisbury, Maryland** ..........................................**147**

Frank And I Get Engaged...................................................................................147

The Engagement Gets Broken..........................................................................152

If You Enjoy Paranoia, Read This!......................................................................155

We Get Re-Engaged ..........................................................................................156

A Series Of My Favorite Moments In Life .......................................................158

Blackmail, False Witness, And The Threat Of Automatic Weapons...............160

A Male Prostitution Ring In My House, A Month Of.......................................164
   Front Page Headlines, Plus The Blackmailer Isn't Satisfied

After That, We Settle Down Comfortably.........................................................166

The Perdue Approach To Social Affairs...........................................................168

"I'm Not Going To Change Anything In The House. I Love It Just As It Is."......171

"To Love A Man Is To Facilitate His Life" ..........................................................173

Undeserved (But Highly Enjoyed) Reputation As A Linguist........................174

My Day Working On The Line In A Chicken Plant ..........................................177

Another Chicken Plant Encounter, Made In Heaven For ..............................179
   Your Basic Boston Debutante

Watching Frank In Action .................................................................................180

Frank As A Romantic .........................................................................................182

Frank As Family Man .........................................................................................183

I Had A Co-Wife .................................................................................................186

Cindy And Greg Downes, And Tammy Cawood............................................187

A Mystery Relationship .....................................................................................188

Jose At Harvard .................................................................................................189

Jose's Methods For Handling Distraught Female Undergraduate................190

Carlos At Berkeley .............................................................................................191

Carlos's Job At Perdue Farms, And Why Poker Was Excellent Training.................................. 192
More Memories Of Frank.................................................................................................. 194
Frank And A Rotten, Terrible, No Good TV News Magazine........................................ 195
Back To Work.................................................................................................................. 201
1993, Driving Across The Country And Back................................................................ 203
Eggscapes(™) Painful Beginnings................................................................................. 206
1995, Frank Is Diagnosed With Pancreatic Cancer....................................................... 209
Was Anyone Ever More Giving?.................................................................................... 211
A Tsunami Of Greed, Fecklessness, And Irresponsibility............................................. 212
The Millennium.............................................................................................................. 214
Frank Perdue's Ethical Will........................................................................................... 215
Excerpts From My Diary................................................................................................ 216
Diary Entries Relating To Dr. Mitzi.............................................................................. 217
Frank's 2000 Brush With Eternity And The Great Thing That Followed...................... 220
9/11................................................................................................................................. 222
A Cruise From Hong Kong To Australia........................................................................ 225
I'm No Longer Employed............................................................................................... 227
One Door Slams Shuts, Another Bursts Open................................................................ 228
Healthy U Of Delmarva Is Born.................................................................................... 229
How I Became Mitzi "The Gun" Perdue........................................................................ 233
2002, Carlos And Gea's Wedding.................................................................................. 235
2003, Jose And Erica's Wedding.................................................................................... 236
Frank's Illness................................................................................................................ 237
Donna Potter, My Internet BF....................................................................................... 239
Frank's Illness, Continued............................................................................................. 241
Sample Diary Entry: December 28, 2004, Three Months Before His Passing............... 242
I Lose The Love Of My Life........................................................................................... 243
Widowhood.................................................................................................................... 244

Chapter Seven: 2006–2009, New York City................................................................ 246
How Many Blended Families Can Match This?............................................................. 247
Frank's Language, A Shock............................................................................................ 248
Girl Friends.................................................................................................................... 248
Summing Up................................................................................................................... 249

Appendix I: Criminal Justice Academy...................................................................... 252

Appendix II: Of Course, This Book Contains A Chicken Recipe.............................. 256

About The Author........................................................................................................ 258

# Prologue:

## *September 1967*

*Ernest Flagg Henderson II*
*(Ernie)*

The week before my father, Ernest Flagg Henderson II, died, I had a lovely and meaningful conversation with him. We were sitting in the ballroom at Knollwood, our summer home in Dublin, New Hampshire, and even though no one realized that his end was mere days away, we got to talking about what he had learned in his seventy years. He reminisced about founding the Sheraton Hotel chain, and about what he had learned about life. Two of the things he said that afternoon have had an enormous influence on how I treated my two sons.

The first of these was that if he had his life to live over again, he would have spent more time with his children. He said that at his age, he could remember how sweet the times were that he did spend with them, and he knew how much he had missed out on, not taking more time to enjoy his family.

With my sons Jose and Carlos, I tried to allocate my time so that at the end of my days, I would never have that terrible, searing regret that Ernie—which is what we children called him—had at the end of his.

The other thing that I most remember from that long-ago conversation—it must have been in November of 1967—was that even at age seventy, he still missed his parents.

He said he often thought of them, and one of the things he missed most was, they were no longer there to answer questions. He would have loved to know, as an adult, more about who they were and what was important to them.

These words that I'm writing now are the second result of that conversation with Ernie. I began writing this book because I wanted my family, both present and to come, to know where they came from, and that there is someone in the past who is reaching into the future to greet them, with the hope of maybe satisfying their curiosity, and to let them know that they were cared for and loved even before they were born.

Er, that was my intention.

But then friends began telling me that others might be interested in a peek behind the scenes at what life was like in an ultrahigh-net-worth family. It was so different from what you read in the tabloids or in *People* magazine. I thought, why not tell the story? Yes, why not?

The format for what you are about to read, Dear Reader, follows the splendid pattern discovered by the great Dutch aphorist Cees Nooteboom: "Memory is like a dog that lies down where it pleases." Although I've made an attempt to be chronological, as you'll discover, my memories do tend to settle down wherever they please.

*Knollwood, our summer home in Dublin, NH.*

# Chapter One:

# *1941–1952,*
# *Lincoln, Massachusetts*

My earliest memory occurs in the house where the Henderson family lived in Lincoln, Massachusetts. Today, in 2010, it's the location of the Thoreau Institute, but back in the early 1940s, it was home to Ernie, Mother, Ernest, Vicky (now Victoria), Penny (now Augusta) Barclay, Daddy Jim, and me, Mary Stephens-Caldwell Henderson (now Mitzi Henderson Ayala Perdue).

The memory was, strangely, a foretaste of my future. The family was going on some kind of trip, but we couldn't leave until someone finished combing my hair, and someone else put the finishing stitches on an outfit I was wearing, a navy blue coat-and-bonnet set trimmed with lovely pink braid. All the family members were in the hallway leading

*Llanover, our country home in Lincoln, Massachusetts.*

1

to the door outside, except those on a stairway, and they were all watching the combing and the stitching. One of the weaknesses from which I have never recovered is a delight in being the center of attention. Perhaps this trait began at that moment.

I was a war baby, having been born on Thursday, March 27, 1941. Other memories of that era include watching Mother shovel coal to heat the furnace in the cellar. The coal man would come in a big truck, deliver several tons of coal down a chute in the basement, and Mother would, as needed, shovel coal into the furnace. Since she was later the acknowledged *grand dame* of Boston society until her death in 1969, I cherish the memory that this grand and even noble lady was not above shoveling coal.

Since this was during the war, I'm guessing that fuel must have been scarce. I can remember times when it was so cold that a pan of water near the window in my bedroom would freeze. The pan was there because it was thought that in the New England winters, the inside air would be too dry for good health.

When the house was really cold, Mother would come to my room in the middle of the night with a hot-water bottle. It wasn't like the standard orangey-red hot-water bottles you'd typically see today. It was white, and although the same size as one of today's hot-water bottles, it was cunningly shaped to resemble a rabbit. The hot-water bottle had inch long white ears coming out the top of it, a bunny face painted on the top third of it, beneath that was painted a little blue bow tie, and its tummy was where most of the hot water was stored.

*Mary "Mitzi" Henderson, taken by Ernest Henderson II.*

I thought this wonderful device was the neatest thing that had ever happened in the world. I also thought Mother was an angel for rescuing me from the cold. Funny, a lingering effect from all of that is, I can sleep as comfortably in a 50 degree room as I can in a 70 degree room. If you asked me which I preferred, I wouldn't have an answer. It wouldn't make a difference.

Another war-years memory is being terrified when airplanes flew over our property. If I were out in one of the fields near our house, I'd run and hide under a tree. As a four year old, I knew enough about the war to know that planes dropped bombs.

Not having any grasp of geography, and knowing that the war was happening in Europe, I had no reason to think that the planes flying overhead might not be coming from Europe. Distances had no meaning to me, especially since I knew about some cat who could put on seven league boots and could traverse immense distances in a single stride.

Victory in Europe (VE Day), May 7, 1945 was exciting for me. We went to the attic at Llanover (our name for the house) and set off Roman candles. People seemed deliriously happy, but the happiness was tempered by the fact that we were also waiting for VJ Day, that is, Victory over Japan Day. I kept asking when VJ Day would happen, and was disappointed that what had seemed like the all-powerful adults in my life couldn't control whatever VJ Day was.

A few months later, my father called me into the living room at Llanover and said to listen carefully because something of immense historic importance was happening. I now know the date was August 6, 1945. I'm trying to remember who was broadcasting the immensely

*Family members listened at the far end of this room, near the fireplace, to the historic broadcast of August 6, 1945, announcing the dropping of the atomic bomb.*

important events, but it could have been Gabriel Heater or Walter Winchell or Edward R. Murrow or maybe Lowell Thomas. Father followed them all. The event was the bombing of Hiroshima, which we understood would end the war. I don't remember a single word of the broadcast, only that Ernie wanted his family to hear it.

Father said that he wished he had spent more time with us, but in fact, a lot of my memories feature him and Mother. He must have spent a lot of time with us.

For instance, he organized a family band, and each of us played an instrument. Barclay was studying either the trumpet or coronet, and I was trying to play the recorder. I think (but really am only guessing) that sister Penny played the piano. Or maybe she sang. Mother was tone deaf, but participated even so.

Ernie (that is, my father) was a big believer in having his children learn languages. While I was still a toddler, he used to play French language records for Barclay, Penny, and me. We'd sit in the living room and practice saying what we heard on the record such as, "*La plume de ma tante se trouve sur le bureau de mon oncle.*" We also had a Swiss cook and an Italian handyman, and part of the motivation for choosing them was to expose us to more languages.

Ernie himself spoke five languages: German, French, Italian, Spanish, and English. However, he spoke them with the vocabulary of a child. The reason? Grandfather was a historian and each year, he'd park his children in a different school in a different European capital. Incidentally, later on I tried to expose my kids to other languages, but on a smaller scale. For years, I'd put them in summer camp in France or Germany or Austria, and they attended schools in Spain for a couple of years. By the way, my brother Barclay and his wife Minako were more ambitious: they had my nephews Kevin and Eric spend summers in Japan.

We also used to have family picnics. We would pack a feast and then the entire family, including Uncle George, Aunt Frances, and Aunt Edith, would trek into the woods and eat a picnic in a clearing in the middle of the forest surrounding Llanover. At these picnics, we would play a game called, "What did they put in the old man's soup." To play, you had to repeat whatever ingredients everyone else had already "put in the old man's soup."

It could go something like this. The first speaker puts a fur coat in the old man's soup. The next speaker puts a fur coat and the kitchen sink in the old man's soup. The next person puts a fur coat, the kitchen sink, and a carrot in the old man's soup. And on and on it would go. Whoever couldn't remember all the preceding ingredients was out.

I was thrilled with this game, and I particularly liked that all ages could play. I think I have a lousy memory in general, but back then I'd often end up a finalist. Ernie always won.

Another game from those early days was, "Hill Dill Come Over the Hill, Or Else I'll Catch You Standing Still." We played it on the front lawn. There were enough of us chasing each other that it was a joyous, rambunctious time. There was also "Prisoner's Base" and "Parson, Parson Lost His Cap," and "Red Light" and "Simon Sez." We'd also play "Family Pounce," a card game, as well as canasta and Monopoly.

We had time for those family games because television wasn't yet available. And of course there was no fast food, so all meals would be shared together, often three meals a day, at the family dining room.

It's clear that Father (Ernie) put a lot of effort into us kids. He enthralled us with what he called the "bottle-spiel," which consisted of quart-size glass milk bottles hung from a rack that he had devised, each bottle with just the right amount of water to make it, when hit with a

*Mary (Mitzi), Penny (Augusta) and Barclay
Henderson in the dining room at Llanover*

drumstick, resonate to the pitch of a given piano key. He was able to duplicate, in pitch, an entire keyboard, and would enthusiastically play tunes for us.

He also built a stage and wrote a marionette show for us kids to perform at the local county fair. My character was a policeman, maybe a foot high, and I learned to make my marionette "walk," "wave his hands," and "nod his head."

Looking back on Ernie and his efforts with us, I think he was a remarkably engaged dad. He also must have been unusually creative and even a little eccentric. Who but Ernie would create a bottle-spiel? For that matter, how many fathers of the era had their children call them by their first name? I thought the whole relationship was remarkably special.

Mother clearly adored motherhood. I can remember once sitting on her lap and asking her if she loved me. She held me tightly against her chest and said, "I love you more than tongue can tell," or another time, "I love you more than two shakes of a lamb's tail."

If you were to parse this last grammatically, it doesn't convey a lot of meaning, but I knew exactly what she meant. It has to be related to my telling my kids, "I love you more than all the bats in all the caves in all of China." I think they got what that meant also, even if that statement wouldn't win any prizes for precision logic.

Mother was always into fun projects. For instance, we'd harvest the Concord grapes from the wild vines that Daddy Jim had tamed and cultivated, and then we'd all make grape jam. Or we'd make strawberry shortcake from fresh strawberries, again from plants grown by Daddy Jim.

Once, when we were all sick with the mumps, she'd entertain us by teaching us to make pot holders, or dolls' clothes. I can still remember a little green doll's purse she helped me sew. It was maybe two inches in size and the material must have been something close to leatherette, unless it was real leather. I remember with wonder how good she was at helping me make the stitches. To this day, I love sewing and almost any kind of needlework.

Mother must have been a wise woman. One day, according to my Aunt Frances Henderson, my brother Barclay decided he didn't want to go to school. Mother didn't argue with him. She said it was perfectly okay with her, but then she handed him a bucket and a scrub brush and told him it was now his job to clean the dozen or so toilets in the house.

"But I don't want to scrub out toilets," Barclay wailed.

"If you don't go to school," Mother answered, "that's all you'll be qualified to do."

My brother Ernest, the oldest, was seventeen years older than me. He always seemed incredibly worldly wise. Barclay and I went through his drawers when he returned from his service in the Navy after World War II, and were fascinated by the coins he had brought back from China. He also brought back grass skirts from Hawaii, which I thought were unbelievably exotic.

The thought of those grass skirts went wonderfully with a small bit of doggerel that Barclay and I used to sing to scandalize the grownups: "Oh they don't wear pants in the sunny side of France, but they do wear leaves to protect them from the breeze."

I guess what impressed me most about "the brother I'd never met before," was that he had dozens and dozens of 45 rpm records and an automatic record player. Since I was used to a Victrola and maybe one or two 78 rpm records, this was just too awesome.

I have a particularly tender memory of Ernest when he first returned from the war. In those first few days when he was back, I had a cold, and didn't understand this strange thing that had befallen me. He explained, in the kindest, gentlest way, that this was a normal thing, and it was by no means the end of the world that I couldn't breath out my nose, and that it happened to lots of people, and that I would surely live through it.

My memories of my sister Victoria, fourteen years my senior, are equally tender. She was the one I went to more than Mother when something was troubling me. She was simply always there for me, whether it was an upset tummy or wanting to know how the world worked, or craving a story.

She was also more successful than Mother had been in explaining the facts of life to me. Mother had tried, and we both thought she succeeded, although in retrospect it's clear something was lacking in our communication.

Mother had asked me one day if I knew where babies came from. Well of course I knew where babies came from, I told her. *Everyone* knows that, I insisted.

She was satisfied with this answer, but would have been less so if she had realized that the knowledge I was so sure of was that the stork brought babies. I could even visualize flocks of them flying over cities at dusk, carrying in their long beaks little pink or blue blankets which, sling-shaped, had cute little babies nestled inside. I was a little fuzzy over what happened next, but I was pretty sure the babies ended up under cabbage plants, and beyond that, I never inquired.

My sister Augusta, or Penny as she was known back then, has always been my idol. She had an endlessly sunny disposition, and she seemed to combine the brains of our father with the warmth of our mother. I also felt that she was a happy middle between Victoria, who was intuitive and mystical, and myself, who was (and am) more of a nuts-and-bolts kind of person, one who only believes something if it seems provable and logical. In most cases, I'm immune to intuitive and mystical things, and in comparison to Victoria, I'm a complete skeptic. Victoria and I agree that Augusta achieved the happy middle ground between us.

Brother Barclay was my friend and pal. We used to love exploring the surrounding countryside and both had a huge love of the outdoors. I also remember when the two of us witnessed time-lapse photography for the first time, and how enthralled we were to watch a seed turn into a plant in a matter of minutes. We also couldn't get enough of *Ripley's Believe It or Not.*

I think Barclay was the most philosophical of my siblings. From earliest times, he was interested in the transcendent. In retrospect, I think he was a nascent Thoreau.

As for me, I think I showed a cerebral bent early. I loved reading and couldn't get enough of it. Trips to the library were an unadulterated joy, and still are. There were few things I enjoyed more, as a child, than reading. I loved reading about role-model women, such as Marie Curie or Florence Nightingale. I also loved all the Black Stallion series, fairy tales, knights of the round table, and all the Albert Payson Terhune books. I adored stories of Indians and woodsmen.

My other big love was Bessie, a beautiful Morgan Arabian horse that belonged to Penny. Bessie was black with a white star on her forehead. Her stablemate was Tansie who, for some reason, never captured my affection the way Bessie did. I'm not sure where Augusta was in this, but for long periods, I was in charge of feeding the horses and mucking out the barn.

I remember joining 4-H to learn more about horse care, and I also remember the bags of Wirthmore Feed, that would occasionally attract rats. An angry rat, baring its teeth as it defends its grain supply, and looking as if it's about to leap from the sack of grain straight toward you, is for a ten year old, a scary thing.

I also remember how difficult it was for me to keep the records that 4-H wanted its young members to maintain. In later life, I think I could be described as meticulous in record keeping, and that particular bent must have had its origin there. Thank you, 4-H! But this was a skill that did not come naturally to me.

When things went wrong in my life, I'd go to Bessie and put my arms around her neck and sometimes cry. I've wondered since why I didn't go to Mother or Father. I don't have an answer to this, but I sometimes think I have a large lone-wolf component to my personality, and maybe that began back then also. (My sister Augusta told me, after reading this, that she also used to go to Bessie and cry when things weren't going right.)

Also, I've rarely cried since childhood. I might blubber in a movie, but I can't think of a romantic entanglement that ever resulted in tears. The one time in my life that I did cry a lot was after Frank's death. But that's later on in this story.

## How To Horrify A Mother

A favorite memory I have of my brother Barclay is one that must have horrified my mother. Barclay and I discovered one winter, when playing around the horse barn, that even when there was four or five inches of fresh white snow on the ground, we could see little vents of steam coming from the manure pile.

How interesting.

Certainly this deserved further investigation.

We dug in the manure and discovered that just a few inches down, it was positively warm, and if we dug down a foot or so further, and buried ourselves in it, that even on a freezing New England day, we could feel warm and toasty.

I can't remember, and for that matter, I can't even imagine Mother's response to us when we came back to the house. Can you think what it must have been like to have two manure-marinated children come back into the house?

She must have been vastly more flexible and tolerant than I was with my kids, and for that, I admire her greatly. My darling sons never confronted me with anything like that. *(Thank you, Darlings!)*

Barclay and I used to love to work in the greenhouse on the property. We'd plant lettuce and other foods and, in the process, we'd also talk about life. Often we'd talk about such things as where did space end, and if it did end, what was behind that? A great big wall? Well, what was behind the great big wall? And where did time begin? Would there be any way to go back in time?

We also tried some agricultural experiments, such as seeing if the strawberry plants which we had liberated from our neighbor Tom Adams' garden, would grow in the deep shade. Ernie's wrath at this transgression and Tom Adams' fury gave Barclay and me an appreciation of property rights that we had entirely lacked before.

One of my father's hobbies was photography. To this day, I have a peculiar relationship with the camera, one that I've only recently come to understand. The understanding, by the way, came from reading Tina Brown's description of Princess Diana's relationship with her father.

Tina Brown said that Diana learned early on to pose for and enjoy the camera because for her it was a guaranteed way to get her father's attention. All she had to do to get lavish paternal attention—the attention he customarily withheld from her—was to behave winsomely in front of his lens. For Diana, according to Brown, the camera represented one of the few ways she had of experiencing paternal love.

I don't think I'm as extreme a case as Diana was, but when I'm being photographed, it brings back some of the good feelings that I got when my father was paying attention to me, taking pictures of me. Today, when I see a camera pointed at me, my associations with it are entirely positive. I like the camera. I don't think I crave it, the way Diana did, but I am definitely comfortable in front of a camera and actively like it. As I'll explain later, this comfort with the camera played an unexpected role in my television career.

## Growing Up in a Hotel Family

We siblings grew up defining ourselves as being the opposite of the Hiltons. Specifically what I mean by that is, we didn't admire Conrad Hilton senior's approach to marriage (for New England Puritans, he was too casual about it) and we made fun of Nicky Hilton's marrying Elizabeth Taylor. I remember after Nicky married the actress, my brother Ernest asked my father, at the dinner table, "Would you please buy me one of those?" This was greeted with hilarity.

And when Conrad Hilton named a hotel after himself, my mother said teasingly to my father, "Would you please name the next hotel The Molly Henderson?" Again, gales of laughter.

## Why Sheraton Is Called Sheraton

This brings me to the story of why Sheraton Hotels were called Sheraton instead of Henderson Hotels. I think Ernie would have had a genuine horror of doing something so egocentric as naming the chain after himself. That kind of attitude is, I think, very New England.

I actually asked him about this once, and he answered that he had never seriously considered naming the hotels after himself. Further, he said that he didn't think having the hotels named Henderson would have been good for us children, and on top of that, he didn't think the name Henderson was "euphonious."

The name he used for his hotels came about because, when he was founding the chain in the early 1930s, along with his brother George and his roommate from college, Bob Moore, it was clear to the three of them that for advertising purposes, if you have more than one hotel, having just one name saves on advertising costs.

They had bought one hotel in Cambridge, and with the profits they made from that one ("I figured out where to put the right padlocks," Ernie said to explain that success), they bought another. The third hotel was in Springfield, Massachusetts, and it had a large $10,000 neon sign proclaiming that its name was "Sheraton."

Ernie liked the sound of the name, and in addition, as a good New England Yankee, the idea of tearing down a perfectly good $10,000 sign bothered him. He simply left it up, and named all his present and future hotels Sheraton. And that, dear friends, is how Sheraton got its name.

Given that Father worried about the effect it would have on his children if he had named his company after himself, I wonder how my parents would have felt today, if they could have read about Paris Hilton.

I think they would have been glad all over again that they sent their children to public schools and that we knew how to muck out barns and shovel coal. I think they would have been glad that their typical response to a request for something we wanted, was: "Earn it!"

## A Rockefeller and How, Most Unfortunately, He Broke His Budget

We didn't want to model ourselves on the Hiltons, but we were taught to revere the Rockefellers. The admiration came, at least in part, because of the following piece of Henderson family lore.

My brother Ernest attended Belmont Hill School (as did Barclay), and one year, his birthday was celebrated at Llanover, our family estate in Lincoln. One of his classmates was a Rockefeller, and at the end of the party, all the little boys were picked up in their chauffeur-driven limousines. That is, they all were except the little Rockefeller child.

Mother noticed that he was hanging around looking lost, so with her kindly and maternal instincts, she inquired if she could help. "Can I telephone your driver for you?" she asked.

"No, Mrs. Henderson," replied the boy. "My parents give me twenty-five cents a week allowance, and I have to save five cents of it and I have to give five cents of it to charity. I'm supposed to use the rest of it to cover my expenses, but this week I spent it all on candy and now I don't have bus fare home."

The Henderson family cherished that kind of frugality.

## Nursery School and Gaming the System

My first school experience was at the Brooks School in Concord, Massachusetts. I discovered then that if I had done something that got me in trouble, such as being disruptive or uncooperative, an absolutely foolproof way of getting out of my difficulty was to appear as if I had no idea what I had done wrong.

"Do you know what you did wrong?" the principal, Mrs. Brooks, would ask sternly.

"No, I don't know why they sent me here," I said with practiced innocence, and then adding, for good measure, "I think the teacher doesn't like me."

Time after time it seemed to work with my teachers and with the principal. In later years, I realized that this particular manipulation was not a nice thing to do, but until then, it and I, had a good long run.

I remember a lot from the Brooks School. I remember the art appreciation efforts the teachers made to teach us the beauty of, for instance, Raphael. Somehow, even though I have earnestly tried to appreciate art, and have been exposed to it since childhood, it wasn't until age sixty-nine that I feel I'm even beginning to get the hang of it. In the time since, I've been to what must be hundreds of museums, been dragged to art lectures by Mother, occasionally been complicit in dragging my own children to art museums, bought and studied books on art, watched programs on TV, and generally made a sincere effort.

I've wondered if some people, myself for example, are simply not wired for taking much of a visual approach to the world. I appreciate real-world beauty, such as a vista of the sea or mountains or a magnificent building, or even a beautiful woman or handsome man, but my mind seems too literal to process whatever other people get out of art. And yet, I truly like Emily Cheng's art. But then I start wondering if that's because I like Emily Cheng, and maybe wouldn't like her paintings as much if I didn't see them, in a way, as an extension of her.

Ah, but I have digressed! Back to the Brooks School. Some of the things they taught there did stick. I remember in first grade loving writing, and being ecstatic when my fellow students seemed to like a serial that I wrote each week about a chickadee. I remember the last line of it was, "…and the trap snapped shut, but the chickadee was safe." The teacher back then said I was a prolific writer, which, comparatively, must have been true because I was writing a weekly serial when the others were writing single sentences. Funny, how bents, such as enjoying writing, begin early.

Actually, to this day, writing is important to me. You know how some people feel off-center if they miss a day of exercise? I feel funny if I let a day go by without writing. It's almost as if I need to write.

Heck, I *do* need to write. If I don't, my fingers itch and feel restless.

The next school, for the fourth and fifth grades, was Concord Academy. I've learned since that this school was founded by Henry David Thoreau. Back then, it was a girls' school, and I remember enjoying it and enjoying learning.

There was something then, though, that influenced my relationship with math. I could do the math so easily that there was no effort to it at all. It took no more effort than reading. After only a few weeks in the fourth grade, I had nearly completed the sixth grade math book.

I was proud of this, but got reprimanded for it. One of the teaching assistants said I was being conceited and showing off. I settled down and tried to act more like my classmates and not be a show-off. I wonder how different my life might have been if someone had encouraged me in math rather than making me see it as a source of disapproval.

Actually, I think math should have been a strong point for me because later on, in high school, I heard that I was the only student who got perfect scores on the three-hour math exams. Unfortunately, I still thought of math as slightly shameful and part of being a show-off. I never pursued math, although knowing what I now know, I would have pursued it with all my heart. And whenever I have a chance to encourage anyone to pursue math, I do.

I was never in the sixth grade, but instead started Lincoln Public School in the seventh grade. Mother and Ernie wanted all their five children to attend public school at some point in their lives, and I think this was because they worried about having children who would, as my mother used to put it, "Be tumbril material." She didn't want out-of-touch little aristocrats who couldn't make their way in the real world. Public school was a way of helping prevent that.

Before entering Lincoln Public School—I was twelve then—I spent a sleepless night, worrying that no one would like me. The next morning, I went to our parent's bedroom and Ernie sensed that something was wrong. I told him about my concerns, and he comforted me by saying that, first of all, I was likable so my new classmates would like me, but second, you only needed a few friends. In his whole life, he told me, he had only one really good friend, Uncle Bob, and that was enough.

I enjoyed Lincoln Public and in spite of my initial fears, did make friends. I still keep in touch with some of them.

I mentioned earlier that my parents had a reason for sending their children to public school, and it's one that I consider incandescently beneficial for me. They wanted their children to experience a broader part of life than would have been the case if we had only attended private schools. I cherish the fact that my closest friends back then included the son of a policeman, the daughter of a dairyman, and the daughter of a clerk who worked behind the counter at, I think, Gilchrist's department store.

Later in life, when Frank and I would be going through the chicken plants, I felt a comfort level talking with the workers on the line and a respect for them that I'm not sure I would have had if my background were limited to private schools and being a debutante. Thanks, Mother! Thanks, Ernie! I wouldn't trade that gift that you gave me for diamonds or pearls. Even big diamonds and big pearls.

## Asthma—Horrible Asthma

At Lincoln Public, I began having health problems. I had developed fairly severe asthma. When the weather was cold, I found that I couldn't breathe, and instead of asking for help, I'd hide in the restroom, struggling for air. Somehow, I thought this weakness was shameful and didn't want to let anyone know. I remember one of my classmates told a teacher that I couldn't breath and she rushed into the restroom to help. I wouldn't come out of the stall, and kept saying, when I could speak, that I was fine. The problem was, most of the time I was gasping for air and couldn't speak.

I wonder why I thought it was shameful. I don't have an answer.

In the next two years, the condition worsened enough so that because of coughing and struggling to breath and coughing blood, I finally ended up with a collapsed lung. I was hospitalized for a week at the Peter Bent Brigham Hospital, and part of the treatment for uncollapsing my lung was a bronchoscopy, or sticking a large tube down my throat to do whatever they did to reinflate my lung.

I still remember it vividly more than half a century later. I was already having severe trouble breathing, and putting a tube down my throat made the breathing more difficult and, frankly, more agonizing and scarier than ever. Further, the tube was large and amazingly painful. I'm wondering if possibly they didn't have a pediatric-size tube. They strapped me down for the procedure, expecting me to struggle.

I made up my mind that even if I passed out from pain and inability to breath, that rather than struggle, I wouldn't move a muscle. During the procedure, I noticed that my right arm wasn't completely strapped down, so gradually, gradually, so the nurses wouldn't be alerted to prevent it, I slipped my arm out of the restraint and then held it at my side, as immobile as if it were still strapped down. It was a point of pride that I could stay still without being strapped, and I suppose this helped me think of something besides what I was going through.

This happened fifty-eight years ago, but even after all this time, I found myself just now taking a deep breath to reassure myself that I still can take a deep breath. In fact I just took three more deep breaths because the fear of not being able to breathe has never really left me. I suspect that a week of my life doesn't go by without my taking a deep breath, just to reassure myself that I can.

What I just described turned out to be the end of my asthma. I have not had an attack since. I think I outgrew it, although I've had asthma experts say that you don't outgrow asthma.

There's room for disagreement on this point because my sister Victoria also had asthma severe enough to cause hospitalizations but, as of now, she hasn't had an attack in many decades.

This is an aside, and not sequential, but I remember when I was in college, Victoria was hospitalized with a severe asthma attack and I went to see her. Part of my reason for wanting to be with her was knowing that asthma involves fear; you desperately want more air and can't get it, and the more you struggle, the more catastrophically worse it gets. I spent the night in Victoria's room, hoping that being near someone who loved her would ease some of Victoria's fears.

The problem with spending the night in her room was that visitors weren't allowed overnight. I was supposed to leave when the visitors' hours were over, but I hid in the bathroom, and I think I recall even hiding under the bed, to escape being thrown out. It was a time of great closeness for us. I wonder if she remembers it the way I do.

In one way, I'm grateful for having had experience with asthma. I think it made me better able to deal with Frank Perdue's breathing difficulties many years later. Again, this isn't chronological, but around 1995, Frank had triple bypass surgery which, as a side effect, caused him to have post-sternotomy syndrome, the condition from which most bypass surgery patients die. Part of the syndrome includes getting many quarts of fluid seeping into the lungs, and in our case, it meant twenty-one days of hospitalization with terrible breathing problems.

I never left his side during this period because I remembered my own experience and my sister's with the absolutely claustrophobic feeling a person can get when every breath you take is shallow and less than you need. I'd tell him stories or read to him, or even at three in the morning, when it was the worst, we'd watch Ken Burns' baseball series, and all of these helped distract him.

My experience with asthma meant that as a child and up until my mid-thirties, I had no use for sports. The memory of having trouble breathing meant that any exercise that could cause panting was, to me, detestable.

I have completely reversed my attitude and at age sixty-nine, cherish physical activity. I would generally prefer to walk up eight flights of stairs to taking an elevator. There are few days in the course of a year when I'm not at the gym or taking ballroom dancing lessons, or doing some form of exercise.

## The Functional Equivalent of a Ghost Story

During the period when my asthma began, the family was still living in Lincoln, Massachusetts. Something happened then that would prove, as Dr. Watson of Sherlock Holmes' fame, would have described it, as "not without interest later on." We had a summer place in Dublin, New Hampshire, and the drive there was one that Mother must have made hundreds of times.

One day, Mother and I were driving to Dublin when she veered off the usual route and began going up one country road and down another. This was so different from her usual routine that I asked her, "Where are we going?"

She answered, as we turned onto yet another back road, "I don't know. I just felt this urge to take a side trip."

This was so unlike Mother that it was making me uneasy. What was going on? True, Mother was a spontaneous kind of person, but this was different from anything I had seen. To drive up one road and down another with no goal in mind? It wasn't her!

We kept driving and then suddenly we saw on the right an old, weathered gray barn with a little blue flag coming from the second story. White lettering on the flag said ANTIQUES.

Mother stopped the car, we entered the dimly lit barn, and as our eyes adjusted to the darkness, we saw an endless array of dusty junk, including rusty horseshoes, old kerosene lamps and... And! And one of the most beautiful pieces of furniture I've seen in my life, either before or since.

It looked like a chest of drawers, maybe four feet high, four feet wide, and a couple of feet deep, but actually it was a desk. It had fabulous, ornate carvings, including what I now know was a de Medici coat of arms, carved from mahogany.

Mother fell in love with it, but the price was far more than she could pay with the money she had with her. We got in the car, drove back to Lincoln, and I still remember her conversation with my father when we got back.

Telling him she wanted it, she said, "I don't need a fur coat, you can skip Christmas presents for the next ten years, and I don't care about a European vacation. Just please, please buy me this desk!"

The desk arrived in our Lincoln home soon after. Mother used to spend hours lovingly showing me the inlay patterns, speculating how much skill and effort it must have taken to create something so beautiful and intricate in a time before power tools.

I ended up loving it too. I remember filling a vase with goldenrod flowers to put on the desk, partly to please mother and partly because I felt the desk deserved flowers.

I'm thinking I must have been around twelve at the time and didn't know that flower vases can leave rings on wood. It did leave a ring, but I don't remember Mother ever scolding me about it. In the end, I'm glad for that water mark, for a reason I'll get to in a moment.

I grew up loving the desk, but after Mother's death in 1969, the desk was sold to an antique dealer. I wanted to get the chest back, but when I asked the antique dealer if I could buy it back, he answered that it had been sold to a decorator.

I tracked down the decorator and learned that she had sold it to a young couple who were using it as the centerpiece of the decor of their apartment and they would never give it up at any price.

This was a source of sadness for me. The Venetian desk, as we called it, was so much a part of my childhood and my memories of my parents that I hated having it go out of my life like that.

I think the desk was sold in the late 1960s. Maybe fifteen years later, I was visiting New York and got a strange urge to go up one street and down another. I didn't know why I was doing it, and this is wildly uncharacteristic of me. In my normal life, I tend to have each minute spoken for, and to wander with no purpose in mind is, I would say, pretty close to alien possession.

I walked and walked until I saw on the north side of the street, on the West Side of Manhattan, a blue flag that said AUCTION TODAY.

I walked inside and found that they were auctioning Mother's desk! I could be sure it was her desk because the water mark from the flower vase was still visible on the top right-hand side. I bought the Venetian desk for roughly one-third of what the family had sold it for, fifteen years earlier.

What are the odds of selling a desk in Dublin, New Hampshire, and buying it back at an auction fifteen years later in New York? What are the odds of my being there at the right time? I'm not superstitious, but these do strike me as unusual odds.

And this makes me think of Victoria again. In her book, *Mystic in the Making*, she talks about how her life leads her more and more strongly to mysticism. In my life, the longer I live, the more I become a nuts-and-bolts person who is immune to pretty much anything that can't be explained by science. And yet…an experience like this threatens my belief in science as the explanation of everything. I mean, the odds of my being there at the right time to get the desk again are so slim. It feels like a ghost story.

It threatens my beliefs, but not enough to change them. I just swallow hard and tell myself, "Well, it's a one in a half a billion chance, but one in half a billion chances, by definition, do happen."

## The Largest Antique Buyer in the World

The Venetian desk had another interesting consequence, one that ended up changing the decor of many hundreds of Sheraton Hotels. I don't think Ernie had been particularly taken with antiques up to this time, but I know he was impressed by the Venetian desk and how little it cost in comparison to its amazing workmanship and great age.

He and Mother began attending auctions at the local auction house, learning more about the bargains to be had. Soon he was buying books on antiques and studying them. I still have his copy of *Nutter's Antiques*, but he had a whole shelf of reference books on antiques.

And then an idea came to him. Back then, in the 1950s, when antiques weren't as much in vogue as they became later on, it was possible to buy important antiques for just about what you would pay for top of the line modern furniture. He asked himself, "Why not furnish the presidential suites with antiques?"

Ernie knew that the presidential suites of all his hotels needed to be furnished in a manner that would entice guests to return. The ambiance had to be outstanding and gracious and tasteful, and that meant the top of the top of the line for furnishings. The problem with the modern furniture was that it generally had to be replaced in ten years.

Ernie calculated that for the same price he had been paying for furniture that would be losing its value with each passing year, he could buy antiques that would increase in value each year, and on top of that, give his guests an even more pleasing experience.

Furniture had started out as a hobby for him but by now he had a professional interest in it as well. He began attending the New York auctions, the Newport estate auctions, and eventually, the ones in Paris and London as well. I'm not sure how many hotels he was furnishing, but I think the number was heading toward one thousand. I'm told that during the 1950s, he was the largest antique buyer in the world.

I personally benefited from one of these purchases, and here's how it came about. There was a three-day auction of one of the great estates in Newport, and he was there, busily vacuuming up the items for use in the Sheraton Hotel presidential suites.

The last minutes of the last day, a terrible storm came up. It was an outdoor auction, and as the skies darkened and the wind was blowing stray newspapers twenty feet in the air, people in the crowd began fleeing for their cars, clutching their coats around them and holding their programs over their heads, trying to protect themselves against the heavy raindrops that were now splatting down on them.

The rows and rows of folding wooden chairs were rapidly emptied, and soon only my father remained, sitting comfortably in the front row. The heavens opened up and great sheets of rain began hitting the ground.

Ernie's attitude about rain was, "I'm not made of sugar; I'm not going to melt." He sat there, alone with the auctioneers on the stand in front of him.

The auctioneers, unlike Ernie, hated being out in the rain. The head auctioneer announced (to the crowd of one), "In view of the terrible weather, we are going to consolidate the last three items, the best that we had been saving for last. We are offering here a nineteenth century Erard Concert Harp, a Washburn guitar (the Stradivarius of guitars), and a Steinway grand piano, in perfect condition. The starting price is $5000."

He began chanting, "Do I hear $5000? Do I hear $5000?"

Ernie sat quietly, the rain sleeting down on him.

"Do I hear $2500? Do I hear $2500?"

Again Ernie sat immobile, as the rain continued to drench him—and the auctioneers.

*Sixteenth century de Medici desk that once belonged to a cardinal. Since this was the time of the Inquisition, who knows what depredations against mankind began with documents signed from this desk!*

"Do I hear an offer? Any offer at all?"

Ernie raised his rain-splashed paddle.

"State your offer, sir."

"One dollar," Ernie called out.

"Sold!" the auctioneer barked, slamming his gavel.

I inherited the Erard harp and for several years took harp lessons. I adored it and still love to look at it, but by now because it is so antique, I can't tune it to pitch—the 2,000 pounds of pressure that a fully tuned harp exerts on the sounding board would cause the sounding board to buckle.

# Chapter Two:

# *1952–1959, Boston*

Lincoln Public School had been fun and educational and I'm totally glad that I went. The next school was Winsor in Boston. The family had moved to Boston in 1952, and our home was 8 Louisburg Square on Beacon Hill.

I remember the trauma of going from being a country girl to a city girl. Formerly, I had used to pity city girls who had to breathe "second-hand city air," and I wondered whatever there would be to do in the city, since at every moment there were so many wonderful things to do and explore in the country. Surely life in the city couldn't be as exciting and full as life in the country?

However, later in life, I've always felt it was a blessing to have had both a country background and a city background. It was like having a foot in both camps, and I have a certain comfort level with both.

I have mixed feelings about Winsor. I value it because it provided me with one of the things I most wanted in life, and that was to be accepted at Radcliffe/Harvard. The education was academically rigorous, and for that I bless Winsor. I also made close friends whom I cherish to this day: Gay Vanner, Judy Innes, Jennie Clark, Corkie Issacs.

On the other hand, I basically hated everything about the school, even up to and including the reunions decades later. I'm trying to think of a time when I felt as depressed as I did at the one reunion I attended. Being in those dour, dreary, cold halls reminded me of the Stalinist period of my life.

## Recognition that Humanity Is Paper Thin

One of the things I learned there, which Miss Winsor's Seminary for Young Ladies presumably didn't intend to teach, is that basic humanity is paper thin. As president of the Spanish Club and the Science Club, I was on the Student Council, and one day, the other members decided that the rules about no talking in the halls (when we were lined up for assembly) were not being obeyed sufficiently. Out of the blue, with no warning, offenders were given notices to appear in front of the Student Council to explain why they weren't obeying the rules.

It was an operation in sadism. The student leaders wouldn't rest until they had reduced each victim to humiliated tears. I told my fellow Student Council members that this was intolerable, but no one else seemed to have figured out that this was completely and totally wrong. I said I wouldn't be a part of this and I was going to tell the rest of the school exactly what was going on.

At this point, the faculty advisor got mad at me, and my response was to say that I was going to write the whole thing up and post it on the bulletin board. This won me no points with her, but the exercise stopped.

This experience gave me an opinion on how totalitarian regimes come to practice the most vile and inhuman cruelties: first, they can, and second, there's a group feeling of being drunk with power and self-righteousness.

I think that having witnessed this, I have an inkling of what makes possible a Robespierre or a Pol Pot: the capacity for evil so easily cohabits and feeds on our sense of virtuousness. I'm pretty sure that my fellow Student Council members felt wonderfully virtuous, because all they were doing was enforcing the rules and helping to encourage an orderly society.

If what I just described could happen in a girls' school with young women who were from privileged families and given a good education, then vicious abuse of power can happen anywhere.

My time at Winsor was mainly spent trying to get good grades so I could be accepted at Radcliffe. I think, at that point, this was pretty much the organizing principle of my life. Mother couldn't understand that I didn't want to come down from my room and be a part of her fabulous social life, but instead chose to spend pretty much every spare second studying.

Part of my studying wasn't even related to school. When I was twelve, Ernie (that is, Father) gave me an expensive set of language records and bet me a guitar that I wouldn't finish it and learn Spanish. I desperately wanted a guitar, so this was excellent motivation.

For almost a year, I dedicated half an hour or more a day to listening to the records and doing the exercises, and then correcting the exercises, using the accompanying text books. Looking back on this, I think I was both student and teacher to myself.

The effort paid off because even to this day, I'm pretty fluent in Spanish and people have told me that they're surprised that I can do such things as use the subjunctive accurately and without hesitation. I'm pretty much at home in Spanish. I've been at dinner parties in Spain where no English was spoken and I hardly noticed what language we were speaking.

Further, this was the beginning of a lifelong love of languages. There are even a fair number of people who see me as a linguist who can speak more than a dozen languages, but as I'll explain later on this reputation is undeserved.

The studies were definitely worth it, but I was disappointed in the reward my father gave me for my year's worth of effort. He had told me he'd get me a guitar, but I guess, not wanting to spoil me, he got me a $27 Stella guitar, which was at the time, the cheapest, tinniest guitar to be found. It had the feel and resonance of plywood and was little more than a toy. Eventually, using money I had earned as a file clerk, I bought a $100 Gibson guitar and for decades, it was the joy of my life.

I wanted to take music lessons, but I quickly came across a problem that made me and music lessons not get along. (By the way, Ernie was willing to pay for music lessons because he had a rule that money spent on tools or on education was always money well-spent.) I guess a guitar, in his view, didn't count as a tool.

**Visual Problems, Music, and the Great Faces and Dancing Agony**

The problem with studying music was, I think I have some kind of dyslexia that keeps me from translating notes on the page to what my fingers do. I could reproduce whatever the teacher wanted me to do, but I'd do it from "hearing" it and not from looking at the page. Thus it would make no difference, when I was doing a lesson, whether I was looking at the page or had my eyes closed. The information just didn't come to me by way of my eyes.

This irritated the teacher and after a few weeks, he said he couldn't work with me. He found me stubborn and uncooperative. My own view of myself was that I wasn't being deliberately uncooperative—I just couldn't seem to do it the way you're supposed to.

For years, I believed this was my own unique little problem, but just recently, I was talking with my son Jose and learned that he has exactly the same issue. Both of us know how to read music, as in, we know which notes on the page correspond with which notes are on an instrument, and intellectually we know the mathematics of the timing of the notes, but there is absolutely no connection between that knowledge and what we play. We play by reproducing what we hear, not what we read. Written music bears no more relationship to our playing than ornithology plays in enabling a bird to sing.

I wonder if this eye-ear problem is connected with dyslexia. I don't know left from right, and can only dial a phone number by saying the number to myself; if I attempt to dial a number without saying it to myself, it's guaranteed that I'll reverse numbers and dial it wrong. I'm guessing that whatever makes me unable to dial without "hearing" the numbers made me unable to play notes without "hearing" them in my head first.

Even today, when I'm taking ballroom dance lessons, when the teacher shows me what to do, it doesn't sink in. Actually it's worse than that. It's that I have no idea what I just saw the teacher do or how to reproduce it or even to remember it. For me, it's somewhat like trying to see the individual blades of an eggbeater in action; it's all a blur.

However, if my instructor says in words, "Keep your shoulders down as if you had two-pound weights on each of them, hold your chest out as if you were displaying a diamond pendant, hold your fingers as if you were holding a champagne flute between your thumb and middle fingers, put your heel down rapidly, as if you're squashing a bug," I get it instantly and can reproduce it at least somewhat competently.

In fact, now that I think of it, I wonder if that's the basis of an enduring problem I have with face recognition. If there were some way I could "hear" a face, I have no doubt that I'd be able to recognize people's faces. As it is, it's as hard for me to recognize a face as it is for me to read music or copy a dance step by looking at it.

## Why Mother Was Afraid I Would Never Marry

Well, back to my days at Winsor. One way or another, I was so absorbed with studies, whether school or Spanish, or music, that Mother was afraid I was too bookish ever to marry. But she also, I learned later from my late sister-in-law, Mary Louise Henderson, had noticed that in general, the men who attracted me were almost always what she termed "exotics."

They were either much older than me (John Wittlesley was a freshman at Yale when I was thirteen; Jorge Cilia, whom I liked at fifteen, was South American and probably twenty-five, and Richard Wade (whom I liked from fifteen to seventeen) was a student at Oxford. This is jumping ahead, but my first husband Francisco Ayala, fit the pattern: when I met him—he was not only a Catholic priest, but also a Dominican monk and he was from Spain. And honestly, Frank was pretty exotic: he was twenty-one years older than me and possibly the most unique, *sui generis* human being I'll ever meet. As I write this, the person I admire most is Washington SyCip, a Filipino national who is ethnically Chinese and twenty years older than me. (This doesn't really count since our relationship is friendship, not romance and I only see him a couple of times a year, given that he lives in Manila.)

On the subject of older and exotic men, it was probably Mother who put Ernie (my father) up to a poignant conversation that led exactly nowhere. I was thirteen at the time, and I remember on a drive from Lincoln to Concord, Ernie told me that it would be better if I were interested in guys my own age. I told him that they bored me. He said that I had probably had a bad experience with someone my own age once and should be more open-minded.

It had no impact on me. For the rest of my life I've always found older guys more interesting and more attractive. I have male friends whom I adore, like brothers, but for the major romance figures in my life, they've always been, in one way or another, both older and exotic.

### Ah, My Wonderful Sunday School Teaching Scam

My best friend at Winsor was Judy Innes. She lived around the corner from me on Pinckney Street. We had a similar sense of adventure, similar sense of humor, an equal fascination with the opposite sex, and we both loved writing. I found her sympathetic, insightful, always up for things, and I guess most of all, a good person.

It was she who talked me into one of my most enjoyable teen activities: teaching Sunday school at King's Chapel in Boston.

I don't quite know how it happened, but the Sunday school class that I was given was composed of unusually horrible, unruly, inner-city, future juvenile delinquents. Oh wait, actually I do know how it happened: a succession of Sunday school teachers had quit and no one else was willing to teach the class.

Fools rush in where angels fear to tread. I volunteered to teach this particular class.

So, one Sunday morning, I, with no background in teaching, am suddenly in one of the King's Chapel Sunday school classrooms, facing maybe a dozen twelve-year-old boys, each one of them dripping with attitude, and not one of them intending to obey a thing I said. Also, I was only a few years older than them.

I had only a few minutes with them before we were to line up to enter the chapel for the kids' part of the service. A problem, no?

As I said, they were dripping with attitude. I pretended to be oblivious to this, and mother-hen-like, spread my arms wide and gathered them close to me, telling them in a conspiratorial voice that this class was going to be different from anything they had ever experienced in their whole lives. Their job from this moment on was to amaze the entire congregation. They were to do this by suddenly and inexplicably, in the space of five minutes with Miss Henderson, being transformed into perfect angels.

In the next few minutes, I got them to rehearse how they would march in to the church, single file, heads up, not looking right or left, in utter silence and then, and when they had reached their pew, look for a slight nod from me and then they were all to sit down in unison. During the service, they were to sit still, and no one was even to squirm. They were to look like little statues. Exiting from the pews was to be the reverse of this.

The kids totally got into it, buying into the notion that we were perpetrating the scam of the century. The kids also agreed that, using a slightly woeful voice, they would tell any of the adults who wanted to know what had happened, that "Miss Henderson is very, very strict with us."

They pulled it off to perfection.

Members of the congregation stared at these well-behaved little martinets, according them far more attention than they had ever gotten for being disruptive. I and my co-conspirators totally got off on this.

To the best of my knowledge, my co-conspirators also gave the suggested explanation to all the adults, the one about Miss Henderson being so strict.

It was apparent to us that the adults were simply mystified by what had happened. How could such a transformation come about when I'd only had them for less than five minutes?

I, of course, pretended total obliviousness to what was going on. When a member of the congregation asked, "What on earth did you do to those kids!", I answered, apparently not quite comprehending the question, my face blank and innocent, "Is something different?"

That began a year of teaching Sunday school, and I couldn't have had more fun with the kids. They totally got into the notion of amazing the adults at how good they had become. We put on a holiday play that they helped write, and then they began astonishing me. Their mothers went to extraordinary lengths to sew beautiful costumes, and they seemed thrilled with their angel kids. I bet our holiday play was as well-acted and sumptuously produced as anything that King's Chapel had ever seen.

The kids were using the same skill and ingenuity that before they had used to get attention for being horrid to, instead, being angels. They didn't really want to be angels, as far as I knew, but they absolutely got off on the complete consternation and amazement that this inexplicable transformation was causing with the rest of the congregation.

We even had mini-etiquette classes in which they'd learn to shake hands and look you in the eye and stand up for any adult who entered the room. Oh, and I told them it was important to have a firm handshake. As long as we were fooling people about how good they had become, we had to go the whole way. No "dead fish" handshakes from my guys!

I ended up adoring them all.

Funny, now that I think of it, the approach of fooling the grown-ups isn't too far from what I told Jose when he was in grade school. He had (and has) a strong personality and adjusting to the restrictions of school didn't exactly "come natural" to him. I told him that he didn't have to be agree with the rules, but he had to act as if he agreed with the rules. His willingness to follow that advice saved everyone a whole world of friction.

## The Perils of Not Knowing Musical Conventions

I don't have a lot of memories of Winsor, but here's one, and it has to do with music. Somewhere around maybe ninth grade, I got the lead in a play, a singing part. The play was to begin with me doing a solo. I enjoyed singing, but having had zero training and not knowing any of the musical conventions, I was unaware that you're supposed to wait until the conductor gives you the initial note, and then you launch in, starting with that note.

It's important to wait for the note because if you're not singing the correct note, you're out of tune with the orchestra.

Er, nobody told me this.

For all the rehearsals for the play, I'd look out at the orchestra, and if they seemed ready, I'd nod to them and then I'd start singing. I mean, I knew the play had to start, and I knew I was the first person who did anything, so I simply assumed that it was up to me to see when the orchestra looked ready, give them a little signal, and then start the whole thing by singing.

One of my friends told me later that the music teacher, who was leading the orchestra, was fascinated that I hit the right note every time. Almost as a game, she let me go on each time to see if I'd continue singing the right first note without first getting the correct musical note from her. My friend said the whole orchestra was in on the game of seeing if I'd get the right note.

But then, when it came time for the actual performance, in front of students and parents, the music teacher faced a dilemma. It had never mattered during the rehearsals whether I got the right note because, if I didn't, they could always start over again. After all, what's a rehearsal for?

But now, when it was for real, what if I didn't get it right? But since we had never rehearsed with her giving me the note first, she was afraid that it would knock me off balance if she suddenly, at the last minute, injected something we hadn't rehearsed.

Out of my hearing, she told the orchestra the problem, and finally the group decision was to continue just as we had in the rehearsals. I learned after the fact that the members of the entire orchestra were holding their breaths, hoping I would hit the right note, knowing that if I didn't, there would be an embarrassing and flop-inducing restart.

I was blissfully ignorant of all this. I looked out from the spotlight toward the sea of darkened faces in the audience, and then looked down at the girls in the orchestra, noticing that they seemed hyper-ready, more ready than I had ever seen them, some with mouths open and eyes fixed on me.

Not feeling that this was different from any of the rehearsals, I simply gave my usual nod and began singing. The orchestra kicked in, and the performance went off pretty much the way it had during the rehearsals.

There was one consequence of this. The music teacher told my parents that since I had perfect pitch, I should study voice and make use of this talent. I took singing lessons for years with the good Miss Streeter. By the way, I don't think she caught on that I wasn't reading the music but was simply reproducing by ear what I was supposed to. Actually, come to think of it, I don't know whether she didn't know or it didn't matter to her.

I learned to love vocal music enough so that I rarely missed the Texaco Metropolitan Opera broadcasts. They were on Saturday afternoons, and I made a major effort always to be near a radio, not only to hear the opera, but also to enjoy and revel in the marvelous commentary from Milton Cross. One of his tag lines was, "You can trust your car to the man who wears the star." This referred to the star that the filling station attendants at Texaco wore. By the way, filling station attendants pumped the gas for you back then.

### Lights, Camera, Action—and an Unpromising Start to My Media Career

Sometime around this period, I had my first brush with being in the media. One summer afternoon when my parents were away, a man knocked on the door and asked if I minded if he took a few pictures of the house.

What simpler times those were, when you could answer the door for whoever knocked! The house that he wanted a picture of was Number 8 Louisburg Square, located on Boston's Beacon Hill, and it may have been the most prestigious address in Boston. Number 8 was the only complete house, all the other buildings having been subdivided into apartments. Also, it was the home of the founder of the Sheraton Hotels.

Anyway, when the guy asked if he could take a few pictures, tomorrow, I couldn't see any reason to refuse. "Sure, go ahead," I told him. He quickly pulled out some papers and asked me to sign. I did so, wondering why all this fuss for just a few snapshots.

The next morning, five huge camera trucks appeared, and I discovered that "a few pictures" actually meant that the house would be a backdrop for one of the scenes for a Hollywood movie starring Haley Mills. It was called *The Parent Trap*.

I hung around the sidelines, watching them film the street and the house. Then, unexpectedly the director looked at me and asked if I'd like to be in a movie. I hadn't met him before and I think he was unaware that the house they were filming was mine.

"Well, *yes!*" I answered enthusiastically.

My role was to walk along the sidewalk toward Number 8, so there would be action in the background.

In a few minutes, everything was ready, and as directed, I started walking and they started filming.

"Wait," the director yelled. "Stand up straighter! Don't look down!"

Back to filming.

"No, no, no, *cut!* You haven't got it right. Head up, shoulders back! Walk with determination!"

Again I started walking toward my house. *"Cut!"* the man yelled. "It's still not right. Okay, here's what I want you to do. Pretend you live here! Act as if you owned the place."

The actual resident of the place, me, didn't match their expectations of what someone there would be like, and here the director was, coaching me on how to be myself! I walked back to the starting point and this time strutted my best imitation of how I imagined a Hollywood actress would portray a snooty, spoiled, entitled teenager putting on airs.

*"Yes! YES!"* the director yelled when I finished this take, "You *nailed* it!"

Beaming, he asked me to sign a release form, and then gave me $10 in return for signing the papers. "Go buy yourself something with it," he said magnanimously as he handed me the cash with a flourish.

I took the money, stuffed it in my tan-colored shoulder bag, and then took out the key to Number 8 Louisburg Square. I then walked up the steps to the front door and twisting the key in the lock, opened the door. As I did, I heard the camera men and crew saying "Oh my God!" and "She really does live there!"

*You can see 8 Louisburg Square with the white columns just slightly to the right of the center of this picture. It was filmed as the location for Haley Mills in The Parent Trap.*

## "My Little Friends, the Credit Cards," and Why I Learned to Hate Them

So, I had earned $10 for being on camera. However, my first real job, the kind you get Social Security for, was as a file clerk in the credit card department of the Sheraton Hotels.

I was fifteen at the time and it had an impact on my attitude toward education. The problem was, the job was inconceivably boring. It wasn't just putting in the time; it was that you had to concentrate on alphabetizing the credit cards, and if you got any in your section wrong, you'd throw off a dozen other file clerks. They would justifiably be angry at you.

That meant no daydreaming or composing stories in my mind; instead just endless painful focusing on putting thousands of credit cards in alphabetical order. The result was, I became positively obsessive about getting a good education so I wouldn't have to do this kind of work.

I learned an important concept from this job though and that is, people are staggeringly different. To me, major surgery has been less acutely painful than the boredom I experienced as a file clerk. However, the second week on the job, a woman returned from retirement, losing benefits as she did. The reason? She just couldn't stand being away from "my little friends, the credit cards."

It astonished me that here she was eager to get back to the very thing I was learning to hate. Making sure I'd get an education that would make me eligible for a career that wouldn't involve this kind of boredom became a focus of my teen years.

Because the credit card division was at the Sheraton world headquarters, 470 Atlantic Avenue, I got a glimpse of how important Ernie was. But his being important kept me from forming close relationships with my fellow employees in the credit card division.

It was interesting to be both a worker, hanging out with my fellow file clerks, while at the same time being the daughter of the founder, and having it known (which it was) that I was his daughter. I think most people in an office would like to be "one of us." I sure would have. But in this situation, for me, it just wasn't going to happen.

I know this will be hard to believe (which, er, is why you shouldn't believe it) but who my father was overshadowed my own adorable, sweet, charming personality. (Reviewer Request: don't take this out of context! I'm *joking*!) My fellow employees and I would work together, eat together, tell jokes together, but in the end, there was always a distance that I was powerless to bridge. There was no closeness.

It was lonely, but I guess there was a partial silver lining to the experience. I'm more aware than I otherwise might have been of how lonely it is to be an outsider. Even to this day, I try (I'm not saying I succeed) to make people feel welcome and part of things and not an outsider. Probably I fall way short of this goal, but nevertheless, it is a goal.

## How the Founder of Sheraton Did It

Seeing the blinding awe with which people regarded my father gave me a life-long interest in what it takes to be a high-achieving individual. On the theory that you, Dear Reader, may have an interest in some of the things I observed, I'll mention some.

I used to ask Ernie what made him a success. Over the years, he had a variety of answers, but among them, he felt that he would try 100 leads when his competitors might give up after forty. He was also forever attending lectures and seminars, reasoning that if he got just one good idea from any of them, this would be an important leg up on his competitors.

I remember his telling me about a weekend management course he had taken in a small town in New Hampshire. The attendees were all owners of mom-and-pop enterprises, such as a neighborhood grocery store and one was the owner of a filling station. Ernie, as the owner of an international company that employed 20,000 people, could have seen himself as out of place there. After all, it wasn't as if he were hanging out with his peers.

But *au contraire*, he relished it. He told me that (a) good ideas are where you find them; (b) the topic had interested him; and (c) the experience had given him ideas that he could use. He was delighted that he had gone.

How many heads of Fortune 500-size companies would be so open to new ideas, so diligent in seeking them out, and so unpretentious about where he'd find them?

Another aspect of his success is, he also felt that having a science background (he had studied electrical engineering at MIT after finishing Harvard), gave him an advantage over his competition because he wasn't afraid to use a slide rule and calculate likely results, as opposed to going by whims and hunches.

Another thing, I don't think Ernie was natively good at socializing. I'll have a story about this later on that comes from my brother Barclay, but I knew firsthand that he was at heart a shy and introverted man. Still, the miracle was that he forced himself to learn how to socialize. He took the Dale Carnegie public speaking class and took several other speaking classes as well.

For a shy man, he became remarkably good at entertaining. He knew the importance of it, especially for someone in the hospitality industry. And in this, my mother was an extraordinary asset. She had all the warmth and naturally outgoing personality that he lacked. She could fuss over guests and make them feel important and welcomed and cared about.

Oh, a quick aside about my mother's hostessing ability: she was known as one of the best conversationalists in Boston. One day she shared with me her secret. "Focus your attention on your guest as if he is the only person in the world," she instructed me, "and then, whatever the topic is, ask, 'And what do *you* think?'"

She went on to tell me, "Your job is to make them feel important. But for this to work, you have to mean it."

Mother had tremendous emotional hospitality, and although she was conscious of the techniques she used for making people feel welcomed and important, it was nevertheless sincere and came from the depths of her heart. She *wanted* her guests to be happy and to enjoy themselves, and she knew how to make that happen. She was positively gifted in being able to step outside herself and imagine what the other person was feeling, and then knowing that, figuring out what to say or do.

But back to Ernie and his having transcended his own shyness. He and Mother entertained, probably on an almost weekly basis, and they did it with a purpose. Often they'd entertain groups of Sheraton Hotel managers, to raise their sites on what elegant entertaining could be, and to encourage them to do similar things at special events at the Sheraton Hotels.

These dinners were elaborate, on a scale that I think only a few embassies in Washington could match. The crystal was rare

Czechoslovakian green goblets that Ernie had bought at an auction, the china was antique Royal Crown Derby Imari, the linens were edged in lace, and the center decoration for our heavy mahogany Chippendale table was an antique sterling silver "plateau" that had taken four silversmiths four years to create. Most embassies couldn't have matched the show, although a palace might have.

I remember one evening when, as part of his showmanship, Ernie (Father) served the wine in a manner that I'm guessing the guests will remember to their dying day. The showmanship part had to do with the wine bottle.

Have you ever heard of a Nebuchadnezzar wine bottle? It holds twenty regular size bottles of wine and weighs about 60 pounds. It took two footmen to carry the thing, and I remember the guys, in their waiters' tuxes, practicing pouring from it before the guests came.

It took muscular strength and great dexterity to aim a bottle the size of a Nebuchadnezzar so that the wine poured into a single small wine glass. The two men had to practice in a coordinated way to get it right and not spill.

When it was "show time," that is, when the party was on and the guests had been seated for dinner, the two men, in lockstep, marched into the dining room lugging the bottle between them. The bottle was at least the size of a ten-year-old child. The room fell silent as the guests gasped while the wine-bearers progressed toward the table.

Then they gasped again, as the two men, with perfect aplomb, as if they had been doing this every day of their lives, went around the table of eighteen or so guests, pouring the wine without spilling a drop. It was a bravura performance.

And Ernie, who had orchestrated it all, gave Mother, at the other end of the table, the briefest, barely visible smile. I knew what that smile indicated: "We did it! We pulled it off!" I'm pretty sure no one else noticed, but I was looking for it. Ernie was relishing this.

I also remember another party where they "pulled it off." Ernie was a history buff, as would be predicted from having a father who was a history professor. At one of his dinners, his interest in history enabled him to do something that actually changed history. But alas, almost no one knows about it.

Ah, but in mere moments, you Dear Reader, *will* know about it. At one of the dinner parties at 8 Louisburg Square he entertained the British ambassador, Baron Caccia of Abernant. At the end of the dinner, instead of serving coffee, as would have been usual, Ernie served tea.

But the tea was no ordinary tea. Father had once done a favor for a doctor, who in return gave him a small, blue, antique porcelain jar that contained 200-year old tea taken from the Boston Tea Party.

The men who started the American Revolution by dumping tea into the Boston Harbor were also frugal New England Yankees, and although they did dump a bale or two of tea into the harbor, most of the tea ended up in New England kitchens, heartily enjoyed.

But not all of it. Some of the revolutionaries/thieves, recognizing that the tea had historic significance, handed it down to their children, who handed it down to their children and so on until about a quarter of a cup's worth reached my father.

For the occasion of the dinner honoring Ambassador Caccia, my father served tea with a leaf or two of the original Boston Tea Party tea mixed in with regular orange pekoe. However, as he announced to the British ambassador, he didn't want to embarrass the ambassador by offering him tea for which the duty hadn't been paid.

I heard my father go on to explain that he had looked up the amount of the tax, and it was actually a small amount. Ernie had gone to a coin dealer (he collected coins so this was an easy thing for him to do), and bought antique coins that would actually cover the taxes that America owed on the tea that had been dumped.

Father produced an antique-looking leather purse and with a flourish, handed the purse with its coins to the ambassador.

I watched as the ambassador opened the strings of the purse, poured the coins into his palm, and then counted them. "I accept these on behalf of my government and Her Majesty, the Queen," Baron Caccia intoned in an official-sounding voice, but then added in a graver, and still more official-sounding voice, "However, the interest on the indebtedness means that these coins do not cover the amount owed."

He paused for drama, and then:

"In my role as ambassador, I am allowed to represent Her Majesty the Queen's government in overseas matters relating to taxes and duties.

In that role, I forgive all interest accrued on this debt and pronounce the taxes now paid in full."

And thus history was made.

I bet it was an evening that everyone present remembered a long time. What a gift for showmanship Ernie had!

There's one more part about Ernie and entertaining. As the president of a major hotel chain, he was obviously someone who regularly ate amazing gourmet food. Wherever he traveled, the chefs at the hotels would outdo themselves to impress him, and I know that he personally auditioned most of the chefs for the chain: he felt that a good chef or a bad one was the difference between a successful hotel and an unsuccessful one. Also, when people entertained my parents, the hosts were likely to try to go all out for my parents.

In light of this, I found it surprising that my father's two favorite meals were on Sundays, and it was pretty much always the same thing. For lunch, at least during my teenage years, we were likely to go to Howard Johnson's for fried clams, and for dinner, he'd heat milk for the three of us (my mother, myself, and himself) to pour over Nabisco Shredded Wheat. Dinner was simple, plain, and bland, just the way this world-class gourmet wanted it.

Well, back to Ernie's shyness and his ability to overcome it. When he was president of the Boston Chamber of Commerce, I remember he once had to address 400 or so businessmen on some abstruse topic, like business cycles. The event was being filmed for national television. The crew had to leave for something else and they had asked Ernie ahead of time if they could get a shot of the crowd applauding, so they could have an ending to their segment and still get to their other assignment.

Ernie, with some embarrassment, explained the situation to his audience and then sheepishly asked if they'd be willing to imagine that he had already given the half hour speech and applaud accordingly.

I was in a balcony, overlooking the hall, and I watched in amazement as the whole crowd sprang to its feet, applauding and even yelling and screaming their approval. The standing ovation went on and on. Minutes seemed to go by, and they wouldn't stop.

I loved it because it had seemed like a referendum on him. This shy man, who had struggled to learn public speaking, was able to bring forth such affection and loyalty from a group of his peers, even when he hadn't yet given his speech.

I no longer remember how the actual speech went, but for me, in retrospect, it had been a Sally Fields moment. They loved him. They really loved him.

I've been talking about how Ernie transcended his shyness, but there was another major part of his business success.

Ernie had a curiosity about where his creativity came from. He told me that several times, the company had faced crossroad decisions, where if he got them right, the company would flourish, and if he got them wrong, it would fail. He'd go to bed at night, uncertain about what to do, and then dream that he was talking with his ancestors. In the morning, he'd wake up knowing what course of action to take, and the results turned out to be good. For instance, Sheraton became the first hotel chain to be listed on the New York Stock Exchange.

I also observed that he enjoyed playing a role in the community. He was generous at charity events, buying items for which he would have no use, such as Arthur Fiedler's baton for $700. He did it purely for the sake of being a good citizen.

He also attended Trinity Episcopal Church in Copley Square each Sunday along with the family. Given that he was a lifelong atheist, this surprised me and I questioned him about it. He answered that he supported the institution of religion as a kind of social buttress, even if he didn't believe in it. Mother, in contrast, believed deeply and devoutly.

During this period, Ernie (Father) did something that I will be proud of until I die, and I hope my children and their children keep this memory alive. When Ernie headed the Boston Chamber of Commerce in the 1950s, he did something way ahead of his time for race relations.

Back then, in Boston, the fancier department stores, such as Filene's, Jordan Marsh, and Bonwit's, all had only white mannequins in their store windows. Ernie had the idea that it would break down stereotypes if people could see nicely dressed black mannequins as well in the store windows.

The problem with persuading an individual store to do this was that back in the early 1950s, when overt racism was certainly a very big factor in Boston, there was likely to be a backlash against any store that suddenly started using African-American mannequins. It could cost the store customers and no one wanted to be the first, even if they understood that doing so was the right thing.

Ernie persuaded the entire Chamber of Commerce to buy into the following proposition: on an agreed upon day, all of the stores would suddenly change their display windows so that 10 percent of the mannequins would be African-American. If there were a backlash, no individual store could be targeted since all were doing it.

And so it was that one day, probably in the early to mid-1950s, all of Boston's department stores switched to having 10 percent of their mannequins be black, since that was the percentage of Boston's population that was African-American at the time. Ernest Henderson was the moving force behind this.

He also did something else along these lines that I admire today, although I didn't understand its import back then. I think during this time, or maybe it was the 1940s, we had several hotels in the deep South. Ernie sold them all, which disappointed me because I used to love it when he would take the family away from the New England snow and we'd go to Florida for a week.

When I asked him why he had sold the hotels, he explained that there were people who didn't like each other for very foolish reasons and in the South, they didn't like to stay in the same hotels with people who had a different color skin. He said that he saw no more reason to exclude the 10 percent of the people who had a different skin color, than he would have reason to exclude people whose names began with the first three letters of the alphabet. He sold the hotels because, given that he wasn't able to change the system, he wasn't going to be a part of it.

Speaking of race relations, he had an interesting relationship with Mabel Corker, the African-American cook who created the magnificent dinner parties which Father used for business entertaining.

In the summers, when we were in Dublin, New Hampshire, Mabel wanted to attend her church in Jaffrey, twenty minutes away. The problem was, Mabel didn't drive.

That was fine—Ernie offered to drive her. But as long as he was driving her, there was the question whether she would sit beside him on the front seat of his Cadillac?

Mabel didn't feel comfortable sitting beside her employer, so she chose to sit in back.

So, every Sunday, Ernie would chauffeur her to her church, and then sit in the car waiting until the two hour services were over. He didn't mind the two hour wait because it was a perfect time for him to work and think uninterrupted.

When Mabel would emerge from the church at the end of the services, Ernie, being a gentleman, would get out of the car, smartly open the door for her, and then hand her in.

I've often wondered what it must have done for Mabel Corker's image with her fellow parishioners, arriving as she did each Sunday, beautifully dressed, in a chauffeur-driven Cadillac, handed in and out of her car by her smartly dressed, high-class chauffeur.

I never asked either Mabel or Ernie how they felt about this arrangement. I'm guessing that they each got an equal kick out of the whole thing.

I think Ernie was ahead of his time in social relations, but he was also an innovator in other ways. I learned just recently from my friend Maury Kanbar that it was Ernie who decided to have the little laundry lines that are over the bathtubs in many of the Sheraton Hotels. According to Maury (and I think he read it in some contemporaneous newspaper or magazine article), Ernest Henderson used to like to rinse out some of his clothes when he was on long business trips. Then he thought, "If I wish there were a laundry line, maybe other guests would feel the same."

He was also one of the first to install air conditioning and bathroom scales in hotels. I asked him about this, since it seemed like a tremendous expense, and if no one else was doing it, why did he need to spend the money to do it?

He answered that soon everyone would be doing it, and they'd have to be spending pretty much the same money to do it, but he'd get the advantage of being the first. It would cost the other companies about the same amount of money to copy him, but they'd get very little promotional benefit from it because you don't get very far advertising that, "We are the second to install air conditioning!" Or "We are the second to have bathroom scales in every bathroom!"

Another innovation that he was responsible for had to do with my friend Donald Tober, the Sugar King. Tober owned Sweet 'n Low, the artificial sweetener, but he was having trouble selling his product to anyone. Over and over again, he'd knock on doors but just hadn't been successful at getting a hearing.

But then he went to the Sheraton headquarters at 470 Atlantic Avenue, and made his pitch. The proposal made its way up to Ernie, who thought it was a great idea and made it available to all the Sheraton Hotels. Don Tober told me that he'll be grateful forever that Sheraton had been willing to look into his product, as opposed to rejecting it without a hearing, as the others had done.

Father also felt there was a tremendous value to developing a reputation for being fair, as opposed to being a shark. His competitors could drive harder bargains and could come out a few dollars ahead in many transactions. But because he was known for fair bargains, as opposed to hard bargains, he generally was the choice for people to come to when people wanted to sell their properties. Widows, in particular, would be advised to sell to him because he didn't mind leaving something on the table. The best opportunities kept coming to him first.

What a great business strategy! And by the way, it was one of Frank Perdue's strategies also. Both men were, as far as I ever saw, amazingly fair.

There was another factor that may have played a role in Ernie's success, although I didn't learn about it from him.My brother, Barclay, discovered it accidentally, and it has to do with the ability to relate to people. Ernie was certifiably *different* in this aspect of life.

Here's how Barclay happened to find out about it. When Barclay was in his late twenties, he couldn't figure out what he wanted to do with his life. He'd try one thing and then another, and nothing seemed like an answer. Out of desperation, he went to the phonebook, found the Johnson O'Conner Aptitude Testing Service and made an appointment.

This would have been back in the 1960s, and as part of the test, the guy at Johnson O'Conner asked Barclay to do word associations. Typically, the procedure is supposed to go something like this:

Guy doing the testing: "Tell me the first word that comes into your head when I say the word 'red'"

You: "Blue."

Guy: "Hot!"

You: "Cold."

Guy: "Inside!"

You: "Outside."

With Barclay, the word "red" would make him think of a fingernail. "Hot" made him think of a "windowpane." "Inside" made him think of "a box of crayons."

At the end of a hundred or so of these word associations, the guidance counselor warned Barclay that the kind of person who had such unusual associations with words would have great difficulty communicating with others or even understanding them. To let Barclay know how extreme a case he was, the counselor told Barclay that in his entire career, he had only once come across an individual who had such completely subjective, as opposed to objective, responses.

The counselor went on to say that the other individual had stood out so much that he'd actually saved the man's file, even though it was from forty years ago. The counselor then went over to a row of file cabinets, opened a drawer, and pulled out an ancient file folder.

Scrutinizing the label, he told Barclay, "Isn't this a coincidence, the man had the same last name as you."

He showed Barclay the file. It was labeled, "Ernest Flagg Henderson II."

For Barclay, this had to be a *Twilight Zone* experience. He had just discovered that his own father, at the same age, had also gone to the same counselor, and had a similar extreme score on the word association test.

What are the odds of this happening and Barclay's finding out about it? One in a million? One in a hundred million?

Barclay told the counselor that Ernest Flagg Henderson II was his father. The counselor, after recovering from his surprise, confessed to Barclay, "I've always wanted to know what happened to this man. I recommended that since he was very bright, but lacked all ability to think the way others do, that he should work at a bench in a laboratory, a place where he wouldn't have to interact with other people."

However, as we all know, that man, Ernest Henderson, didn't become a scientist. He ended up in the hospitality industry interacting with numbers of people on a scale that I think only a national politician could duplicate. And as an aside, what happened to Barclay? He also went into the hospitality industry, although in his case, as a mega-successful restaurateur.

Ernie was successful in his career in the hospitality industry, but he frequently acknowledged that his business partner, Bob Moore, was essential to Sheraton's success. As Ernie explained, they each balanced each other's weaknesses.

For instance, while Ernie was a creative and somewhat helter-skelter personality (you should have seen the dozen or so three-foot stacks of papers in his den, with no attempt at filing) while Bob Moore was an orderly, a-place-for-everything-and-everything-in-its-place, person. Ernie felt that one of his strengths was seeing opportunities but that Bob Moore was good at "cleaning up the messes" that Ernie created along the way. He often said that without Bob Moore, Sheraton could never have grown as it had.

It was an amazing partnership. They met their fist year in college and were best friends and business partners from then on. For more than forty-five years they shared the same office and the same secretary.

When Ernie died in 1967, I saw "Uncle Bob" at the funeral. We were just outside the entrance of Trinity Church, standing beside a six-foot high flower arrangement from one of the hotel workers unions. Uncle Bob looked haggard and distraught and, I remember thinking, as pale as if he were half dead himself.

He told me he had lost his best friend. Trying to make conversation, I asked him what the partnership had been like. Did they ever fight?

Uncle Bob answered, clasping his two hands together, "We could no more argue than my right hand could argue with my left hand."

## Family Dynamics

I admired both my parents greatly, but even so, my brother Barclay and I have often discussed our relationship with our parents and how it influenced us. It's funny, both of us determined to be very different parents from our own parents.

Barclay's goal was to be more engaged with his children than Ernie was, and my big goal was to be different from Mother; I wanted to have a warm, give-and-take understanding, caring, "I'm there for you" relationship with my kids. I think I succeeded more than she did. Possibly she had the beginnings of dementia long before it was diagnosed, and as Tom Osborne once told me when I was distressed about not being able to talk with her, she had been better able to do this with my older siblings.

I wanted to be different from her with my kids, but as for her inability to be there for me, the more I think of it, the more I realize that this was connected with her dementia and was not a character flaw.

Even her dementia is complicated. She did have it, but it began, as far as I'm aware, in the mid to late 1950s, when a statue fell on her head, causing a serious brain bleed. I've read that in many cases, people with head injuries end up with dementia. Direct exposure to blood, I've read, is toxic to brain cells, and the poisonous damage blood causes to the cells causes a gradual cascading effect that over the years results in dementia. I think Mother would have been more engaged with me, when I was a teenager, if the statue hadn't hit her on the head causing the brain bleed.

Even so, I treasure things I learned from her. She collected phrases, which she called, "recipes for living." One was, "Put back in the bucket," and that phrase was usually accompanied by a talk on how we had been given so much, and it was important to give back. For her, it was all-important for us "to be good citizens," and that meant contributing as well as getting.

She loved Grandfather Jim's motto, "Do more than your share." Or she'd tell my siblings and me, "If you have an impulse to do something good, do it immediately. You can't count on the impulse returning."

This admonition was often accompanied with "The givers of the world are happy. The takers of the world are miserable," and "If you want to be happy, think of what you can do for someone else; if you want to be miserable, think about what's owed to you."

In a different vein, she also valued buying quality in clothes. "The rich man gets the most for his money," she once told me, as she showed me how to appreciate the texture and "hand" of the well-made Hattie Carnegie dress she had just bought.

But somewhat contradicting that, she adored bargains. She regularly bought designer clothes at mark-down sales at Filene's Basement. I think she liked the sport of it.

She could, of course, have bought her clothes at the fanciest shops on Newbury Street, and occasionally did, but over the years this Southern belle had turned into a true New England Yankee: frugal, bargain-loving, and abhorring waste.

Which brings me to a favorite "recipe for living," that I grew up with. I'm not sure where I first heard it, although it could have come from Mother. Up until a few years ago, I thought it was pure New England, but I've since learned that other regions claim it as well:

"Use it up,
Wear it out,
Make it do,
Do without."

For a good part of my adult life, I was an environmental writer, and my feeling that avoiding waste was a moral issue probably began with the childhood exposure to the notion that waste and excessive consumption was repugnant.

Father also had "recipes for living," but he didn't call them that. He'd tell us, for example, that it was always right to spend money on education or on tools. He particularly valued education, he said, because no matter what happened in life, education was something that no one could take away from you.

He also wanted us to be down to earth and not attached to material possessions. Once in the late 1940s, we were visiting our summer cottage in Dublin, and I watched in fascination as he chopped wood for the fireplace. Someone experienced in swinging an ax does it with an almost balletic rhythm and accuracy, and even as a child, I could see that Ernie was doing this with great skill. He had clearly done it lots.

Near the kitchen door of the cottage, there was a pile of logs to split, and he kept at it for probably an hour. As I watched him rhythmically hefting the ax behind his shoulder, and then powerfully swinging it in a perfect arc so it connected with the log, always in the precise place that would cause it to split, I told him that I was surprised that he, an important businessman, would have this skill. After all, he could have paid someone to do it.

He answered that, first of all, he enjoyed doing it and liked the exercise. But second, he said that if he lost everything he had, it wouldn't rearrange his mental furniture much because he knew he could land on his feet and he wasn't afraid of work.

And this brings me to yet another "recipe for living," although I don't know where I got it. It was just with me for as long as I can remember. It expresses what I sensed and admired in my father, that day he was chopping wood on the side of Mount Monadnock in Dublin, New Hampshire.

"He who loses wealth loses nothing.

He who loses health loses something.

He who loses character loses everything there is."

Ernie was a wonderful father, and I'm grateful that he was my father. I admired him and learned from him, but sadly, our connection was predominantly intellectual as opposed to emotional. There was always something a little aloof about my relationship with him. He lacked Mother's emotional hospitality, although in compensation, he was easy to relate to in matters of the mind. A lot of my conversations with him were about business or politics.

I feel he tried hard to be the best father he could, but that possibly Asperger's Syndrome explains some of why he was not 100 percent effective in developing emotional bonds with us. The people who have Asperger's tend to be facts-and-figures people and they don't really understand how to relate to people. My guess is that it's easier for them to let down and blubber in a movie (something he regularly did) than it is to be emotional in front of real people.

(Hmmm: I never cry except at movies. With the exception of when Frank died, no guy has ever caused me to shed a tear. I'm not, except in extraordinary circumstances, a crying sort of person. Now I'm wondering about me and Asperger's.)

Back to Asperger's. The empathy and understanding and ability to read people that come naturally for most people is a matter of decoding for someone with Asperger's. However, they frequently have a phenomenal ability to focus, and many become great scientists. I wonder if Ernie's inability to be close wasn't only because of his Germanic upbringing, but maybe it could have been caused by the wiring in his brain.

His marriage to Mother was a huge case of opposites attract. Mother was warm and emotional and empathetic, while he was cool, driven, and surprisingly immune to empathy.

I love the story of their courtship, one Mother told us many times. Mother was from Wheeling, West Virginia, and she had met my father at a dance in Cambridge, Massachusetts, when she was visiting a cousin.

Ernie and Mother fell in love, but Grandmother Berta, Ernie's mother, tried to discourage the match. "Don't marry Ernest," she told

Mother. "He can never stick to anything and you'll end up poor."

"I don't care," Mother answered. "I love him." Grandmother Berta von Bunsen Henderson lived long enough to see some of her son's business successes and to know that her prediction hadn't come true.

During one of Ernie's trips to Wheeling, he and Mother got engaged. Being engaged meant that it would be okay to kiss, and Mother waited for this wondrous event to happen. But it didn't, at least not while they were in the parlor of her house.

As he was taking his leave, she followed him to the porch. Still no kiss.

Then she did something that respectable girls didn't do back in 1918—she followed him all the way down to the garden gate and actually went through it, beyond the white picket fence, onto the public street, desperate for the expected, and by rights hers, kiss.

Finally, she just planted herself in front of her fiancé, face upturned, making it Totally Obvious that the Time for a Kiss Was Right Now. Ernie, his face beet red, closed his eyes, aimed for her mouth and missing it, planted the sought-after kiss smack on her nose. "And then he turned on his heel and fled," Mother said, finishing the story.

When they did marry in 1923, she had trepidations about what she was doing. I know this because I have her diary. There's an entry in it when they're on their honeymoon, leaving West Virginia and traveling back toward Massachusetts.

They're in a train, and as it makes its way ever farther north, she writes about how she loves Ernie, but what, she asks herself, has she gotten herself into? She was going to where the climate was cold, the people were cold, and what must have been worst of all, "My children will grow up Yankees!"

In spite of her trepidations, the move had to have been a good one. She was a social success, I imagine in part because Bostonians must have enjoyed her languorous Southern accent, her genuine warmth, her gracious ways, and a deep and unfailing kindness. I never saw her do anything petty or small or disrespectful.

She also had a grace to her. I remember, after her death, the postman for Beacon Hill came up to me as I was walking near the house and condoled with me about her passing. And then he told me, "I used to love to catch sight of her because she always had such elegant posture.

I'd walk three blocks out of my way, just to go by Louisburg Square, hoping I'd see her."

How many women are so appealing to look at that a postman would walk three blocks out of his way on the chance that he might see her?

Oh, and that reminds me of another thing Mother used to say. She valued good posture, and she used to tell Augusta and me, "When you walk, walk as if you were wearing a train."

I was talking awhile back about how Barclay and I had decided that we wanted to be different from our parents. I had wanted to be a different mother, and he wanted to be a different father.

Barclay particularly noticed how Ernie withheld approval. I certainly noticed that. I don't think any of us grew up spoiled, economically (how could we when Ernie was always telling us to earn whatever it is we wanted?) but I think at least the majority of us kids (Augusta perhaps being the exception?) wrestled with self-confidence and self-esteem. I've sometimes wondered if I would have been as driven and as ambitious if our parents had shown more approval and I didn't have to work so hard at manufacturing my own self-confidence.

The shortcomings of Mother and Ernie were small, and their virtues great. All in all, I think I had a paradise childhood, but as my sister Augusta and I often tell each other, we took it too much for granted. We didn't know how lucky we were and we didn't appreciate it enough at the time. We have since vowed to each other that forever more, when things were going well, we would take the time to step back and feel grateful.

Augusta was always the sibling I was closest to. Sometime around this period, I guess around 1957, Augusta and I spent part of spring vacation in New York City. It was April and I remember so well that we wore matching spring skirts with wonderful blue and purple flowers on them. We felt like fashion models. We saw *West Side Story*, and we also went to the United Nations together.

It was there that something happened that was like a vision of the future. Standing in a gallery at the UN, overlooking the seats where the delegates would be if the General Assembly were in session, Augusta said that her dream was to marry an ambassador. She got her wish, because her future husband, Joseph Petrone, did become a UN ambassador. My wish was to be the wife of a great man, and I got my wish too, because Frank Perdue was a great man. It's funny, but at ages twenty and sixteen, we each knew what we wanted and we got it.

## My Continuing Career as a Scam Artist

Another memory from this period was a game that I used to play at Winsor. I had read a book on palmistry, and though I never believed a word of it, people seemed to find my efforts to put it into practice entertaining.

Many people at school wanted to have their palms read and I, wanting to live up to their expectations, was capable of putting on something of a show. I'd solemnly examine the lines in their palms, twisting their hand this way and that to get the light right for the most accurate view, all the while taking my time as I pondered the gravity of what I saw there. Then, my brows knit from the seriousness of what I was about to say, I'd somberly deliver the reading. It was, of course, entirely the product of my own teenage imagination.

The reason I remember this at all is that years later, I found that I had developed an impressive reputation for being a psychic. People whose palms I read had compared notes, and over and over again, when I told people such things as that they would have three children, or that their first marriage wouldn't last but their second one would be happy and lasting, my predictions had came true.

I have two ways of looking at this. First, they probably noticed the things that came true and forgot the ones that didn't. Or second, possibly they arranged their lives to live up to the prophecy. But in either case, I'm as skeptical as ever of the paranormal, having had a brief but happy career as a fraud myself.

Actually, looking back on it, it's unsettling to realize how eager people were to believe. When I was doing it, I honestly thought I was just putting on a show and that they were in on it. It was a shock years later to realize that people had taken it so seriously.

## Richard Wade, First Kiss

Richard Wade, a student at Oxford whom I met in December of 1956, when my family was vacationing in Jamaica, was the first guy I ever kissed. After that, we had an intense relationship by mail for close to three years.

My father was unimaginably supportive because he allowed Richard to work for Sheraton as a summer job, thereby making it possible for me to see him for an entire summer. The next year I saw him in the South of France when I was attending the Ecole du Montcel, and finally, my senior year, I visited him and his family in England.

He studied Arabic at Oxford, plus he had an awe-inspiring knowledge of Greek and Latin, and he shared my love of classical music. I was dazzled by his knowledge and culture. He went on to have a major job at the BBC. We broke up, mutually as I recall, but from my point of view, Arthur Houghton was my reason. More on him later.

## An Event that Formed My Character

During this period, a minor and brief event occurred that has had the most profound influence on my life. It influenced the next fifty years of my life, and I hope it will be a guidepost for the rest of the time allotted me. I'd say it's almost a key to my character.

A woman, a retired opera singer I think, had invited me for tea. She was probably in her late seventies and possibly in her eighties. On the appointed day I was tired and had a bunch of things to do and was tempted to bow out and cancel.

Thank heaven I didn't. When I arrived at her very modest two-room walk-up apartment, I saw that she had gone to a breathtaking amount of trouble over the tea. There were lovely little tea sandwiches and pastries and candies and nuts and, I think, maybe fresh strawberries and cream. She had a coffee table, and the whole thing was covered with wonderful tea things, plus her beautiful tea set and nice china and linens.

If I had canceled, an elderly and lonely lady would have gone to an amazing amount of trouble to be nice to me, and I never would have known it. She would have been disappointed and I wouldn't been aware of what I had done.

Looking back on it, I'm guessing that she didn't have many callers and that she cared that someone would come calling and take an interest in her. Having a caller must have meant so much to her that she apparently cooked and prepared for days and, judging from the rest of her apartment, might even have broken her budget to put on such a beautiful spread.

I made a vow that day that unless I was hospitalized with tubes coming out of me, I would do my very best never to be a no-show. The thought of this dear lady and the unhappiness I could have caused her by being unreliable, is just about too terrible to contemplate. To this day, it touches emotional chords in me, thinking about what might have happened.

Because of her, and the horrible disaster I could have unknowingly been guilty of, I've tried to live my life so that when it's within my control, I'll be there if someone expects me to be there.

## Depression and Then My Debutante Year

My senior year, I experienced the only depression that I can remember that was not the result of something that would normally make a person feel down, such as the death of a spouse. I had wanted more than anything I could name to get into Radcliffe. I had applied for early admission, and the day the acceptance to Radcliffe arrived, I had a few moments of stunned elation, and then hours and hours of total letdown. I had a ghastly sensation that the organizing principle of my life was gone and I hardly knew who I was. It was like being depersonalized. I felt so down I could hardly move. I could hardly breathe. It wasn't until five or six hours later, when I found a new goal, doing well at Radcliffe, that I recovered my spirits.

Graduating from Winsor was the beginning of my debutante year. Because Mother was the queen bee of Boston society, because father was the founder of the Sheraton Hotels, Investment Trust of Boston, Standard Wholesale Supply, a credit card company that he sold soon after its formation, Thompson Industries (which made stainless steel parts for the automobile industry), and probably several more companies that I no longer recall (I seem to remember that he once owned the controlling stock in the Buenos Aires metro system), plus oil and gas wells, my debut was a big deal. I came out in Boston, New York, London, and Paris.

My escort for most of this was Arthur Houghton, a Harvard student. More on him in a moment.

I didn't keep a scrapbook of this, but I remember several years later meeting, on a fall day in Harvard Square, a woman who informed me that I was Mary Henderson. Against a beautiful backdrop of falling yellow leaves, she told me how for years she had been keeping a scrapbook of the newspaper articles and gossip columns that chronicled my doings. I also met a woman many years later who told me that she had followed me as an example of class and style for others to follow.

How amazing.

I had no idea in the world that anyone was paying attention. I was just, to paraphrase the immortal Cyndi Lauper, a girl who wanted to have fun.

I guess a high point of all these doings was the debutante cotillion at the Galerie des Glaces at Versailles. I went back there in 2007 and was reminded of the glitter, the wines, the orchestras, dancing the night away the first time with the Duc de Feltre. I wonder what became of him.

My sister Augusta and her infinitely handsome husband, Joseph Petrone, were living in Paris then, and I stayed with them at their place near Fontainebleau. Joseph thought, wisely, that it would be a good idea for me to learn what it was like to be drunk, so I could know the signs in the future.

*Mary "Mitzi" Henderson, graduation picture*

54

*Debutante party in Boston, 1959.*

I enthusiastically drank the wine they were offering. I've since learned that back then, in the late 1950s, they typically drank Lafitte Rothschild. They liked the taste better than any of the other available wines, and while it cost slightly more than the other available wines, the difference was so small that, as far as price went, they wouldn't worry about the cost of Lafitte Rothschild anymore than they would have worried about the price of a Coke. I wonder if I had the privilege of getting drunk on Lafitte.

I did get totally, falling down drunk, and could hardly get out of bed the next day. From that day to this, I doubt that I've ever had more than three glasses of wine at a time, and it's almost always less. I adore wine, but the lesson Joseph engineered for me has been a lasting one.

Actually, I have been drunk one other time, but it was unintentional and it didn't involve wine. Luis Bunuel, son of the famous movie maker, invited me for dinner and margaritas. It was a sweltering evening in New York and Luis didn't have air-conditioning. I was under the impression that I was drinking lemonade. The hangover the next day corrected this impression.

# Chapter Three:

# *1959–1965,*
# *Cambridge, Massachusetts, and*
# *Washington, DC*

After a summer in Europe, I was ready to start Radcliffe. I loved and still love my alma mater, heart and soul. I loved it as much as I disliked Winsor. There was freedom and ferment and a chance to study subjects that enthralled me.

I expected to be a philosophy major, but after a few government and economics courses, it seemed to me that government was philosophy in action, so government became my major. I also adored the economics classes, mostly because I found anything to do with numbers congenial, but also, I liked that almost no women were in the classes. It's not that I'm against women, but rather, I enjoyed the visibility and professorial attention that this guaranteed.

## The Archetypal Worst Nightmare

My first exam turned out to be the stuff of nightmares. My beloved roommate, Sally Moore (now Sally Gall), had a very serious health problem and the time I had expected to devote to reviewing for the exam evaporated as I drove her to the hospital.

Worse, I thought the exam the next day was at 11:00 a.m., and that I would have an hour between classes to review and at least study a little. However, as I was entering Widner Library to study for an hour, I met a classmate who asked why I wasn't across the campus taking the exam.

56

I realized that I had the time wrong and would not even be starting the hour exam until twenty minutes after the hour.

I raced to the lecture hall, grabbed a blue book, and wanted to start writing. However, my adrenalin was at such a peak and I was trembling so hard that my writing hand wouldn't even stay on the blue book. My last thought, before I became unconscious, was that I needed to use my left hand to hold my right hand to keep it on the page of the blue book.

I came to at the end of the exam, handed the book in, and left the place convinced that I had completely failed the exam. A week or so later, when the exams were to be handed back, I decided to skip the class on the grounds that it would be too demoralizing to start my Radcliffe career with an F, and that I would simply make sure that never again would I be in such a situation. There would be a fresh start.

When that day's class was over, I was outside on the Radcliffe quadrangle, and I saw one of my classmates, Doris Meyer, brandishing a blue book. "It's yours," she said gleefully. "I brought it back for you!"

This was the blue book that I had wanted never to see, and now I couldn't understand how my friend could look so happy when a personal catastrophe had just befallen me. She was grinning ear-to-ear as she thrust me blue book into my hands.

**It had an A+ on it.**

In my college career, I never achieved that grade again. Further, my classmate reported that the professor had held this blue book up in front of the 500 or so students in the class, using it as an example of how good an exam could be. I even think I remember that she said that he read excerpts from it.

I couldn't believe the A+. I examined the blue book, and the first few letters on the page were jiggly, two inches high and illegible. But then the handwriting settled down into the best penmanship I'm capable of. Further, there were perfect, insightful paragraphs, apparently perfect quotes from the reading material, and not a single crossing out or even a smudge. If I had been transcribing somebody's work, I couldn't have created better-looking pages. Further, on reading it, the logic seemed both organized and compelling. What I was reading was completely new to me. It was my handwriting but I have no memory of having written a single word of it.

I've never had exactly that experience since, and I wonder if others have discovered that their unconscious mind can take over and do wonders. However, there's an analog to this that happens to me all the time in my career as a writer. If I mentally "stand aside," and let whatever-it-is simply flow, the writing invariably seems better and less labored than if I had tried consciously to control it.

Ah, which reminds me of an example of what I disliked about Winsor. In writing class, we were supposed to write outlines, then topic sentences, and then fill in the paragraphs. My mind doesn't work that way, not even remotely. That's because I don't know where I'm going to end up until I've actually written whatever it is, and then I know, after the fact, what I wanted to say. At Winsor, I was eternally a square peg being forced into a round hole.

Funny, twenty-one years of my career was as a syndicated columnist, first for California's Capitol News and then for the Scripps Howard News Service. In more than 1,000 syndicated columns, I never once wrote an outline. In every case, I just sat down at my desk and wrote.

## Life at Radcliffe

At Radcliffe, I felt I bloomed. I adored the classes. I adored them so much that I always took five, instead of the required four, and when the president of the college congratulated me on getting good grades when I was taking five courses, I was honestly surprised at her attitude. Why would anyone not take five courses, if it didn't cost anything extra? Here was this stupendous resource that you could get at no extra cost; it would be a waste not to take advantage of it.

In general, I found the courses easy. I remember once when it was time for the final exams, I had finished studying for the exams, and having nothing better to do, started studying some of the course work for the next term. I was doing this in the dining hall during breakfast, and one of my classmates noticing that I was reading from the next semester's book list, proclaimed (not asked) in front of the twenty or so women in the room, "What courses have you taken next term?"

Something that I particularly enjoyed was that my major,

government, was not popular with other women. There were courses, particularly the economics ones, when there were as many as two hundred men and then me, the only woman.

There was a touching moment when one of the professors asked if I could handle being the only woman in his economics class. It was touching because I couldn't process the notion that this was a problem. *Au contraire*, being the only woman in a large class of men was for me the ideal situation, a dancing on the table, swinging from the chandeliers, remember-it-to-this-day source of delight. How dear of this sweet man to imagine that I would find this a problem.

Why was I so delighted? Whatever I did or said would be noticed, which seemed to me an ingredient in success. If I raised my hand in class, it was simply guaranteed I'd be called on. If I had a question after class, I could count on not being ignored. I'm all for hiding one's light under a bushel, as long as it's a transparent acrylic bushel and the light underneath it is a flashing neon sign.

Something else that I loved about Radcliffe: my roommate. I've mentioned her before, Sally Moore (now Sally Gall) but she and I were friends from the moment we met, and the friendship seems as strong forty-nine years later as it was in the beginning. She's awesomely smart, is kind about sharing her wisdom, comes from an academic family that exposed her to culture on a scale that I'd never experienced, and most of all, we were never competitive with each other. I think each honestly rejoiced in each other's successes and wept for each other's problems. I think we were totally supportive of each other and could talk about things with an emotional affinity and understanding that has happened to me rarely in life. Frank Perdue, Gay Vanner, and my two sisters, are the only people I can think of for whom I felt such a depth of friendship.

I loved Radcliffe and Harvard so much that I don't think I ever skipped a single class, at least until my senior year. (More, in a moment, about skipping classes my senior year.) It was a special kind of heaven, listening to brilliant professors and learning things that thrilled me. Plus, I didn't find that the course work took much time, which meant an abundance of time for dating, friendships, concerts, practicing the guitar, decorating my room, trying to dress well, student government, and so on.

However, on a social level, I'm not sure that I ever dated a Harvard guy, with the brief exception of Arthur Houghton. My favorite date back then was Richard de Neufville, president of the No. Six Club at MIT. The Harvard guys seemed too much like brothers; one could adore them and care about them, but romantic love wasn't part of it.

## Arthur Houghton, World's Best Guy—for Someone Else

Arthur Houghton was extraordinarily special to me. He had taken a year off after his freshman year, so my first year at Radcliffe, ours was a long-distance relationship. I looked up to him, admired him, adored his company, but we broke up my sophomore year, when he returned from, I think, California. I've seen him since, after twenty years and then after forty years, and even though I think he's a superb human being, I'm grateful that we did break up. There's zero possibility of our ever having made a life together, no matter how much I cared for him back then. I have a tendency to be attracted to saber toothed tigers, while he was more of a border collie. By the way, border collies are magnificent, so I'm not knocking border collies.

Still, my time with Arthur was joyous. At that period we were in tune with each other. We used to talk about how we "uned" which translated, means, we were doing things that were so unique to us. We explored life and thoughts and romance and music and restaurants. It was intellectual, spiritual, and definitely social as well: my favorite hobby today is still dancing, and oh, the wonderful dancing we did! He was divine in a tuxedo and our dancing was as "uned" as everything else in our relationship.

Another thing that we related to is that we both came from backgrounds of privilege. His family was the Corning Glass family and I was the Sheraton heiress. When two people come from similar backgrounds, socially, educationally, intellectually, and economically, there can be a comfort level and a trust that just falls in place effortlessly. We had the same reference points and deeply understood each other's aspirations to be stewards of our wealth and not to let wealth destroy our lives. We had each seen this happen with others.

Further, we each understood that it was our lot to come across people wanting friendships with us based on wanting things from us. We also came across people who felt the need to flatter us (uh, we could live with that!) but we also endured the tiresomeness of people who felt the need to tear us down, not because of who we were as individuals but because of their projections of us. We each valued people who were genuine, and we shared the experience that this was not always what came our way.

I have a memory of Arthur that reveals a lot about Mother, and too much about me. One day Arthur came calling at our house in Louisburg Square. We entered the living room where Mother was sitting, and she instantly grasped, without his telling her, that he had had a wisdom tooth pulled and was in pain. For her, it was as clear as if she were reading a printed sign. She rose from her chair and came fluttering over to him, putting her hands on his shoulders, looking into his face and cooing with concern and caring, distraught that someone she cared for was in so much pain.

I adored Arthur, but had totally missed what was instantly clear to Mother. Until she pointed it out to me, I had missed Arthur's ashen and drawn face.

My assessment of myself is that I hope I'm an empathetic and caring person, but something is dreadfully missing in my ability to read or even recognize faces.

As I've mentioned before, that's been a lifelong torment to me. I think I just don't see faces the way other people do. I have almost zero visual memory for faces. And although I can decode obvious facial clues, such as a grin or tears, in most cases, I am inept at reading anything more subtle, like someone I loved being in agony from a tooth extraction.

I know that remembering people is important and it's demeaning to people not to remember their faces, but in spite of reading books on training your memory for names and faces and even taking a couple of courses on it, I feel as if I'm almost blind in that particular area. And yet, I think I have at least some ability to read body language, and I can hear a lot in a person's voice. Plus, if I'm paying attention, I can often remember what people say in an amount of detail that later surprises them. I think that helped me no end as a columnist.

Back to Arthur. He was my first love, but it didn't last. I think he would be the perfect husband for someone other than me. I don't have a single bad thing to say about him. The fault was entirely mine, and the fault was, I think, that I was imprinted too much on my father, with his out-size ambition, fabulous energy, and ability to grasp and force into existence opportunities that were invisible to others.

Arthur's personality was more like my mother's: kind, generous, giving, loving, gentle, supportive. I've mentioned this earlier but, with the exception of Frank Perdue, I've always alternated between (or had going at once) guys who were either like my mother or like my father. None lasted, unless I had two going at once. Frank Perdue, however, combined the forcefulness and brilliance of my father, with the loving supportiveness of my mother.

## I Sing at Carnegie Hall

Back to Harvard. A favorite memory I have of this time was one day, I was playing the guitar and singing in my third story room at the off-campus house, Coggeshall. A complete stranger who had heard me through an open window came in saying she had been caught by my music. She turned out to be not only a modern dancer but a modern dance teacher.

She asked me then and there to accompany her with my music and said that she would express in dance what my music made her feel. We went back to her house, which was on the same block, I met her husband, and we tried seeing if such a collaboration might work.

It was incredible. I felt as if my singing called forth the most astonishing expressivity in her gestures and movements. She literally embodied the emotions I was trying to express in music. It may be the most moving, creative, and artistic collaboration I'll ever have.

The collaboration resulted in my accompanying her at dance recitals, and we did well enough at one of these (it was a competition) that we were invited to perform (I still can hardly believe this) in Carnegie Hall.

Actually, that's not nearly as impressive as it may sound. Carnegie Hall has a main concert hall, and that is not where we performed. Rather, the place is honeycombed with dozens of smaller recital halls, and we performed in what was likely one of the smaller ones. But nevertheless, there was a live audience and I was thrilled. It was such an adventure, taking time off from classes in Cambridge and going to Manhattan to play and sing at Carnegie Hall.

The experience gave me a huge lust to perform in front of audiences and for awhile, I even imagined trying for a career as a singer and guitarist. Ah, the road not taken!

In the end, I'm glad I didn't because my career in writing and television was more in tune with my personality. I loved singing and I loved having an audience, but I wasn't at heart enough of a musician for this ever to have had a chance. I can write for ten hours at a stretch and not know it, but I can't imagine practicing music with that kind of commitment and love.

My senior year at Harvard, I did something that I suspect few others have done. I was a full-time Harvard undergraduate, I had an 8:00 to 4:30 job at the Treasury Department in Washington, and I was taking a full course load as a graduate student (master of public administration) at George Washington University.

It came about this way. The summer before my senior year, I had a wonderful job in Foreign Tax Assistance at the IRS headquarters in DC as a summer intern. While there, I learned that their management intern program would begin the following January, and that if I didn't join then, the next class wouldn't be until a year and a half later.

I couldn't stand the thought of putting my career on hold for eighteen months, so I applied for the management intern program that started in January of my senior year. That meant working an eight hour day at a full-time job in DC. I figured I could study for my Harvard

*I made a record of some of my songs, but nothing came of it. Still, it was fun to pose for the cover! It was different from my normal student look!*

classes at a distance, return to Cambridge to take the exams, and graduate in June.

However, once I was accepted as a management intern, I learned that all the interns were eligible for a full scholarship for a master's degree at night school at the George Washington University. Getting a free master's degree appealed to me, and further, I could become a graduate student without any entrance requirements other than the tests I had already taken to become a management intern.

The most delightful part, from my point of view, was that the admissions people at George Washington University assumed that anyone who was in the management intern program was already a college graduate. That meant I could (and did) take a full time-equivalent course load as a graduate student while I was still an undergraduate at Harvard. However, to keep the graduate school scholarship, I had to have the full-time day job at IRS.

It was a slightly harrowing experience, at least at the beginning. The first week of night school classes, I was wondering if I could manage being an undergraduate at Harvard in Massachusetts, a full-time government employee in Washington, DC, and also a full-time master's degree candidate at the George Washington University.

That week, I struggled through the reading assignment, my first as a graduate student, and was staggered by how much they expected of us. I concluded that graduate school was much more difficult than being an undergraduate and I was worried if I could keep up the pace. Still, I got the reading done, while still working on my Harvard assignments.

However, the second week, I realized that I didn't need to worry after all. What I had taken to be the week's assignment at George Washington was actually the semester's assignment.

Even so, it wasn't a cake walk. I found the statistics course difficult, mainly because it assumed that we already knew mathematical concepts that I had never heard of, such as set theory. In retrospect, I think statistics and accounting are the two most useful courses I ever took, with the possible exception of language courses, but they were difficult, given that I had no background.

The Harvard exams my senior year were traumatic. The last final exam I had to take (although this is the first time I've thought about the connection) was in its own horrifying way, a repeat of the first exam I took at Harvard. In both cases, I was drastically late for it.

I remember getting off the plane from Washington at Logan Airport and hearing myself being paged. Since I didn't think anyone knew I was at the airport, this was scary. I got to a pay phone and called the number I had been given in the page.

It was a Harvard official, wanting to know where I was and why I had missed my last exam. It turns out I had gotten the time wrong, and someone from Harvard had tracked me down. My Harvard tutor went to bat for me and said that he may have been responsible for my having the time wrong and I should be allowed to take the exam, if I went straight from the airport to a room near the Radcliffe library, where the exam would be administered just for me.

This was a high-stress situation, because I had counted on having some time to review the course. I arrived at the exam room and was given the blue books for a three-hour exam. But next door was a group of classmates talking and laughing in the loudest manner I could ever remember. They had finished all their exams and were now celebrating *fortissimo con brio.*

I calculated that I could ask them to be quiet, but I couldn't be sure that they would, and it would take time to do that, and the unpleasantness would be an even bigger distraction. Instead, I decided I had to simply tune them out and focus on the job at hand. And that's what I did.

As with the first exam I took at Harvard, I was enough worried about whatever I wrote that I didn't want to find out what my grade was. However, unlike what happened with my first exam, I never did learn. Obviously I passed because the next month I graduated (with honors), although with my job and my night classes in Washington, I didn't attend the graduation ceremonies.

Actually, not attending my 1963 Harvard graduation is something I've regretted. I love Harvard and I would have loved the pageantry. But back then, I didn't appreciate pageantry and the connection with previous generations and with history. I also skipped my George Washington graduation, which would have been in 1965, but in that case it was because, after listening to so many lectures, I had developed a total allergy to sitting still and having people talk at me.

## I Invent the Internet

While getting my master's in public administration at George Washington, I did have a full time day job, working in the Foreign Tax Assistance office at Treasury, so getting my MPA meant writing a master's thesis at night. I decided to write on the future of computers.

The reason I chose computers was that IRS was converting to automatic data processing (ADP), using punch cards. When I was choosing the topic for my thesis, and after watching what was going on at IRS, I was guessing that computerization would be to brains what mechanization was to muscles. The changes computers could bring about seemed far more transformative than the Industrial Revolution had been. I was completely taken by the topic, and have been ever since. To this day, I love everything about computers.

I made a prediction in my thesis. I said that one day, in the far off future (it being 1964 at the time) computers would become so powerful, and they could compress so much knowledge into so small a space, that one day we would be plugging into the wall to get information the way we now plug into the wall to get electricity.

*Behold, the Internet!* And here Al Gore thought he had invented it.

One of my best sources for my master's thesis was John Diebold, who I now think was something of a sociopath. I got romantically involved with him as I was writing my thesis. But alas, he became part of a pattern in my life that scares me.

I think, for most of my life, with the striking exception of Frank Perdue, I've oscillated between really nice guys who bore me and exciting, high-achieving people who are jerks.

John Diebold was in the latter category. He told me that he was divorcing his wife (the first and last time I ever believed that kind of story), that he was hopelessly in love with me, and that we would soon be married.

What's wrong with this picture is that I now know of two other women he was saying the same thing to at the same time. He drove one of them, Marjena Malinovsky, to attempt suicide. I think I got out of this with rather few scars, but the relationship, based on lies, lasted almost a year.

# Chapter Four:

# *1965–1968, New York*

In 1965, after getting my master's in public administration, I returned to Boston briefly, and then Gay Vanner (now Gay Vanner Fairfield Steward) and I moved to New York. I got a job working for Encyclopedia Britannica, and I don't remember what Gay did. What I do remember about Gay was that she was and is one of the kindest, most insightful, most decent people I'll ever know. She could also be hysterically funny and had a slightly oddball approach to life that I cherished—and still cherish.

For example, one day she announced, as she opened the apartment door, having just come home from work, that she had seen a box. It was on the street, and she had seen it as she was walking home.

"It was a BOX!" she told me, as if seeing a box was something really, really important.

"It was a BIG BOX!" she said insistently, making sure I was paying attention. "It was RIGHT IN THE MIDDLE OF THE STREET! It was a box!"

Forty years later it's hard to recreate how funny this seemed at the time. The sheer nonsense of it entranced me. I mean, who else will I ever meet who could make a great big theatrical event out of seeing a box. She didn't tell me a word about how big the box was or what it was made of or what it might have contained, or which street it was on, or what it might have been doing there. Listening to her box adventure was like a Noh play in which you have to supply the details.

I thought, at times like this, that she was astonishingly feminine and enchanting. Her antics were as far from male as possible. By the way, I think some of her approach has rubbed off on me. To this day, with guys

I sometimes go beyond being illogical and achieve complete incomprehensibility. When I do, guys seem to come back for more. I revel in an awareness that this is so much something they wouldn't do. With Frank, I'd sometimes behave like Gay, and he'd look at me as if I had set down from another planet, but he'd look pleased and flummoxed and delighted. And he too would come back for more. I'll give some examples of this later on. (Be on the lookout for my approach to decorating his house or planning our social life.)

Gay and I roomed together quite happily and I don't recall ever arguing with her. Pretty soon, we also acquired another roommate, Lana Friend, who was also easy to get along with, but I interacted with Gay much more. My biggest memory of Lana was that her name became the subject of my best practical joke ever.

### In All Modesty, This Is the World's Best Practical Joke

I love practical jokes, I still keep doing them, but I never again did one this large because, even though in the end it turned out well, the impact it had on peoples' lives was bigger and riskier than I ever want to be involved in again.

It began when one evening, Lana and Gay were out on dates and I was alone in the "63rd Street Settlement," which was the 63rd Street apartment we shared. I have experienced loneliness so rarely in my life that I hardly comprehend the idea, but that night, I had something like it.

I had tried to telephone a girl friend, just to chat, but she wasn't in.

So, I tried another friend, and she wasn't there either.

I tried a third, a fourth, and a fifth. Same result.

It was getting creepy. How could everyone I knew all be out at the same time? Had they fallen into *The Void?*

(You know, of course what *The Void* is? No? The Void is when you're standing beside your best friend, and your second best friend comes up and you need to introduce the two of them, and promptly forget both names. Or you go charging into a room to get something, and then can't remember what you went in there for. Or you dial someone on the phone, and when they answer, you've been thinking of something else and can't remember whom you just called. Or the ever-present, you put something down, and a few minutes later, you absolutely for certain know it's there, but you can't find it. All of these are examples of *The Void in Action*.)

Anyway, with all my friends not answering the phone (and this was before caller ID, and everyone answered the phone back then, assuming they were in), this seemed statistically so unlikely that maybe *The Void* was the explanation. It became seriously important to me to hear someone's voice.

My plan was to open the Manhattan phone book, dial any number, and after I heard the person's voice, say that I had dialed the wrong number. That way I would have heard a human voice and I would have had proof that *The Void* hadn't taken over the universe.

Except.

I reasoned that as long as I was calling a stranger, I'd prefer that it be a male voice. I like men.

And as long as it was going to be male, that meant the possibility of romance.

If there was a possibility of romance, it would be so much more convenient for me if he had the same last initial, and that way, if we married, I wouldn't have to change my monograms.

Ah, but as long as he was to have the same initial, why not the same last name? As a practical matter, it would save me a world of inconvenience and paperwork for getting my name changed.

Ah, yes, important considerations.

So, I wouldn't just randomly pick any name from the phone book, it would be a male Henderson.

As long as I was going to pick a guy named Henderson, it might as well be someone nearby. Dating someone from Brooklyn or the Lower East Side would be, quite simply, inefficient.

So, I went to the Manhattan phone book, found a Henderson who lived on the same block that I did (he was on Madison and 63rd, and I was on 63rd at Madison, and the two buildings actually touched.) The name: Duncan Henderson.

I dialed his number. Since no one had answered all evening, I was shocked and taken aback when someone did answer. I was so shocked that I hadn't prepared anything to say, so I blurted out the first thing I could think of: "Is Lana Friend there?"

"No, she's just stepped out for cigarettes, I expect her back in 15 minutes," an attractive, cultured, intelligent-sounding voice answered.

"Oh. Would you tell her that Mary called?"

"Sure, but why don't you call back in a quarter of an hour. I know she'd like to hear from you."

"Okay. Thanks! Bye."

"Bye bye."

How interesting.

The odds of there being a Lana Friend there had to be close to zero. And the odds of a Lana Friend who would be back in fifteen minutes and wanted to talk with "Mary" had to be exactly zero. The guy was playing!

Fifteen minutes later, I called him back. "Is Lana there?"

"I'm so sorry—she's not back yet, which is unusual for her. Can I give her a message?"

We talked for a minute or two more about Lana, and then I said good-bye.

That should have been that. I had gotten my fix, I had talked with another human being, and I had experienced firsthand, convincing proof that indeed, *The Void* hadn't taken over the world.

Except.

A week later, I was on an airplane, flying to London with my girlfriend, Cecily Clark. To make conversation, I told Cecily about the funny conversation I had with a guy who pretended that Lana Friend was staying with him.

Since I had Duncan Henderson's address, Cecily and I figured out that it would be really funny if we each sent Lana Friend a postcard, care of Duncan Henderson. I think the address was something like 699 Madison Avenue.

When we arrived in London, we told our friends there about this funny circumstance, of sending postcards to a phantom person, care of Duncan Henderson. They loved the idea, and we concocted a whole plot around Lana, Duncan, and Mary.

The plot was to unfold as follows, and everyone had to agree to follow the plot. For the next month, everyone, and their friends, were to send postcards to Lana, care of Duncan. They could be chatty or sincere or anything you might say to a pretty good friend, but they were all, in one way or another, to mention Mary. They could say how she was doing, how pleased they were to see her in London, what an adventurous life she was leading, and so on. No one was ever to mention that Mary's last name was Henderson. (My name being Mary Henderson at that point.) They were allowed, however, to mention that I was on my way to Lebanon and then India, both of which were true.

At the end of the month, all communication was to cease.

Cecily's and my next stop was Lebanon, visiting friends we had made there. We told our Lebanese friends about the Duncan Henderson Caper, and they completely got into it. They agreed with the rules of never mentioning a last name for Mary, but they could mention that Nadim Saffouri considered Mary his and was extremely upset that she was going to see Jaghi Singh in Bangalore. Oh, they could also congratulate Lana on having found Duncan and they hoped the two of them would be very happy together. No one was ever to include a return address or any way Duncan could contact the senders of the letters.

According to the rules, they could elaborate in any way they chose about how Nadim had a jealous and violent nature and was known to carry concealed weapons. As an added bit of spice, by the time I was in India and could be sending postcards postmarked India, they could start writing to Lana Friend telling her that Nadim had left for India and they worried that Nadim might kill Jaghi. They could also start complaining about why Lana never answered the letters and postcards.

We and our Lebanese friends laughed ourselves silly over the plot. Meanwhile, I'm writing postcards and eventually letters to Lana, acting as if I'm completely oblivious to Nadim's intentions and just thinking he's a sweet, nice man. But I'm also congratulating her on her engagement to Duncan and saying that if he's everything she says he is, he most be the most wonderful man on the planet.

We tried to imagine what Duncan must be thinking, being on the receiving end of all this. What I did know, even then, was that Duncan was getting a lot of mail from England and Lebanon.

From Lebanon, our next stop was Delhi and then Bangalore. On arriving in Delhi, we told our Delhi friends the plot and the rules, including that in about two weeks, there was to be an utter blackout. The plot, developed further as we went along. We began having friends write to Duncan directly, asking why Lana hadn't answered their letters.

Our Delhi friends even had the idea of writing to Duncan directly, demanding that he put them in touch with Lana or there would be legal consequences.

Meanwhile, I was merrily writing Lana, telling her how happy I was that she had found true love and wishing her well. I also wrote about what an amazing coincidence: Nadim said that he would be traveling to India. I wrote in apparent innocence of what everyone else has been reporting to Lana, that Nadim had gone insane and intended to kill Jaghi.

In Bangalore, the plot continued, with all Cecily's and my Indian friends writing to Duncan and Lana, but by now, the tone had changed from rejoicing over her new found happiness to deep and dark suspicion of why she wasn't answering any of her best friends' letters. They also told her about how Jaghi was taking me elephant hunting and how they weren't sure it was a good idea because Jaghi was known for his temper.

In Bangalore, I wrote how astonishing it was that Nadim had business in Bangalore and wasn't just coming to India, he was actually coming to Bangalore. "Whatever business could he have in Bangalore?" I asked innocently. But by now, the cutoff point was here, and no one in England, Lebanon, or India was to write one word more. I learned later that in fact, none of our dozens of friends who had written to Lana or Duncan broke the cutoff date. From an absolute torrent of postcards and letters, suddenly there was none.

Actually, life came awfully close to imitating art because there was a point when Jaghi did point an elephant gun at me in a fit of anger and probably jealousy because I liked his brother Biri. It was the closest to eternity I've ever come in sixty-nine years. I know what it's like to expect to be dead in a matter of seconds, and the supreme lightness of finding oneself unexpectedly alive.

Back to the Duncan Henderson Caper. Cecily and I did go on the elephant hunt, and as I've hinted, it was not uneventful. However, eventually we returned to New York and often laughed over this fabulous practical joke.

Until.

Until a couple of months later, Cecily Clark's parents decided to put on a small dinner dance for her in Oyster Bay. It was black tie with engraved invitations, and suddenly we got the insane idea, wouldn't it be fun to address one of the invitations to that adorable couple, Duncan Henderson and Lana Friend.

Cecily mailed the invitation, and two days later, got a phone call from a guy with a most attractive voice saying that he was Duncan Henderson, he'd like to accept the invitation, but unfortunately, Lana Friend couldn't accept because she had moved to Anaheim, California.

Cecily called me, and we laughed ourselves sick over this. We were finally going to meet Duncan Henderson. That evening, I looked up Duncan's number in the phone book and called him.

I told him that I had heard from Cecily that he would be attending her party, and I wondered, if we didn't live too far away from each other, if I could get a ride with him to Oyster Bay. He said yes, by all means, but who was he speaking with?

"Mary," I answered. Now "Mary" is the person he had been hearing about as being the center of a whirlpool of international intrigue, danger, and possible murder. Now suddenly this Mary is on the line.

"And your last name," inquires Duncan Henderson.

"Oh, my last name—," I say innocently, with just a moment's dramatic pause, "—Henderson."

"Mary," he says, quite smoothly, I thought, under the circumstances, "I've been having some issues with Lana, and I really need to talk about them with one of her friends. Would you be willing to have a cup of coffee with me tonight, even though it's late?"

I answered, "Sure, I'd love it, as long as you don't live too far away."

"Okay, where do you live?"

I answered, again, all innocence, "27 East 63rd Street." That happens to be in the building that touches the building he lived in at 63rd and Madison.

He had to be shocked. The mysterious Mary has the same last name as he did and lived literally around the corner from him.

*We were on the Assam border, illegally, and got to see troop movements between Red China and India.*

We agreed to meet at a nearby coffee shop, and now it was my turn for surprises. Duncan Henderson was my age, a Yale graduate, 6'2", and had the body of a lifeguard, which in fact was his summer job as a teenager. Further, he was in real estate, and had actually been negotiating with my father over a block of property my father owned near Wall Street!

Truth is definitely stranger than fiction.

During that first coffee date, neither of us admitted that Lana didn't exist. But we did get to talking about other things, and I found that I liked him. Er, a lot. We went out a couple of times, and he actually brought me to Greenwich to meet his parents before the two of us admitted that there was no Lana.

In the next few months I grew to like him enough to bring him to Dublin to meet my family, all of whom adored him. He could talk business with my father and brother, and was generally charming with everyone. He could even charm my aunts, talking about dogs. It even turned out that my aunts knew his mother, since all were active in the Westminster Dog Show.

At this point, I learned what the impact of what I thought was the World's Best Practical Joke had been on him. It was severe enough that I have never played a major practical joke on anyone since. It turned out to be beneficial, but it could have been catastrophic.

The fact is, at the height of the practical joke, he'd be getting eight to ten letters every single day. They obsessed him and he couldn't wait to come home from work at night to discover what was going on that day.

But the difficulty in all of this was, he was engaged to be married. How do you convince a fiancée that all these letters congratulating him on his happiness in finding Lana Friend didn't refer to something real?

His fiancée, who visited him on weekends, couldn't be made to believe that there wasn't a real Lana Friend in his life. How could there not be, with this avalanche of letters and postcards congratulating her on her happiness with Duncan?

The engagement broke up.

If that were the end of the story, I would have thought that through meddling, I had done something catastrophically unforgivable. The mere thought of such a thing has made me forever more tone down my practical jokes.

But it turns out that this wasn't a bad thing. He had gotten engaged because he had been driving when there was a car accident that was severe enough so that the woman he was with was diagnosed at the hospital as never being able to walk again. In an agony of guilt, he proposed marriage to her, saying he would take care of her always. They told their parents, the engagement was made public, and if the Lana Friend letters hadn't happened, he might be married today.

However, a few weeks after they were engaged, she began recovering the ability to walk. And meanwhile, Duncan, who was prepared, out of guilt, to spend his life with the woman he had caused to become an invalid, no longer felt the same crushing obligation once it turned out that, after all, she could walk. He no longer wanted to marry her.

Still, breaking an engagement wasn't easy for him to do. He was having difficulty, trying to bite the bullet. He couldn't just tell her, "I only proposed to you because I felt sorry that you were a cripple," but still, this wasn't the woman he wanted to spend his life with. It was in the middle of this that the Lana letters began arriving.

In the end, the Lana letters caused Duncan's fiancée to break the engagement. She felt that he was lying to her when he said there really, really was no Lana and he had no idea where all these letters were coming from. They had a terrible fight over his "lie," and that was the end of the engagement. Duncan felt the letters were a *deus ex machina,* getting him out of an agonizing difficulty.

He said that the letters were his one escape from this sad and difficult situation. But they also worried him because he felt that there was an imminent murder about to take place, and that he, as the only one who was hearing from all the participants, was also the only one who could put all the pieces together. However, he couldn't do anything about it because there was never a return address or a last name.

He told me he even went so far as to try to contact law enforcement people in India. He really believed that a murder was imminent.

Eventually I confessed my role in the entire thing and both of us admitted that the whole thing had been, for both of us, a high point. We became close enough so that I think our relationship might even have progressed to an engagement. He was there for me when my father died in November; he attended the funeral, supported me through it, but then in January, my life totally changed.

## 1968–1971, New York City, Marriage to Francisco Ayala

I had met Father Ayala at Sally Moore's birthday party the summer before, but there hadn't been much interest on either side. I thought he was fascinating, but I also knew he was both a parish priest and a Dominican monk. However, in January of 1968, he telephoned me to wish me happy new year. We somehow got together and since he had a background in pastoral counseling, he helped me deal with my grief over my father's passing. I found it easy to tell him everything and he seemed kind and soothing.

We began seeing each other in mid-January and got engaged February 13th. The whole thing was so sudden that when I called up my brother Ernest to say that I had gotten engaged, he said, "Wonderful! Put Duncan on the line so I can congratulate him!"

Ooooops!

## Father Ayala Leaves the Church

Francisco's leaving the church was complicated, from my point of view. I'm going to make a great effort to be as objective as I can about it, although in doing so, I will be simplifying and glossing over important points.

Although it appeared to many that I was the cause of Francisco's leaving holy orders, I believe that while I may have been the proximate cause, the ultimate cause was different and more in the spiritual realm. I could say more on this, but he is a public figure, and since he has not chosen to be public about his reasons, I'll respect his privacy.

Somehow, I didn't realize at the time that his leaving the priesthood was as big a deal as I now recognize it to be. Back then, things just kind of happened, and I was swept up in the events without ever stepping back and assessing things. It's amazing how the immediacy of day-to-day events can obscure the big picture.

For the rest of my life I'd every now and then get a clue that this was a big deal because people at parties would come up to me and say they wanted to meet the woman who caused a priest to leave orders. Or once I met a world famous scientist who knew the story and said some flattering things about understanding why Francisco did it. The only thing is, in the end, it wasn't that flattering because I know in my core that I wasn't the real reason he left.

We married on May 27, 1968 after a courtship of three months.

## How the CIA Paid for My Being Courted by a Spanish Priest

The courtship itself had some fun features. Among these, the CIA paid for almost all of it.

You are, I hope, wondering why the CIA would pay for a hotel heiress's courtship?

The answer is, my CIA is the *Cigar Institute of America*. I had written an article for *Cosmopolitan Magazine* on "the Gigi Touch," or how to offer a cigar to a gentleman. Once it was in print, I leveraged that into a glorious, mad scheme in which I proposed to the CIA that they give me a virtually unlimited budget to go to eight of New York's fanciest and priciest restaurants, make myself visible by sending back the finest wines and other attention-getting behavior, and then at the end of the meal, to take out a cigar and smoke it.

By the way, everyone smoked in restaurants then. For younger people, this may be hard to imagine, but there was a time when restaurants were filled with smoke.

I told the CIA I would write about whatever experiences I had, and they could try to place my stories in newspapers throughout the land.

Would you believe, they bought it?

Well, yes!

Francisco and I would go to places like the Four Seasons, send back zillion dollar bottles of wine, explaining that of course we'd pay for it, and then I'd proceed to order the most expensive things on the menu ("What, this caviar is *pressed?* Send it back!") and

*Father Francisco Jose Ayala in his laboratory*

finally, true to my CIA agreement, I'd pull out a cigar and smoke it.

At every restaurant, something amusing would happen. For example, at the Four Seasons, the owner himself came bounding up the stairs toward me when Francisco lit my cigar. (We had, of course, practiced this move to perfection.) I was sure the owner would throw us out, but instead he said, "Madam, I am overjoyed to see such an elegant lady as yourself smoking a cigar. My wife smokes cigars in private and now I will tell her that it is okay to do so in public."

After each restaurant experience, I'd write it up and submit it to the CIA. The PR people at the CIA placed the stories in an ongoing series that was picked up by hundreds and hundreds of newspapers. My temporary boss at the CIA would show me clippings and also lists of the newspapers that were carrying it. I think they got their money's worth, and Francisco and I got to sample (is "pillage" a better word?) Manhattan's fanciest restaurants while having a total blast doing so.

**Marriage to Francisco Jose Ayala**

Francisco and I married at the end of May in a lovely ceremony in the ballroom at Knollwood, the family house in Dublin. My marriage to Francisco was not, however, a happy one. Nevertheless, I'll always be grateful for it because without that marriage, the very best part of my life would not exist, which is my two sons, Francisco Jose Ayala and Carlos Alberto Ayala.

I'm wrestling with how to deal with the question of an unhappy marriage. Philosophically, I am in favor of honesty in an autobiography, but philosophically, I'm also in favor of not wallowing in things that didn't go right or in casting blame. I've made a sincere effort for forty years not to bad-mouth Francisco to his children or, to the best of my ability, to anyone else.

Also, there are a lot of good things to be said about Francisco and the marriage. I admired his intelligence, and I cherished his European approach to child-rearing, which is much stricter and more demanding than the American approach. We saw eye-to-eye as parents on the importance of education, languages, manners, self-discipline, high standards, not making things too easy for children, trying to make sure they weren't spoiled or fussy or entitled. We were fine with the notion of giving the kids small allowances, and I think both of us were more than comfortable with telling the kids that we didn't care what so-and-so's mother or father allowed, we weren't so-and-so's mother or father.

I said on the first page of this autobiography that memory is like a dog that lies down wherever it wants, and right now a memory occurs to me which isn't quite chronological, but it did date to the second year of my marriage to Francisco. It involved one of the most traumatic things that ever happened to me.

## I Break the Law and Risk Jail Time

When Jose was maybe seven or eight months old, we left him for the evening in the care of a babysitter. When we returned, the doorman of our building at 230 Central Park South asked if we were okay and if I needed to sit down.

I had no clue as to what he was talking about, but I soon learned. Jose had been taken to the nearest hospital, Roosevelt Hospital, with burns to his face.

We rushed to the hospital and learned that he had third-degree burns on his face and they were so severe that the eyelashes had come off. The doctor informed us that when burns were this severe, it usually meant blindness.

There's no way to recreate the agony of hearing this, or the agony of the rest of the night. This was a less humane time than today, but they wouldn't even let us stay with our child. The visiting hours were enforced.

By the way, the burns, I was told, came from Jose's having pulled a pan of boiling hot water over himself. To this day I wonder if that's the whole story because I don't think he was tall enough to reach the handle of a pot on the stove.

Anyway, the next day we learned that a doctor had checked Jose's eyes and he wasn't blind, but the injuries were severe enough that he would need skin grafts from his legs, and he'd be hospitalized for a couple of months.

Only he wasn't. I was thinking, as I watched little Jose, used to being nursed, lying on the pediatric bed, his feet and hands tied in a spread-eagle position, unable to see, torn from his home and his parents, and in pain, that whatever his physical injuries, the psychological harm that two months of this would do to him would be even worse.

Then I noticed that even though he was in an isolation ward and we had to don sterile garments and face masks and gloves before coming into his room, the cleaning lady was going from room to room with a mop and no sterile precautions. Jose's rooms had large glass windows and I watched in horror as the cleaning lady, pushing her mop ahead of her, left the room where there was a pediatric diphtheria patient, crossed the hall, entered Jose's room, and started mopping. Although we had to cover every inch of our bodies with sterile garments, this woman was simply going from room to room with no precautions at all. It looked like a guaranteed way to spread infection.

Since burn victims are extraordinarily vulnerable to infection and need to be kept away from the kind of germs the charwoman was bringing in with her mop, this situation was beyond intolerable. I told the hospital doctors that I wanted to take Jose home and away from all this. They said absolutely not and that if I tried I would be jailed for child endangerment.

My next step was to telephone Jose's pediatrician, telling her that I was going to take Jose home. I asked her what I needed to do to prepare our apartment to be as sterile as possible, and would she come by each day to see him.

As with the doctors at the hospital, she informed me that what I was planning was illegal and that I risked jail for doing this. However, if I did do it, she'd do her part. She said the way to prepare the room was to spray it with disinfectant and then cover every surface with commercially

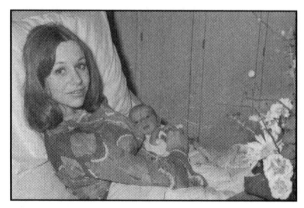

*Mitzi wih baby Jose*

laundered bed sheets, since these would be sterile. She also said to cover the interior of the taxi that we took Jose home in with bed sheets.

I prepared the apartment, and got a sympathetic cab driver to agree to having his cab sprayed and then having the back area draped in freshly laundered sheets. Everything was ready to go except for the question of how to get Jose out of there without officials stopping me. I often think of myself as having the backbone of a limp noodle and I'm basically fearful of authority and, on top of that, I have an almost immeasurable horror of being a lawbreaker. But in this case, with my child's health at stake, I was ready to do whatever it took.

I went to the hospital, and while the cab waited outside, prepared with white sheets covering the inside of the cab and sprayed with disinfectant, I rode up the elevator and got out at the isolation wing of the hospital. There was a Prussian-looking nurse there, guarding the entrance of the wing. This was not visiting hours, but I breezily told her that Dr. Smith had given me permission, and then briskly walked in as if I was supposed to be there.

I went to Jose's room, quickly untied him from the restraints that held his hands and legs, and then scooped him under my dress, put a cape around us both, and waddled out as if I were suddenly nine months pregnant. But just before leaving the room, I told Jose not to cry—that it was the most important thing in the world to be absolutely silent. To this day, I wonder how a preverbal child knew not to whimper or make a sound. It's as if somehow he understood and didn't make a sound.

I marched out of the isolation ward, past the nurse, toward the elevator, all the while praying that Jose would be quiet and that nobody would notice that I had come in not pregnant and was now waddling out about-to-deliver-pregnant.

I was hyper-aware that things could go wrong. What if one of the attending doctors happened to come by? In particular, what if one of the ones who had told me I couldn't do this saw me? What if Jose started crying? What if my face, which I was trying to make look relaxed and pleasant, revealed the anxiety I was feeling inside?

I kept remembering that at least two people had already emphasized that it is literally against the law to remove a child from the hospital without a doctor's consent. I rode down the elevator with several doctors, thinking each second that something could go wrong. Meanwhile,

Joselito was being quiet as a mouse.

I walked through the Roosevelt Hospital lobby, down some steps, and into the waiting cab. Once inside the cab, for the first time in hours I could take a deep breath. We got home, and once home, I called the hospital and told them what I had done. The person I talked to was appalled and made threats, but as I thought would happen, they never followed up.

I held Jose in my arms for the next twelve hours. The pain from his burns must have been ferocious, but from then on, I'd keep him from crying by nursing him whenever he'd start to cry.

Avoiding crying was monumentally important because by now his entire face was covered with thick brown crusts and any movement of his face meant separating the crusts from the recovering skin underneath. Not only would that be painful but it would also increase the scarring.

This story has a happy ending because, when the crusts came off, his face was free of scars. Further, he was essentially completely better in a couple of weeks, as opposed the couple of months that was predicted if he were in the hospital. He also avoided the skin grafts.

The pediatrician said that the speed of his recovery was a miracle, and that being at home must have made an extraordinary difference in the speed of his recovery.

I don't see any debilitating emotional scars in Jose, although I bet there might have been if he had spent two months in the hospital. As it is, for many years, he wanted me to tell him the story over and over again. I bet I've repeated it to him fifty times, if not a hundred, so it did have an impact on him. I'm not quite sure what message he takes from it, but I think it must mean a lot to him that Mommy was ready to risk jail in order to do what was best for him.

# Chapter Five:

# *1971–1988, Davis, California*

By early summer of 1971, we had moved to Davis, California, where Francisco taught genetics at the University of California at Davis. Theodosius Dobzhansky came with us, his wife having recently died from a heart condition.

Now, back to what I was saying about how Francisco and I were in agreement on child-rearing. One of the outstanding areas of agreement was on schooling. Francisco and I shared the attitude that we weren't in the business of making school easy for the kids.

Back in the 1970s, in Davis it was fashionable to keep kids back a year, with the idea that being the oldest in the class meant that the child would have an easier time of it. We on the other hand, rejoiced in having our kids skip grades; we wanted them to stretch and be challenged. We didn't want "soft kids."

*Jose was always tremendously curious*

At one point, our nicknames for the them were "Rough Enough" and "Tough Enough," which was not in sync with most of California's softer approach to child-rearing. I remember when other parents were telling their kids, "It's cold, make sure you wear your hat," we'd be telling the kids, "Don't you dare put on a hat! If you do, you'll grow up soft and need to wear a hat!" I remember one fall and winter, Jose made up his mind that he wanted to wear sandals to school instead of shoes. People reacted with horror to my permitting this, and probably suspected child abuse. I, on the other hand, was thoroughly delighted. I loved it that he was into toughness and wasn't going to be bothered by the cold. The funny thing is, it's only very recently that I've gotten a glimpse into where my own attitude on toughness came from.

The clue came when a couple of weeks ago, I was visiting my New England friends, John and Carol Cabot. My visit was in the dead of winter, 20 degrees outside and six inches of snow and ice on the ground. John Cabot helped carry my suitcase from my car, across the parking lot, and up the path to the stairs leading to the front door of the house. But there was something glaringly wrong with this picture.

In weather so cold that I was hugging my fur coat as close to my body as I could, John Cabot was walking through the ice and snow barefoot.

*Barefoot!*

I don't believe he was showing off; I think he was just expressing his native attitude that being tough is good for character, and it's how one ought to be. He simply took being tough for granted. Maybe this is a New England thing and I, having grown up in New England, unconsciously and unknowingly transmitted this to my kids.

Anyway, Francisco and I were definitely not into coddling the kids. I remember with glee a threat I used to deliver to the kids. "Don't *do* that or you'll grow up fussy." (As in, what could be worse than growing up *fussy?*)

## Prodigies

As I've said, Francisco and I encouraged skipping grades. I'm told that Carlos was the youngest graduate ever of the Davis School system. And Jose was attending university-level math classes when he was in fourth grade. The courses were upper-level university classes and the other students were all math majors at UC Davis.

I remember the professor called me at home one day and said, "Mrs. Ayala, I thought you might like to know what the class with Jose in it is like. I start the hour by going to the board and writing a problem. Jose then raises his hand, gives the answer, and we spend the rest of the hour trying to figure out how Jose got it."

Jose took the SATs when he was twelve years old. The results that came back showed that he scored high enough to be eligible for most of the colleges and universities in the country. I remember the fun of it, when Jose went in to take the exams, surrounded by eighteen-year-olds. He was so small in comparison, and they were amazed that someone so young would be taking the exams. His IQ, according to one test back then was ten points higher than Einstein's, and according to another, something close to 200.

For Jose's entire high school career, his mornings were spent taking classes at the University of California at Davis, and then in the afternoon, he'd bike over to the Davis High School, and do the sports or other age-appropriate things that he couldn't get at the university.

Actually, I am beyond joyous at the program Francisco and I jointly approved for Jose. I think other parents might have simply sent the kid off to university at age twelve, but we were at least as interested in his being a normal (er, at least somewhat normal) boy who could enjoy life and learn the life skills that you learn in high school. As I write this, he's

*Theodosious Dobzhansky, the famous geneticist, with Jose and Carlos Ayala. Dobbie, as we called him, was a dinner guest at least three times a week.*

forty, and I think he's as much a genius at social relations as he is in science and math. If I want insight into what's going on in a relationship that I'm in, Jose (or often Carlos) would be whom I'd go to for the advice that I most believe and trust.

(By the way, I don't know the results of any IQ tests Carlos had, but I do know that in later life, when he was applying to Wharton, his test results were so high that he single-handedly raised the average for his entire class. And as I think I've mentioned elsewhere, he was the youngest graduate of the Davis school district ever. I always felt that both kids were equally bright, but in different ways.)

The funny thing is, from the vantage point of sixty-nine years old, my kids' successes seem to me to be astonishing. But while they were going on, they seemed so normal in the scheme of who they were that I think I wasn't fully conscious, or even half conscious, of how amazing their performances were. I know I was proud of them, but I wasn't keel-over-and-faint proud of them as I am right now, thinking of them.

I started a few pages previously describing my marriage to Francisco. There were a number of good things about the marriage, and most of them center around how he was as a parent. I think that no matter how badly we were getting along (and one woman who interviewed me for a book she was writing about bad marriages said that ours was the worst she had come across after interviewing 200 people about their marriages), we always put the well-being of our kids ahead of our personal dislike of each other.

A perfect example of this was when Carlos was being considered for skipping a grade, Francisco and I were in the middle of a lawsuit against each other and, trust me, there was no love lost between the two of us. However, for Carlos to skip a grade, the school wanted to know that both parents supported it. We sat in the principal's office and put on the best show of being united, loving parents that Hollywood could have imagined. I think both of us have some actor's instincts, and while we didn't overplay it, play it we did!

Here we are in the principal's office, and he's just asked us some detail about Carlos:

Mitzi: "What do you think, dear?"

Francisco: "Yes, that's exactly right. We're both in total agreement."

And then we look at each other and exchange loving glances, followed by us each finding the other's hand and giving a quick surreptitious squeeze.

We colluded to perfection because that was what was needed for the good of our child. This happened during a period in which I think both of us would have sincerely liked to rip the other's lungs out through their throats.

I have many times thought that, if we could have seen eye-to-eye in the rest of our marriage the way we did about our children, there never would have been a divorce. But this was not the case.

My relationship with Francisco wasn't a happy one, but my children were the greatest source of joy to me that I've ever known. Watching them unfold and grow was endless delight.

Jose, for instance, showed all sorts of traits that he still has to this day that play a role in his being a scientist. From infancy, he had a tremendous drive for being orderly. When he was too young even to crawl, I once put him on his stomach on his father's large, flat-topped desk, while I was writing out address cards for people who had asked for reprints of Francisco's articles. When it was time to start dinner, I was about to scoop Jose up in my arms and take him downstairs to the kitchen, when he let me know through the most intense squirming that he didn't want to be picked up.

Curious as to why, I set him back down on the desk. He squirmed over to the twenty or so three-by-five inch cards and arranged them in several rows so they looked neat instead of helter skelter. Once he had finished creating order out of the chaos, he was perfectly content for me to turn him over, pick him up in my arms, and take him down to the kitchen.

When he wasn't old enough to walk, but was old enough to pull himself up to see over the edge of a drawer in a cabinet, he discovered maybe a dozen plastic baby bottles. With tremendous focus and determination, he set about arranging the bottles by color, so that the blue ones were beside each other, and likewise for the yellow ones, and the transparent ones.

Where did this craving for order come from? I didn't teach him because I'm a lot more casual in my approach to orderliness. As far as I could tell, it seemed simply to spring out of his nature. And it stayed with him in childhood and as an adult. I would bet that if you could open his desk drawer today, you would see the pencils all lined up with the nicely sharpened points facing the same way. (I emailed him right after writing the preceding sentence, asking if at this moment the pencils in his desk were all facing the same way. He answered, "Of course.")

I could have worried about obsessive compulsive disorder, but his sense of order didn't take him in that direction. Once things were neat and to his taste, which he achieved quite quickly, he moved on to other things so, on balance, I concluded that being orderly improved his life as opposed to complicating it.

There were all sorts of reasons to think that Jose was smart. In addition to being physically coordinated enough to walk at nine months, he was, as I've already said, preternaturally aware of pattern and order.

He also was capable of spatial reasoning as a toddler that I am not capable of today as an adult. Here's an example: at an age in which young children still love stuffed animals, he wanted me to make him one, but in his case, it was one that he designed himself. He wanted me to sew him a mammoth, a two feet long by one foot high mammoth.

I enjoy sewing, so I was happy to sew a stuffed mammoth for him out of fake fur. I showed him my best effort at drawing a mammoth, which I sketched on some old newspaper. I was planning to use the sketch as a pattern from which to cut out both sides of the future stuffed animal. My expectation was that when I sewed the two sides together and stuffed them with cotton, Jose would have his own "mammoth."

However, when I showed the sketch to Jose, he pointed out that it wouldn't be able to stand. As a two-dimensional figure, it would have only two legs, while he wanted a mammoth with four legs.

I told him I had no idea how to draw the parts of the mammoth that it would take to create a three-dimensional mammoth. I mean, how on earth do you translate a two-dimensional, two-legged drawing into a pattern that creates a three-dimensional stuffed animal that stands on four legs?

Jose's response was to take over and do it for me. He looked at my drawing carefully, and then drew a very strange shape that went in and out in odds ways, and then drew four inch-and-a-half circles and a couple of four-inch cone-shaped things.

I didn't understand what he was trying to do. "What are the circles?" I asked him.

"They're for the bottom of the mammoth's feet," he answered.

"What about the cone-shaped things?"

"When you sew them together, using cream-colored silk fabric, they'll be the mammoth's tusks."

"And what about the rest of the thing you sketched?"

"Cut it out of the same material you'll be cutting out the other two sides of the mammoth, and then, where I show you, sew it to the sides of the mammoth."

"Jose, it will never match up. This can't possibly work."

"Yes, it will."

Following his directions, I cut out my two mammoth-shaped pattern pieces, and then the incomprehensible design that he had just drawn. I would have bet my inheritance that what he had designed wouldn't match up with what I had drawn.

But when I pinned his parts together, every single piece fit perfectly, right down to the bottom foot pads of the mammoth, plus, of course, the tusks. I sewed the thing together, stuffed it, and suddenly, we had a three-dimensional toy mammoth that could stand on its four individual feet.

To this day, I don't understand how he could visualize what the pattern would have to be, and then on top of that, get the sizes right. To this day, I couldn't even start the problem, let alone get it right.

I have trouble imagining that one person in a hundred could translate a flat drawing into a three-dimensional creature, and maybe not one in 10,000 who could draw it the first time and get it to fit, and not one in 1,000,000 who could do it at age three.

Other clues that he was smart included that he also loved math from his earliest childhood. I used to feel that a powerful method of controlling Jose with rewards was to talk math with him. By the way, normal methods for influencing a child had little impact on Jose.

I wish I had a record of how old he was when he learned to tell time—and this was before digital watches, so a kid back then had to tell time from the dial of a watch. However old he was, it was an age when I couldn't conceive that this little tiny child would have an interest in it, let alone be able to get it.

Nevertheless, he wanted to know, so I did my best to explain how there were 60 minutes in an hour, and that when the minute hand was on 12 and the hour hand was on 3, that it's 3:00 o'clock. Then if the minute hand is on 3, it was quarter past 3.

This is fairly abstract for an adult, but what could it mean to a very, very young child. I expected that I was talking over his head and that what I was saying must have been meaningless to him.

I was in for a surprise. "Mommy, does that mean that when the minute hand is at 6, that it's half past? And when it's at 9, it's quarter of?" *What?!*

How could he get something so abstract with so little background? As I said, I no longer remember how old he was, but I do remember that it was years and years sooner than his peers would get it. At the time, it was inconceivable that this little mite could get it.

I also remember teaching him the rule about how to multiply by 9. You know it. It's the one about if you're multiplying a number 1 through 9 by 9, you don't have to memorize the answer. You just subtract one from the number you're multiplying and then calculate the number you would have to add to make 9. Those two numbers are the answer. For example, you're multiplying 5 by 9. You take 1 from 5 and have 4. To make 9, you would need 5. The two numbers are then 4 and 5, or 45. Thus, $5 \times 9$ is 45.

Jose got the principle instantly, just by my telling him. And by the way, I was telling it to him while we were in Madrid, walking along the city street, Gaztambide. I didn't even have to write down what I was telling him—I just told him the rule and he got it and began using it, as we walked along, him giving me examples of how it worked.

I could handle that, but what stunned me was, during this same conversation, he wanted to know what rule you could generate for multiplying 9 by numbers larger than 9. When he had explored this to his satisfaction, he grinned up at me and said, "Oh neat, now let's see if we can generate rules like this for other numbers!"

As we were discussing this, he didn't have a pencil and paper with him, plus there was traffic whizzing by. Even so, he was able to get fairly far in his calculations by doing it all in his head.

I was impressed by his ability to focus. Most of all, I was charmed that he was so attracted to math that, far from being a burden for him, it was a treat.

I mentioned a moment ago that using math as a reward was a way of controlling Jose. When we'd be going on a long car trip, I discovered that the perfect way to keep him engaged for hours was to give him a math book to study. Before I hit on this, nothing ever worked. He was astonishingly difficult to control by the usual methods parents use. I remember reading books on parenting and thinking whoever wrote those books hadn't met my Jose.

Initially, his teachers found him not just difficult to control but impossible. In first grade, his teacher told me after the first couple of days that he was only to be allowed to come to school for an hour a day. "I can control the class, or I can try to control Jose, but I can't do both," she informed me.

I asked what he was doing that was so difficult. I learned that she'd do things like ask the class to line up and follow her. Jose, standing on the other side of the room, would then announce, "No, line up and follow me!" and half the class would follow Jose.

This necessitated a man-to-Mommy talk. I told Jose that this just wasn't working and we needed a different approach. I told him, "You don't have to be like the others, and you don't have to agree with them, but you do have to pretend to be like them."

He bought into this, but there still wasn't much love lost between him and his early teachers.

I wanted Jose to be tested for the gifted and talented program. His teacher told me that Jose was the last child she would ever consider for the program. I think I remember her telling me that she almost fell off her chair with laughter at the mere suggestion of such a ridiculous thing.

Nevertheless, he was tested. The woman who administered the test asked to talk with me about it afterward. She told me that in thirty years, she had never come across anyone, not even adults, who had been able to answer all the questions correctly. Jose, however, had.

She showed me the last question and said that no one had been able to answer it before Jose. I read the question, and even though I'm a Harvard graduate and like math, I couldn't follow what the question was, let alone give an answer. The teacher told me that answering the question involved higher level math that Jose could not possibly have studied yet.

In theory, he should have been unable to get the answer because he hadn't studied the calculus and other types of math needed for solving it.

Since it was certain that he was too young to have studied calculus and the other upper-level math courses he would have needed to answer the last question, the woman asked Jose how he had gotten the right answer.

"It's like a Crazy Eight Ball," Jose told her. "I looked inside my mind, and the answer came floating up."

By the way, this wasn't a multiple choice question. It's one that had a precise number for an answer, such as (although this wasn't it) 4289.122. It's not one that a person could possibly get by guessing.

I'm struck that he described the answer as "floating up," because Einstein used to say that answers came to him in such a form that he knew the answer in his mind before he had the words for it.

Jose had something else in common with Einstein. Both spoke late. Jose didn't speak a word until he was two years and nine months old,

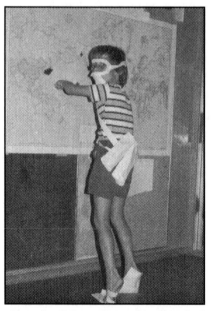

*Jose made paper "goggles," "oxygen mask and tanks," and "flippers" in preparation for "diving" into the Pacific Ocean. This was in the family room of our home at 747 Plum Lane in Davis, California.*

causing his father and me to worry that he might be deaf. I suppose in more modern times, as opposed to the early 1970s, we would have packed him off to a specialist to find out what was wrong.

I'm glad we saved ourselves the time and money because he eventually developed into a gifted speaker. I've since learned that many scientists who have unusual mathematical gifts speak late. A theory for why this is so is that the math-processing part of their brains is so large that it crowds out some of the language-processing parts.

Looking back on what Jose was like, it's clear to me now that I had a prodigy on my hands. Yet while Jose was growing up, I think I was surprisingly close to oblivious of the fact. I was more interested in playing with him, seeing who his friends were, and just enjoying his being a boy. Whatever he did simply seemed normal for him, and therefore, unsurprising.

As an aside, as I look back on my life so far, I'm struck by how often things that seem to me to be amazing today, didn't seem so at the time. They were just part of daily life as it unfolded, and it takes distance to see them in context.

Carlos was in his own way, equally amazing. I have a lot to say about this, and I'll say it in a moment, but first, a quick story about Carlos' name. On my side of the family, Carlos has a great, great, great, great, great grandfather (that's five greats), Baron Carl Christian Josias Bunsen (August 25, 1791, to November 28, 1860). I admired von Bunsen enormously, for many reasons which I read about in the *Life and Letters of Baroness Bunsen*. He was brilliant, a world renowned scholar, a family man, and generally embodied goodness. That plus he had what has to have been one of the world's most romantic stories.

Carl Bunsen was the son of a landless farmer, but early showed signs of academic brilliance. He studied, as a boy, Hebrew, Arabic, Persian, Norse, and later wrote three volumes on hieroglyphics. Because of his brilliance, he was chosen to be the tutor of William Blackhouse Astor, John Jacob's son, during the young man's grand tour of Europe.

However, when they were in Rome, the younger Astor received word that his father had died, and he had to return home. Carl was left stranded in Rome but his brilliance quickly landed him a job as secretary to the Prussian envoy to the Papal Court, Barthold Niebuhr.

At this point, one of the great heiresses of England, Frances

Waddington, was traveling with her mother in Rome as part of the Grand Tour, something fashionable ladies did when they finished school. Carl and Frances came across each other at the Colosseum, and since Carl knew so much about it, he was an entrancing guide for Frances.

Initially, both understood that the social gulf between them was, in principal, unbridgeable. He was the son of a peasant and she was an aristocratic heiress. She was unthinkably wealthy, while his father had been so poor that he had to give up farming and join the military. Also, at that time, the prejudice against international marriages, except in the case of kings, was greater than the prejudice against racial intermarriage was in the 1950s. People referred to the results of international marriages as "mixed breeds" that didn't belong to any world.

Nevertheless, the two fell deeply in love. For Frances's mother, Georgina Mary Ann Port Waddington, this was a catastrophe. How could she let her daughter marry the son of a penniless farmer? On the other hand, how could she destroy her daughter's happiness?

She went to Niebuhr and asked his advice. Niebuhr answered that Bunsen's character and intelligence was worth more than any amount of money in a bank, and that the marriage should proceed. In July 1817, it did.

Bunsen's diplomatic career skyrocketed. He had become close friends with Frederick William IV, the Prussian king, after the king visited Rome. People said of the relationship that the king showered Bunsen with every possible recognition other than adopting him as his son!

Years later, when the king needed to appoint an ambassador to the Court of St. James, he would have liked to appoint Bunsen, but protocol dictated that he appoint someone with a noble title. To do less would be an insult to Queen Victoria.

To get around this problem, the King did something unique in all of diplomatic history: he offered the Queen three nominees, Prince so-and-so, Count so-and-so, or the commoner, Carl Bunsen. Bunsen's reputation for brilliance, charm, and sagacity was well-known by Queen Victoria, and she chose him, a commoner, for the ambassadorship.

It was a moment of triumph for Bunsen. The night before he was to present his credentials to the queen, he wrote to his mother-in-law, to thank her for entrusting her daughter to him twenty-five years before, saying that he hoped that today, he had justified Mrs. Waddington's faith in him back then.

What a love story! Rich heiress and penniless scholar find true love and happiness! I have two marble statues, one of Mrs. Waddington and one of the baron. I hope they stay in the family a long, long time.

Well, Dear Reader, this has been a long diversion, but it's family lore, and I wanted you to know about where Carlos' name came from. I wish I knew stories like this from my mother's side.

Back now to the focus on Carlos. A favorite memory I have of him is when he was not yet able to walk and probably not yet able to crawl, he made friends with a stray cat.

What astonished me about this relationship was that he demonstrated an empathy that seemed (and seems) preternatural. While still in his high chair, he'd hide little bits of chicken or whatever other food he could under the rim of his plate and then when the cat was near, he'd feed the cat.

How could an infant in a high chair know that the cat would be hungry and be aware enough to save food for it?

When I'd set Carlos down on the green couch in our living room, he wasn't old enough to crawl, but he was nevertheless able to lift the cat up beside him. He did it with the gentleness of a veterinarian. I would expect a child to pick a cat up roughly, or by its ears, or in one way or another, to cause discomfort to the cat. Carlos had such perfect empathy that he did it just right, although to the best of my knowledge, he'd never seen anyone handle or feed a cat. It seemed innate. As an adult, Carlos still seems to have extraordinary empathy.

I was also charmed by how he acquired language. I remember once when he was still a toddler, he asked for a "Kleeneck." He had obviously generalized the rule that if you want to make something plural, you add an s and if you want to make something singular, you take away the s. "Kleenex" to his ear must have sounded as if there were an s at the end of it, so if you want just one of these things, you naturally ask for a Kleeneck.

Both kids had a lot of fun with going to "Yourami" when we told them that we'd be going to "Miami." The also loved to talk about how a door cannot be ajar. A jar is a jar, not a door.

But back to Carlos and his unusual abilities in relating to animals:

I have photographs of butterflies landing on him, and also one with a sparrow in his hands.

How did Carlos happen to have a sparrow in his hands? The family was spending a few days in Washington, DC. In 1976, when Carlos was only four and a half years old. While in front of, I think, the Lincoln Memorial, Carlos asked if it was okay to catch a bird.

We knew that it was impossible for a child of four to run after a bird and catch it. "Sure," I said. "Go ahead," Francisco said. A minute or so later, Carlos appears with the bird nestled in his hand. It was unbelievable. No one can just catch a bird in his bare hands.

I asked Carlos how he had done it, and he said something that didn't make sense to me, something about sneaking up on it. Still, I have the photograph of him with the bird. And by the way, it was a healthy bird because when he let it go, it flew away.

(Funny, after I wrote that, I asked Carlos if he remembered catching the bird, and if so, how he did it. Carlos did remember, and his answer was that he just very carefully snuck up behind the bird and grabbed it. But the thing is, normal people aren't able to do this. They just aren't.)

On that trip he did something else that was memorable. While we were visiting the aquarium, it happened that a local television crew was doing a live remote from there and the host, on camera, was talking about the fish in the tank behind him. Before we could stop him, Carlos walked up to the host and began telling him, occasionally turning to the camera, about the fish that the host and the camera were looking at. Carlos had been studying fish on his own, so he, with the aplomb of a little broadcaster, simply shared his knowledge with the host and the camera.

The host was obviously charmed. He interviewed little four-year-old Carlos with the sort of seriousness he would have used when interviewing an adult. Little Carlos responded with equal seriousness and I, who later had a career as a TV hostess, can say that Carlos probably gave the guy the human interest, attention-getting interview that a TV host dreams of.

Where did Carlos get the instinct to do this? He wasn't much beyond the toddler stage. It's been a gift that stayed with him because to this day, he is remarkably good at explaining things with poise and clarity. As far as I can see, he is devoid of the kind of stage fright or fear of public speaking that most people have.

He also had a gift for business. During a time when I think I was paying five cents an hour for chores, Carlos got a couple of honey bee hives, and made something over $300 per year from the honey he got from the hives.

I remember one day he got stung several times on the face, including on the lip, and there were tears in his eyes. I expressed surprise because I can't remember ever seeing either of my children cry. He explained that it wasn't that his face hurt (although it must have) but because he was afraid his father would make him stop having the hives.

He got through that particular episode, but I learned just recently, from his wife Gea, that on another occasion later on, his father did catch him with bee stings and did end his career as a beekeeper. Carlos had just been stung numerous times and to hide this from his father, had hid under the covers in his bed. His father, noticing that Carlos was in bed during the day, came into the room, uncovered the situation, and got rid of the bees.

*Carlos caught this bird in his bare hands. I thought it must have been injured or something, but when I asked him to let it go, it just flew away. He said he held it gently, as you would a butterfly.*

I had a moment during Carlos's beekeeping period that made me at least temporarily lose my enthusiasm for beekeeping. When a wild hive swarms, this is an exciting time for beekeepers. There are beekeepers everywhere who would like to capture the swarm, so on the extremely rare occasion when a swarm lands on one's property, it's time to call the county extension people to let them know the excellent news that a wild swarm is available.

One summer evening, a wild swarm arrived on one of the trees at the front of our house at 747 Plum Lane. We called a county extension agent and had the privilege of watching how tame the swarming bees were and how easily he could put the bees into a sack and take them away.

The kids and I watched and it should have been an awesome experience.

Er, it wasn't.

The bees weren't in an angry mood and it seemed safe to be ten feet or so away to watch. It's true, they were pacific, but that didn't stop one of them from becoming exploratory.

*While visiting the National Aquarium at the Commerce Department during the summer of 1976, we happened on this TV crew, filming for the evening news. Carlos walked up to the interviewer, and began explaining about fish, including that they had gills and could breathe underwater. Now and then, he'd look at the camera, letting the viewers in on this important information. Carlos was four and a half years old.*

I was wearing long trousers, and a bee somehow got under my pant leg and began crawling up my leg. I couldn't brush it off or defend myself in any way because I knew that if I scared it, its instinct would be to sting.

The thing kept crawling and crawling. I could feel each of its little insect legs as the bee progressed up mine. In horror, I felt as it got closer and closer to where I would least like it to be.

When it got there, it stopped. *Eeeeek!*

I told the county extension guy my problem, and he had no idea what to do either. Not being able to think of anything else to do, I just stood there, very, very, very still.

Time dilates at moments like this. I think three years went by.

But more likely it was sixty seconds. Eventually, the bee started down my other leg, reached the cuff and daylight, and finally flew away.

In the end, I still like bees, but that's an experience I'd just as soon not repeat.

When Carlos had to give up his beekeeping business venture, he substituted another that wasn't entirely problem free either. Some wretched awful person gave Carlos a female boa constrictor, and someone equally awful and wretched gave his friend David Nielsen a male boa. The two youngsters, probably age ten, figured that if you put the two together, a blessed event might occur.

I didn't know about this plan at the time, but what I did know was that Carlos all of a sudden desperately wanted, as a Christmas present, an incubator for quail eggs. At his request, I got him one that would hatch thirty eggs at a time.

I didn't know what was going on until after the fact, but Carlos and David had timed the hatching of the thirty quail eggs to coincide with the time when the baby boa

*Carlos caught this tiger swallowtail butterfly with his bare hands. It stayed with him for a couple of days*

constrictors would hatch (although his snakes were viviparous, so hatch isn't the correct word). Carlos had figured out that these darling little birdies were just the right size to make a meal for a baby boa constrictor.

I'm scared of snakes to begin with and having two adult boa constrictors and maybe sixty or seventy baby ones in my home was not something that appealed to me greatly. However, Carlos was able to sell them to local pet stores for $50 each and again he thoroughly upset the wage scale that I had for paying for chores.

Actually, although I once had a genuine phobia of snakes, I'm now pretty well able to tolerate them. It was Carlos who cured me. He did it in the following way.

He'd have a snake in his hands and he'd be standing maybe twenty feet from me. He'd explain that it wouldn't hurt me, and I was to come gradually closer but the moment I felt uncomfortable, I was to stay still until I had adjusted to being that close. In the space of maybe half an hour, I was able to touch the snake, and all the while Carlos was keeping up a steady stream of, "You can do it, it's okay, it's not going to hurt you," and so on.

How did Carlos know, without reading books on it or taking a course, how to get me over my terror of snakes? But he did. Carlos was a "Mommy Whisperer."

Actually, there have been many times where I felt my children were the grown-ups and I wasn't. I'd often ask them for advice and the reason I did it was that I felt they had better answers than I did. I still feel that way. Nothing has changed. They're smarter than me.

A couple of years ago, I asked Carlos, "Did you and your brother mind not having a grown-up for a mother?" He answered, "No, we didn't mind. We love you just the way you are."

For me, being the mother of Jose and Carlos was the best gift that life could offer me. There were so many fun parts to being their mother.

For example, they each had their own rooms, but I turned a two-tier bunk into something we called the "Dreamland Express" that both of them used. I got a neighborhood kid who was good with woodworking to make a shell over the bunk bed in the form of a London Bus. We painted it bright red and then I cut out yellow felt letters that spelled out the name DREAMLAND EXPRESS. The kids could crawl through the windows of the bus to get into their beds. I think it was the marvel of the neighborhood.

I also had the bus traveling on a "road" which was painted in curves across the floor to a "stop light" that I painted on the room's wall, and beside the "stoplight" was "the Magic Story Telling Tree." I made it using paint and green felt. At bedtime, we would sit under the Magic Story Telling Tree and I'd read them stories.

*Carlos and Jerry Marston.*

An arch-favorite of both kids was *Good Night Moon*. The kids loved seeing what changes they could find from page to page.

I know a lot of moms read poetry to their kids, for instance Robert Louis Stevenson poetry or nursery rhymes. My kids were perfectly immune to nursery rhymes or poetry. There was simply no traction with them. Possibly this was because I never learned to resonate to nursery rhymes or poetry either, and therefore wasn't able to transmit whatever is magical about nursery rhymes.

*Carlos the Snake Whisperer.*

Jose told me that years later, when he was a proctor at Harvard, he and his fellow proctors were reviewing the case of an undergraduate who was "a perfect Christopher Robin." Jose had no idea what they were talking about. His fellow proctors were aghast! "What, you don't know who Christopher Robin is? Everyone knows who Christopher Robin is!"

Nope. Not if you had Mitzi Ayala for a mother. Actually, to this day I don't know who Christopher Robin is. I've picked up over the years that he's an A. A.. Milne character, but as to what his personality would be or what someone who is a perfect Christopher Robin would be like, I have no idea.

Both kids were sociable creatures and would often bring home friends. I used to serve a snack that turned out to be popular with the neighborhood kids, and I think it earned me a reputation among their mothers. The snack, which the neighborhood kids helped invent, was ground up cashews and dried fruit, such as figs, raisins, and apricots. When this mixture was whirled in the Cuisinart, the result was a gooey paste which, when dropped in spoonfuls and then rolled in shredded coconut, yielded an unusually yummy morsel.

The neighborhood kids had all helped with the "discovery" of this mixture, suggesting we add this or that to it. When we were done, I told them that since this was new, we needed to name it.

I carefully explained to them that the goal of the name was that when their moms heard what they served at Jose and Carlos's house for snack, they (the mothers) would all feel inadequate and have to serve fancier snacks themselves.

The kids totally got into the goal. After many attempts, we settled on the perfect name: *Pork Chops and Caviar.* They all swore that when their parents asked them about their day, and what was served for snack at the Ayala's, they would truthfully answer that snack at the Ayala house was Pork Chops and Caviar. It's just that our "Pork Chops and Caviar" wasn't exactly what their parents thought it was.

An ongoing relationship during this period was my friendship with Father Antonio Moreno. I adored him in ways that had a harmonic back to the time when my father was still alive. As with my biological father, Father Moreno's favorite hobby was photography.

I believe he was also a monk and, as a monk, there was no way he could afford the cost of a model. I used to pose for him, and it was sort of a recreation of my childhood experience of having my father's attention when he was taking photographs of me. In the end, this comfort with the camera helped my television career enormously, but I'll get to that later.

Father Moreno used to visit the family at least once a month. I so looked forward to seeing him because it meant time with a good and kindly man who valued me. I had something to give him (posing), and he had the world to give me, in the form of gentle kindness. Without him and Dobzhansky and Fran DuBois, I wonder what would have become of me.

Sometime around this phase of my life (actually, it had to be 1974), a trick knee that had always bothered me was giving me increasing

*At night, I would read Jose and Carlos stories under the Magic Story Telling Tree, and then put them to bed in the Dreamland Express.*

trouble. I used to be able to push it back into it's groove, but one day, when it had slipped out and I gave it an almighty shove to get it back, something went wrong. There was a tearing feeling and then, in addition to ferocious pain, I was no longer able to bend the knee.

I learned later that I had split the cartilage in my left knee and it had folded up underneath itself, forming a wedge that kept the knee from bending. Surgery cured the problem, but I remember feeling frantic from pain before the operation. Since then, something neat happened. My trick knee was cured, and that meant a whole world of mobility that I hadn't known before.

Before, I had always been slightly afraid of its giving way at an inopportune moment, like if I were standing near the edge of a cliff or climbing a ladder. Now, I could do everything without fear of having my knee buckle. My knee has not given me a day's problem since then.

I took up jogging, and have kept that up pretty much every day since then—except today, instead of jogging, I do ballroom dancing. But I have been into exercise ever since.

During one of those jogs back in the 1970s, I had something close to a mystical experience. I had been running longer and farther than normal, and suddenly the flowers that I was passing began to glow with the most enchanting, dazzling radiance. They had the beauty, I swear, of the Holy Grail. At the time, I was even thinking of the Holy Grail. And

*Kids as magicians*

then a voice asked me if I would like to know the nature of good and evil.

I allowed as I would, yes.

The voice told me, "Good is that which feeds on happiness and growth and healing. Evil is that which feeds off of pain and suffering and stunting of growth."

The experience was so gorgeous and it seemed so enlightening that the hope of getting it again kept me jogging for years.

And then one day, years afterward, I again during a jog found that the flowers I was passing by were beginning to glow like the Holy Grail. A voice inquired if I would like to know the meaning of life.

"Well, yes!"

The voice told me, "It's to give and receive love."

Years after that, I had one more experience, and have never had one since. The third time, when the flowers I was running by began to glow with their magical colors, the Voice asked me this time if, now that I knew the meaning of good and evil, and now that I knew the meaning of life, would I like to know the purpose of life.

Again, yes, I would, thank you very much!

"The purpose of life," the Voice responded, "is to serve one another."

I'm pretty sure that these experiences are just examples of the runner's high, but having a chance to learn the nature of good and evil, and the meaning and purpose of life seems like a worthy thing to me. I'll take it.

I'm not sure when the following happened, but it was during this time period. I had a dental emergency that was so traumatic that to this day, I still have a hyper-sensitive tooth that always feels as if it's just on the edge of hurting. It doesn't actually hurt, but it's as if all the nerves are primed to be too sensitive. Several times a year, I probe that particular

*Mitzi Perdue, photograph by Father Moreno.*

tooth with my tongue, just to assure myself that it's okay. In fact, I did it just now.

But what's curious about this is, the dental emergency didn't happen to my tooth. It was Francisco's. He had had a root canal during the day and had been feeling really bad all evening. By 2:00 a.m. he was in such agony that I was wondering if someone could die of pain.

His face had turned so white with pain that I felt I could see the skeleton underneath. Today, we would have gone to a hospital emergency room, but back then, in the country, and not near a hospital, we were on our own. Something desperately needed to be done.

I went to my sewing machine, removed the needle from the sewing machine, having decided on that kind of needle because it's sharp, tough, and has a flat edge at the top that I could use as a handle. Francisco drank some brandy, and then using the needle, I "operated."

It took half an hour, but using the sewing machine needle as a "drill," I scraped and scraped and scraped with the goal of removing the filling so that the pressure would be released.

Each scrape was agony for Francisco, but it was also agony for me because I could so empathize with him, knowing that unbearable pressure on his nerves was being added to with each one of my scrapes. It may have been the longest and most unpleasant half hour of my life. I kept at it because giving up wasn't an option, and I could see I was making progress in scraping through the filling

Then suddenly, I broke through the filling and there was an explosive puff of a perfectly ghastly, unimaginably fetid odor. This ended the pressure, and with it, the torture we both were suffering. A dentist fixed Francisco's tooth the next day, but today, thirty-five or so years later, I can still sense in my own mouth which one it was in Francisco's.

By the way, this may sound like the interaction of a loving couple who adored each other. Actually, we couldn't stand each other, but I had enough respect for his humanity to suffer at seeing him suffer.

Sometime around 1978 Francisco had a sabbatical year, and decided that the family would spend it in Madrid. I highly endorsed this, since I thought the chance for the kids to become totally fluent in Spanish was not to be missed. At the time, Carlos would have been seven and Jose nine.

For me, the time in Spain was among the happiest in my life. (My time with Frank Perdue and our two families was the happiest time of my life.) The ingredients of it were what I imagine life might have been like 100 years ago. Francisco's family embraced me and it was the sort of thing that when Jose had a cold, I'd get phone calls from five different family members each day, worrying about him. I had simply never experienced such caring and such closeness.

Several times a week, the brothers and sisters, including Francisco and I would get together either to eat at sister Maria Rosa's and brother-in-law Gerardo Gil's house. The assistenta Maruja would have spent most of the day preparing the many-course meal, and each morsel was admired and praised. It was relaxed and caring and full of interesting conversation, usually about food or culture.

After the meal, we'd sit in the living room and often the guys would talk politics and the women would sit quietly and sometimes embroider. It's hard to express why this was so enjoyable, and by women's lib standards, it must seem appalling. But for me, it was enchanting. There was nothing competitive, just appreciation of who we were and what we were about. It was simply a relaxed state of highly enjoyable being. I loved my time in Spain.

Since I was so happy, I've wondered since why I haven't tried to recreate it. I guess the answer is, happiness isn't all there is. Maybe it's that there was an element of infantilism to it, an absence of effort and self-expression. Even though mightily enjoyable, it wasn't complete.

In my case, I need to feel active and that I'm expressing myself through activity. I was amazingly happy there, but I wouldn't want to go back to that life because I wasn't using whatever abilities I have. For me, lasting happiness has to include using the abilities you have at their highest level in a cause you believe in. There has to be the possibility of success, but it has to involve effort and striving.

Speaking of effort and striving, in Madrid, I had an "attitude experience" that has influenced me ever since. It's one that makes me forever admire that great late twentieth century philosopher, Miss Piggy.

When Miss Piggy is about to go on stage in front of an audience, she pauses for a second, looks in the mirror, preens, and then announces, "I feel beeyootiful!" Then, shoulders back, head held high, she swoops onto the stage to makes her grand entrance.

My own Miss Piggy Enlightenment came one day when I was walking up the Gran Via in Madrid, feeling tired, hungry, lonely, unfashionably dressed, and in short, the essence of an ugly American.

This attitude was definitely not working for me, so what to do?

Attitude change needed! Miss Piggy to the rescue! I decided that I was a movie star in disguise.

I stood up straighter, shoulders back, head erect, with posture that I imagine I would use if I were royalty reviewing the troops. My walk, I hoped, was a cross between a most restrained and lady-like version of both a model on a catwalk and Marilyn Monroe.

Suddenly the Diane von Furstenberg black dress that had seemed so out-of-place a moment before felt like an amazing and gorgeous fashion statement. I felt as if I were radiating glamour from every pore, and that every cell in my body was vibrant and enchanting! I felt my face transforming and then a gracious smile was impossible to suppress!

*The Spanish artist, Joaquin Pacheco, took these photographs. I always thought he would become famous, but as of 2010, he apparently hasn't.*

The results were stunning. As I progressed along the Gran Via, heads turned—all of them. It's as if I had a small force field surrounding me in which people wouldn't get too close, but they were all staring, just as if I really were a movie star in disguise. When I asked for directions for a store four blocks away, the guy I was addressing bowed and said he would be honored if I would allow him to show me the way.

It was amazing. From one second to the next, I went from a dowdy, frumpy ugly woman to a head-turning movie star. It was memorable. And enlightening. The Buddhists say, "Attitude is everything," and experiences like that one make me believe it. I was the same person, wearing the same clothes, but with a different posture, gait, expression, and attitude, I became a different person.

## 1983–1988, Single in Davis

Francisco and I were married from 1968 to roughly 1985. I'm a little unclear about exactly which year it ended because our divorce was bifurcated. The actual divorce, leaving him free to marry Hanna, which he wanted to do quickly, happened before the property settlement. I think all aspects of it were over by 1985.

When Francisco and I separated, we had joint custody and, again, even though we had legal battles with each other, to my knowledge, both of us enforced the other's behavior rules. Neither kid could ever go to the other parent and say, "Daddy lets me do this" or "Mommy lets me do that." I found him reasonable and accommodating and couldn't have asked for more in our joint custody arrangements.

I know women are frequently unhappy about being divorced. For me it began a period of euphoria that has never stopped. I would describe my life as basically fabulously happy from the day we ended our marriage until today. There can be times of feeling down, such as after Frank's death, but with the exception of that, the background is basically upbeat and full of rejoicing. On a scale of one to 10, with 10 being the happiest possible, I would describe my life as routinely somewhere around a 9 to a 9.5.

## What You Won't Read in This Autobiography

This is a side note, but it has to do with what I write in this autobiography. I know the commercially successful autobiographies have plenty of dirt and wallow in the things that have gone wrong and the terrible mistakes the author made. Here would be the place for me to talk about why my marriage to Francisco broke down, which it did almost within hours of our wedding. However, I'm not capable of doing that. I'm not into wallowing. It's almost my religion to be upbeat, and as someone who enjoys being happy, I don't think I'm capable of focusing on the bad things that have happened to me.

In fact, I don't think you'll be reading a lot of examples here of when I fell on my face. It's partly because I almost don't process this. I always wanted to emulate Babe Ruth's approach to life. When someone asked the Sultan of Swat what he was thinking about when he struck out, he answered simply, "I think about hitting home runs."

I think either through habit or wiring, I'm given to thinking about hitting home runs rather than about striking out.

I imagine a psychologist could read this and talk about my being in denial. However, my view is that life is short, and you have a choice of focusing on the wonderful or the horrible. I actually can't understand why people would voluntarily focus on the horrible. For free-floating wallowing in the bad things of one's life, why would anyone put one's energy and focus there? By the way, in the case of something like grieving for a death or being anxious about a loved one's health, I know there's no choice. I'm only talking about when you do have a choice, such as dissecting a rancid marriage.

That makes me think of something else. I don't do guilt either. I think that whatever I've done, I did my best, given my abilities and the information I had at the time. I don't ask myself to do better than my best, so if something didn't work out for the best, well, that's the universe at work, it's not something I can feel guilty about.

That may make this biography less interesting, but it will make it more true to who I am and what I am about. That's why I'm almost incapable of talking more about why my marriage to Francisco didn't work out. Oh, and there's another factor. No matter how unhappy the marriage, and no matter how much we came to dislike each other on a personal level, I still have enough respect for Francisco Ayala to believe that washing our dirty linen in public was and is unthinkable. And besides, given that he did such an excellent job in producing such wonderful children, my overall attitude is gratitude.

Actually, that's not exactly right. My real attitude comes from *Fiddler on the Roof*: "May God bless and keep the Tsar, far away from us!"

Well, Dear Reader, back to the story.

Being divorced meant an explosion of career success for me. Part of this came about because of overcoming shyness. While Francisco and I were married, I had developed an almost pathological shyness. Heck, it wasn't "almost," it was pathological.

I was so shy that it was difficult for me to use the telephone. I remember, when I had to make a phone call to one of my kids' teachers, I'd be sitting on the edge of our bed, rehearsing each word, aware that I could handle the first few words, but then worrying what I would say in response to what the person on the other end of the line would say next. I was afraid I'd say something dumb or that they wouldn't understand what I was saying or that maybe I wouldn't be able to answer anything at all. I'll have more to say on this in a moment when we get to an organization that changed my life, the Business and Professional Women's Clubs.

It's as if the minute Francisco and I separated, a spell was broken and my self-confidence began to return. I felt pretty much ready to take on the world. But to explain all this takes a very long, as in several-page, digression. It has to do with my career as a rice farmer, and how it progressed to a career in television, radio, newspapers, and extensive public speaking.

## Well, Yes, I Really Was a Rice Farmer

Here I need to jump back to 1974, which was the beginning of my career as a rice farmer. Being a rice farmer was a somewhat solitary occupation and I rarely had to speak to or be with more than one person at a time.

I got into this because I bought agricultural land with some of the money inherited from the sale of the Sheraton chain. Before buying the land, I spent several years auditing courses at the University of California at Davis, learning about such things as agronomy, rural appraisal, and agricultural accounting. I also tried to learn as much as I could about farm management. I'd spend days with different farmers, and more days with the county extension agents, looking at land and learning the pros and cons of each piece.

Each night, I'd write notes on everything I'd seen and heard or studied, and by the end of this, I had something pretty close to a book on rural appraisal. By the end of this process, I think I could have written a doctoral dissertation on land values. It got so that one of the land-tax guys in Sacramento would regularly ask my opinion on the value of parcels of agricultural land that he was appraising.

I bet I did in depth analyses of thirty-five different farms before finally selecting one. I was picky because I believed that good farm land rarely changed hands, and that generally, it was the lemons that came on the market.

For example, I remember a piece of property that looked wonderful and passed the thirty criteria on my checklist. The soil was class one and "so deep you could dig it with your fingers all the way down to China." The usual weed problems were manageable, the water rights secure, its production record beyond excellent, and the walnut trees in the orchard were at peak production and disease free. It was a beautiful piece of property, with a gorgeous river frontage. I lusted after this farm.

I was about to make an offer on it, but decided to check with one more expert. I had noticed that the riverbank on the far side had a new reinforced embankment, and I wondered why. I asked a guy from the Army Corps of Engineers to come have a look at it with me.

We stood on the property, looking across the river at the construction on the far side. The Army Engineer explained to me that the reinforced embankment had been constructed because the river had just slightly changed its course, as rivers will do. Unfortunately, the new circulation pattern meant that there would be a new flooding pattern.

While this farm had never been flooded in the past, we could expect that roughly one year in five, this farm would be under water. The flooding, in addition to destroying that year's crops, would bring in noxious weeds that would take five years to bring under control, and a severe weed infestation can quickly cause a farm to become uneconomical.

In other words, this farm had now become a lemon. The real estate agent had told me the farm was for sale because the owner was having marital difficulties. I suspect the real reason had more to do with the river's changed course.

Eventually I bought a rice farm in the Natomas area of Sacramento. It proved to be excellent on all counts, and I got it at a fabulous bargain because there was a monumental difficulty attached to the title, but one that I could afford to deal with. The land was jointly owned by a syndicate of twenty-eight teachers, and each one of them had to sign the land sale document. They had been disagreeing with each other for years, and during that time, the land hadn't been cared for. It was a fixer-upper and getting title was a process that took months and months, and until the last person signed, I never knew if I would get the property. But dealing with these hassles meant I got an excellent piece of property at an almost give-away price.

Since I wasn't going to farm the land myself, I also wanted to make sure that I got a good tenant. My approach was to ask all the landowners I knew who were the best three tenant farmers in the area were. I got dozens of names, but one name kept turning up on every list: Fran DuBois.

## Fran DuBois, My Anti-Role Model

I arranged to meet him and asked, before I made an offer on the Natomas property, what he thought of it, and would he farm it. He agreed and he became, other than Frank Perdue, the best friend I ever had. He was also terribly important to me at the time because he helped rescue me from the emotional devastation I felt after Theodosius Dobzhansky's death. (Dobie, as everyone called Dobzhansky, had been an emotional life-line for me, and I hardly knew what to do with myself after his death.) Fran was warm and kind and endlessly understanding. As with Dobie, I always felt I could be myself with him and didn't have to be on guard.

Fran had many, many things going for him, in addition to being the best tenant in three counties. He was a good and decent man, but on top of that, he had an IQ over 200. He was one of the forty original Whiz Kids who were used to calibrate the Stanford Binet IQ tests. I believe Washington SyCip and possibly Murray Gell-Mann might have higher IQs, but I'm not sure.

He was wincingly honest, far-sighted, and I felt that walking the rice paddies and listening to him talk had to be among the great pleasures that life has afforded me. Listening to him gave me the same feeling of awe that exploring Chartres Cathedral gave me. His intelligence was endless and monumental. The eight years when we worked together were for me, one of life's greater treats.

I adored Fran, but he became a role model for what I didn't want to make of my own life. He had these fabulous gifts, but he used to describe himself as "the World's Greatest Underachiever." I've sometimes wondered if fear of failure was what caused him not to make use of his gifts.

He told me that his goal in life was to write a book that would be his gift, in gratitude for the good fortune of having the IQ that he had been granted. He wanted to put together all the wisdom from science, history, and literature to create a book that would help people live their lives to the fullest.

He had this idea in his twenties, but it was entirely clear to him that at that age, he was too green and wet behind the ears. In his thirties, he came to the same conclusion. Same for his forties, fifties, and mid-sixties. However, at sixty-eight, while he was my tenant, he was diagnosed with terminal heart disease and the doctors were in doubt if they could keep him alive long enough to schedule open heart surgery at the Mayo Clinic.

He refused the surgery. He knew that his odds of being alive two years later, given the amount of damage his heart already had, were close to zero, and further, he'd be in significant pain through most of that period. He decided to die.

He was depressed as anyone would be who has been given the diagnosis he had been given. Compounding this was the unbearable grief of knowing that he would never write his book, the one he had been spending his whole life preparing for.

At this point, I did something truly presumptuous. He was in my office at 747 Plum Lane, and he being too weak and depressed to stop me, I called up the Pritikin Clinic in Southern California and signed him up for a month. The Pritikin Program had a track record of helping heart patients, and I was grasping at straws.

Fran went to the Pritikin Clinic, he had a diet of unrefined foods, lots of fruits and vegetables, hours of daily exercise, plus stress reduction exercises. After a month of this, he lost probably 10 pounds (eventually 20), and his chest pains vanished. Although before, he couldn't walk across the room without crippling pain, now he was walking five miles and ready to tackle double that.

His heart, he learned from his cardiologist, had revascularized and he was, in effect, cured. I told him, "Fran, this is wonderful, I'm so happy for you! *Write your book.*"

"Yes, yes!" he answered, "Now I'm going to do it! I only need a little more research before I start!"

I knew at that moment that he would never write his book, and that I would spend the rest of my life working to make myself into the opposite of this man whom I otherwise so much admired. I vowed right then and there that I would avoid the trap of always planning and never doing. I adopted the motto, "Ready, Fire, Aim!", as in, I would just do it and maybe plan later. I didn't literally "plan later," but I made very sure not to spend so much time planning that I never acted.

Incidentally, Fran lived another thirty years, and never did write his book.

## Rice Farming, or Wouldn't It Be Fun to Transform World Food Production

I thoroughly enjoyed being a rice farmer. It felt like important work in part because being near the University of California at Davis, I could make part of my farm available for experiments with rice culture. Because rice was a staple for more than half the world's population, even small changes in its culture could have phenomenal impacts on world food.

One such change involved azolla, a plant that's part fern, part lichen. I read about it for the first time when I was reading one of Francisco's anthropology magazines. The author of the article told about how in Vietnam, certain villages are prosperous and others are hard scrabble, and it all had to do with how secrets are kept in the village. The secret for prosperous rice crops would be handed down to the sons but never to the daughters.

The reason?

Daughters would marry outside the village and could be counted on to reveal the village secrets for lush rice crops. Therefore, they were never told the secrets. The author said the secret had something to do with a scum called azolla that grows on the surface of the paddies.

When I was reading this, I wondered if just possibly the secret might involve nitrogen-fixation. Could azolla be the wetland equivalent of alfalfa, which fixes nitrogen for dry land crops such as corn? If there were a plant that could fix nitrogen for dry land crops, why not one for aquatic ones.

I showed the article to one of the botanists at UC Davis and learned that yes, azolla does fix nitrogen. However, as he explained to me, it wouldn't do us any good in California because where azolla was known to grow, Vietnam, it lived in an acidic, jungle environment. It could take many decades to acclimatize it to grow in California. And further, it could take 100 years to be sure that it had the right predators and wouldn't over-run the country.

I was disappointed, and told Fran about the situation. I handed him a picture of azolla, and Fran studied it closely. Turning it this way and that, Fran looked at the pictures of azolla that I had brought and told me, "I believe I've seen this plant before. If I'm right, it grows twenty miles from here at Gilsizer Slough, near the old China camp."

He was referring to one of the old camps where Chinese workers lived while constructing the transcontinental railroad. Fran drove to Gilsizer Slough, got samples, and showed it to the UC Davis professor. The professor concluded that we had a strain of azolla that had acclimatized, that had achieved a way of keeping itself in check, and that did fix nitrogen.

*Theodosius Dobzhansky and Mitzi at Harvard.*

We started culturing it in my paddies. It had the tremendous advantage that not only did it fix nitrogen, it also grew so thick that it entirely shaded out any weeds that competed with the rice plants. If you inoculated the paddy with azolla after the rice seedlings had pushed through to the sunlight and oxygen, you could prevent weeds from growing behind the rice seedlings.

It was a success, but not a total success. The limiting factor in rice culture is often nitrogen, and if you don't have access to any artificial nitrogen supply, azolla is fabulous. But for commercial culture in the US, azolla didn't produce enough nitrogen to make an optimum crop. However, it did have a use in other countries.

## The Business and Professional Women's Club Changes My Life

Being a rice farmer, except for my friendship with Fran, did not involve a lot of socializing. And as I said earlier, I had developed a terrible case of shyness. Except when I was with Fran or Father Moreno, or before that, Dobzhansky, I thought that I was stupid, and that I expressed myself so badly that people wouldn't understand what I was trying to say.

And as for public speaking, when I had to give a fifteen-second announcement in church about where the energy conservation bus tour would be leaving, it ruined my whole week; all I could think of was how scared I was of having to stand up in front of the sixty or so members of the congregation.

I'd stand in front of the bathroom mirror and repeat aloud, "The energy conservation bus tour leaves from 5th and G Streets at 2:00 p.m." Or I'd be driving, saying the same thing, hoping I wouldn't forget the line when it actually came time to give the announcement in church.

The day when I had to give the announcement, I doubt if I heard a word *Kids as scientists.* the minister said during the church service. All I could think of was how much I dreaded the idea of standing up and speaking.

And this wasn't a case of talking in front of strangers. I knew every member of the congregation well.

I think my lack of self-confidence was complete. This was not unrelated, by the way, to a marriage that, as I've mentioned earlier, would

be difficult to describe as supportive. I felt at this stage in my life that I hardly deserved to take up space on planet Earth.

Somewhere around 1980, things began to change. It began with a cold-call phone call from a volunteer for the local Business and Professional Women's Club (BPW). The speaker on the other end of the line wanted to know if I'd like to sign up for BPW's individual development class. She said I could learn public speaking and parliamentary procedure.

Since I was at this moment traumatized by how difficult it had been to give the fifteen-second announcement in church in front of people I knew well, I realized that something was wrong with me, and that I needed to do something about what had become a phobia.

"Yes," I answered. "Sign me up."

The night of the first class, I remember sitting in my car outside the building where the class was about to be held, realizing that if I crossed the threshold into the building and entered the room where the class was being held, that my life was going to change.

The sun was setting at this moment, and as I looked at the long, thin clouds on the horizon, each ablaze with neon oranges and reds, I had the strongest sensation that if I entered the room, the sun would also be setting on my marriage.

And it was. As you've seen, I did not have a happy marriage and getting involved with outside influences was an extreme act of rebellion. In the end, it was even more: it was like breaking a spell.

Holding my breath, I walked into the classroom and saw maybe fifteen other women sitting in chairs, waiting for the class to start. I felt out of place, and petrified at being with these strangers. The teacher, Robbie Robinson, told me later that she sized up my case immediately. She realized that she had on her hands someone who was "insufferably shy."

I found a chair in the back of the room and then heard with horror that we were going to start off immediately by having to speak.

"Everyone is going to stand up and say her name and where she's from," began Robbie.

I was so shy at that point in my life that, while I knew I could say my name, and I knew I could say that I was from Davis, I wasn't at all sure that I would be able to say both. As I've said, my lack of self-

confidence at this period in my life, was total.

"For this first evening," continued Robbie, "when you stand up and give your name and where you're from, just this once you can hang onto the back of the chair in front of you." She was looking at me when she said this.

When it was my turn to speak, I clung to the chair in front of me in a grip of death. "My name is Mitzi Ayala." I was ready to blank out, but then realized that maybe I could do it. I formed the words, "And I live in…Davis."

Hmmmm. That wasn't so bad.

By the end of the first class, I was feeling less shy. In the course of the next few weeks, I even began to enjoy the experience of talking in front of my classmates. Robbie was a magnificent, kindly, fun, inspirational teacher, and she had an abundance of phrases that helped.

"Fear feels worse than it looks. Even if you're dying inside, your audience probably won't know it."

"When it comes to confidence, fake it until you make it."

"All speakers get butterflies: your job is to make them fly in formation!"

Her technique was to make everyone feel good about her attempts at speaking, no matter how unpolished or primitive. She said that a rose has to start out as a bud before it becomes a fully opened rose, and we shouldn't get mad at ourselves because we were still buds and not yet roses.

As the classes continued, I felt I was starting to get the hang of speaking in front of other people. Surprisingly, I not only liked it, I was starting to love it.

## The Beginnings of My Career as a TV Hostess and Producer

Somewhere around five weeks into the course, an amazing thing happened. I had written a political article arguing that rice growers shouldn't be forced out of business because of burning their stubble but instead should be given a year to put their own house in order. It had became the cover story of a local in-flight magazine, and because of that article, I had been asked by the CBS affiliate in Sacramento, KXTV, to be a guest on the local farm show.

I wanted to be on the show, to tell the rice farmers' side of a controversial issue, but for a person who a few short weeks before had been too shy to use the telephone, this was an unthinkably big step. My knees were literally wobbling as I told Robbie and the class about my dilemma.

Robbie responded by saying, "We're stopping the class right now. This is important. It's time for a *buck up Mitzi session!*"

Gathering my classmates around me in a circle, she directed each of them to say things that would help me get through the TV interview.

"I know you can handle it," said one.

"We believe in you," said another.

"You've been able to speak with us; just be yourself, and pretend you're talking with us!" said a third.

It's an amazing experience, being surrounded by a group of supportive women, each of whom is saying something that in one way or another, expresses faith in you.

The exercise worked and I felt genuinely "bucked up." When it was time for the interview on KXTV, the voices in my head that were telling me that this was too scary and that I couldn't do it, were drowned out by the voices telling me that people believed in me and were pulling for me and that I could do it.

When you're in a TV studio and it's a live show, at least back then, there's a little red light on top of the camera, the tally light, and it lets you know that the camera is live and that you're going out over the air. When the tally light came on for my interview, I experienced one of the greater shocks of my life: When that light came on, I came on!

As in, I came alive! A camera lens, focusing on me! I was in my element. Life was good! It felt like the times with Father Moreno, or my own father, when I was posing for them. I felt utterly natural and at home!

My shyness and fear vanished. I found that I loved talking on camera. I had something I was eager to share, and this was a heaven-sent opportunity to communicate things I believed in. The words flowed smoothly, and though I know this must sound hard to believe, I was more comfortable on camera than I normally would be off camera. It was as if I was completely in my element.

I loved every single thing about the TV studio. I loved the mild tension, I loved knowing that I was sharing with tens of thousands of people things I cared about, and I enjoyed the hyper-alive adrenalin rush that meant that the perfect words were coming to me. I even felt that my features were "up" and naturally smiling and eager, yet comfortable.

At the end of the show, the manager, who had been watching, pulled me aside and said, "Did you know that you are a natural for TV? Would you like a job hosting the farm show?"

I think at that moment there were few things in life I could have wanted more. But I also think it was one of the greatest shocks of my life. I, who was under normal circumstances too shy to use the telephone, had been asked to host a TV show?

Within the week, I was hosting and producing *Focus on Farming*. I, Mitzi Ayala, who had absolutely no experience in hosting or producing television was suddenly doing it and getting paid to do it! Unbelievable.

By the way, my new and unexpected self-confidence did not have a wholesome effect on my marriage. Francisco asked for a divorce shortly after this. This was not unwelcome news, as I'll describe later.

Back to television. For the first show, I decided not to make it easy for the station management to get me out of there. I announced an ongoing contest and promised the viewers that I'd give the winner's name a week later. I think the contest was something silly, like asking, as I held up a five-pound bag of almonds, how many almonds were in the bag.

For the first half year, I had contests where viewers were to write in and win bragging rights for coming closest to the answer. In short order, I actually had sponsors for the contests, something I calculated would really make it hard for the station to get rid of me.

The show's name eventually became *Mitzi's Country Magazine*, but meanwhile, hosting the farm show wasn't quite the honor it seems. For one thing, it had virtually no viewers. It was early in the morning, and the records at the station didn't indicate that a single person watched it.

It occurred to me that the problem was, farmers didn't want a farm show that told them how to farm. Radio was far better for giving current news and crop reports. "What if," I asked myself, "what they really wanted was a chance to talk about farming to the non-farm public?"

That week, I printed 100 prestamped postcards addressed to me, with a questionnaire on each. I attached these to a letter to the 100 farm representatives on the California State Fair Advisory Committee, and asked them, to fill in the blanks on the postcard, indicating whether agriculture would rather have a half hour TV show once a week directed to farmers, or instead, have farmers telling their stories to the urban public.

I got back ninety-eight of the postcards and every single one of them said they favored using the time to talk with the urban public. I brought these postcards into the station manager, Monk Henry, and asked his permission to recast the entire farm show.

No longer would we be telling the tomato growers how to fertilize (which they know anyway), or giving them the farm report (which they'd get hours earlier on the radio), but instead, I created a format in which I'd invite, say, the tomato farmer to talk about what it takes to grow tomatoes, I'd show him on the tomato harvester, and then typically I'd have his wife demonstrate great ways of selecting, storing, and serving tomatoes.

In other words, every word and every visual in the show would be aimed at the non-farm public. Further, I created a rule for all my shows. They had to be useful to the viewer. If I couldn't tell the viewer something that would save him or her time, money, or help with nutrition, or show them better ways to feed their families, that show didn't happen.

For example, with tomatoes, I could show the fascinating Volkswagen-bus-sized tomato harvester at work harvesting tomatoes. I could tell why you shouldn't refrigerate a tomato ("It will lose it's flavor, texture, shelf-life, and nutrition. Nature never meant for it to encounter the chilling temperatures of a refrigerator. Science knows of almost 100 temperature-dependent chemical reactions that go on inside a tomato, and cold temperatures are bad for all of them.") (Funny, thirty years later I can still recite, probably verbatim, lines that I said during that particular show.) (If only my memory for faces were like my memory for words! This is a small aside, but I looked up almost nothing when writing this book; if it's in words, I can probably remember it.)

Finally, I'd end with the farmer's wife showing how she selected, stored, and served tomatoes. The salad of tomatoes would be beautifully arranged and, I hoped, viewers would copy it themselves.

## My Near-Death Experience on Camera (and I'm Not Kidding!)

Since I was not only hosting the show, but producing it as well, I had a simply splendid time doing things that I hoped would interest the viewers, and that I knew would interest me. For example, being somewhat comfortable with honeybees, Carlos having kept hives, I did a show on honeybees.

Honeybees are fascinating, including how they communicate, how to avoid getting stung, why they're crucial to agriculture, and so on.

However, the show didn't go as intended. The plan was to start off the show in an almond orchard that was in bloom, knowing that there would be countless honeybees in the vicinity. I had the "come here" bee pheromone on my mike, and as I talked, the bees would start alighting on my mike.

Visually, it had the potential of being spectacular. I began my "open," with "Good morning, and welcome to *Country Magazine*. I'm Mitzi Ayala, and this morning we're going to be exploring the fascinating world of honeybees."

By now there's a tennis ball size clump of honeybees covering my mike, and I pretend to notice them for the first time, as if they've suddenly caught my attention. "You may wonder what these bees are doing on my microphone, and why I'm not getting stung. For answers to this, and other questions, and to learn how honeybees touch your life, join me in visiting with world famous bee biologist, Dr. Norman Gary!" (Again, I bet I'm reciting this verbatim, after not having heard or seen these words in thirty years. If only I could remember faces the way I remember words!)

The camera pulls out to reveal that I'm standing near Dr. Gary, and I spend the next fifteen minutes interviewing him. But once the interview is over, I learn from the cameraman that for some reason, it didn't record, and we have to do the interview over again.

This kind of thing happens now and then and it's not normally something that would bother me.

It did in this case, though.

There's no "off-switch" for the "come here" pheromone, and the bees were coming to my mike in ever greater numbers. We start the interview again, but I have to hold my mike away from my body, and

I've already been carrying at least 10 pounds of bees.

Have you ever tried holding a ten pound weight in an outstretched arm? It's easy for the first few minutes, but it gets heavier and heavier as the minutes go by. I already had had my arm out for maybe twenty-five minutes, and the weight was getting heavier by the minute, as bees from all over the orchard kept adding themselves to the mass of bees on my mike.

What's wrong with this picture is that the way to avoid getting stung is to be perfectly still. But my arm muscles were rapidly turning to what felt like water. I couldn't brace my arm without squishing many bees, and killing even one would cause the "Mortal danger! Attack! Attack!" signal.

The swarm of bees was rapidly growing from the size of a football to something approaching the size of a basketball. They were covering not only the mike and my hand, but by now, they were weighing down my whole arm as well.

I was conducting the interview the second time completely on automatic pilot because every conscious thought was focused on the fact that my arm was starting to wobble. I didn't have the strength to hold it steady and pretty soon, it was going to collapse, thereby alarming the bees and probably ending the Mitzi show.

Er, I'm not referring to the television show, I mean me.

While I was conducting the interview, my thoughts were on the imminent possibility that 10,000 bees might soon be stinging me, and that if they did, I was almost certain to die a particularly unpleasant death, and I didn't want to die because I loved my children and wanted to live for them. I think I was as scared as I know how to be.

Somehow, I lasted through the second interview, and then Norman Gary used a smoker to disable the pheromones, and I was able to shake the bees from my hand and arm. Somehow, even remembering this terrifying event is making my heart contract with fear, even though it happened more than a quarter of a century ago.

There's a P.S. to this story. I know how scared I was. But when the show aired, I watched it with friends, and they were complimenting me on how fearless I was. For that matter, I myself couldn't see how terrified I was.

This proved to me how right Robbie Robinson had been during the

BPW individual development class when she said, "Fear feels worse than it looks." I was almost dying of fright but the camera didn't pick it up.

## Attention-Getting Shows

As I said earlier, it was genuinely fun to plan shows that would get attention. I did hundreds of things that at least back in the 1980s were not usual television fare. I showed a horse having surgery using acupuncture. I showed a calf being born. I showed on camera, live, how a cell could be enucleated and substitute genetic material could be put in. I made use of scientists and county extension agents and rodeo queens, and bratty, adorable, little 4-H kids who would confide on camera how they'd try to distract the judges so the judge would miss areas where they weren't doing well … and on and on.

A fun ongoing motif that just happened by accident was that farmers who were talking about their animals would bring ones in that they had named after me. It started with Mitzi the Pig, and went on to Mitzi the Lamb, and Mitzi the Dog, Mitzi the Chicken, and eventually (and incredibly) Mitzi the Queen Bee. A beekeeper had somehow managed to write the name Mitzi on the back of a queen bee. At my guest's direction, the cameraman zoomed in on it, and yes, there at a microscopic level was my name on the queen's back.

*When my TV show came on, this is the first picture the viewers would see. Ah, yes, we Boston debutantes are really country girls at heart!*

I did one show on the importance of bed and breakfasts to rural economies, and the point of this particular show was that the owner had created a nice business by staging murder-mystery weekends. But we didn't just talk about murder mysteries. I opened the show, standing on the set and looking into the camera, and began with my usual cheery "Good morning, and welcome to *Country Magazine!* I'm Mitzi Ayala and today we are going to…"

But my opening monologue was cut short by the crack of a gunshot. I convulse as if hit by a bullet, and clutching at my chest, red fluid spurting out from between my fingers, I sink to the floor of the set, prostrate. But then seconds later, I rise up on one elbow, and laughingly finish the opening monologue by explaining that, no, this wasn't a real murder, but today we're going to learn how a popular new form of entertainment, murder mysteries, is helping the local economy.

The big question I have when I look back on those times is, could it be legal to have so much fun?

I'd get hundreds of letters from people who seemed to enjoy these kinds of antics. People seemed to love the little schtick things like the animals being named after me, and it felt like the show had aspects that were almost like being a family.

*Kids in country.*

This gets back to my theory of communication, that the camera is like a mirror: what you send out to the audience gets reflected back to you. I know this because letters I got proved it. When I was looking into the camera and feeling I was talking with a best friend, I'd got the most wonderful friendship letters back. When I was feeling romantic and would look into the camera and imagine I was talking to someone I loved, I'd actually get love letters!

Further, I'd meet people in the supermarket or at county fairs or wherever, and they'd say they looked forward to breakfast with Mitzi and they felt as is I were a close friend, and they wanted to know what surprising or amazing thing I was going to do that morning.

## The Show that Never Aired

One of what should have been my best shows never aired, alas. There was a guy who appeared on TV a lot back then, stating that his produce, which sold throughout the state, was completely organic. He was like a prophet, telling people to buy his organic produce, and proclaiming that all other farmers should copy his example.

I thought it would make a fantastic story, to visit his farm and see how he could be so productive and profitable without chemical intervention. What wonderful methods had he pioneered? What a public service I would be performing, spreading the word about his chemical-free produce.

I took a camera crew, but I also included Boyd Burton, from DuPont Agri-Chemicals. Boyd had a Ph.D. in organic chemistry and his specialty was agricultural chemicals. I included him because I wanted his opinion of the seeming miracle that Mr. Famous Organic Farmer had achieved.

We arrived at the farm and I, for one, was dazzled. There were hundreds and hundreds of acres of weed-free melons, tomatoes, green beans, and other summer fruits and vegetables.

As far as the eye could see, the growing plants were lush and beautiful. It was a visual feast, to see such vigorous and healthy plants. It was the kind of sight that does the heart good. This was going to make amazing viewing for my audience.

But after a minute or two, Boyd Burton pulled me aside and pointed to the veining patterns on, I think, the string beans we were looking at. I'm no longer sure which plant it was, but Boyd began listing the telltale signs of Round-Up, and half a dozen different pesticides and herbicides. He could also point out the salt-like discolorations that (again, I'm not completely confident of these details) indicated artificial fertilizers. He said that this man was a fraud, and that he was probably using twice to three times the chemical intervention of the average commercial grower.

I wanted to air this story as an expose of a complete con artist, but KXTV didn't want the hassle of law suits. They knew we would win because, legally, truth is an absolute defense, but the station didn't have anywhere near the extra manpower that would be needed to devote to an unnecessary lawsuit. Mr. Famous Organic Farmer continued to preach his con in advertisements everywhere, and to my knowledge, nobody ever did expose him.

## How I Got to Be Assemblyman Greene's Mother—and What Happened Next

One of my favorite guests was the dean of the California State Assembly, Leroy Greene. I had recently become a member of California Women for Agriculture (CWA). As a member of CWA, we were each supposed to participate in the "Adopt a Legislator" program, which meant making friends with a legislator, including inviting him or her to visit our farms while giving him or her the opportunity to meet dozens and dozens of their constituents. We'd also work for their campaigns, whether Republican or Democrat.

I was assigned Assemblyman Greene, which was something of a problem because the article I had written about agricultural burning went directly against the bill that he was sponsoring to ban agricultural burning. Still, I had a job to do, so I got an appointment to see the assemblyman.

*Look at the mike that I'm holding in my right hand. It's covered with thousands of bees, and surrounding me and Norm Gary are thousands more. This was for one of my TV shows.*

When I first entered his office, he sat behind his desk, arms folded, face scowling, looking as pleased to see me as he would be pleased to see a cockroach crawling up his arm. Every vibe said that I was someone whom he profoundly wished would go away, and soon.

This was predictable. After all, the article which began my television career probably cost him votes, and he undoubtedly knew this.

Of course I ignored all of this, and instead pranced in, cheerily informing him that *I was his mother.*

He did a double take. *"My mother?"*

"Yes, Assemblyman Greene," I answered, striking a pose and tossing my long hair just slightly, "I'm from California Women for Agriculture, and the organization has decided that you are my adoptee from the Adopt a Legislator program."

I now flash my best smile, and watch as he tries to absorb all this. Initially he seemed not to know quite what to make of this, or for that matter, me. I think he's starting to conclude that I've set down from another planet.

"Since I've *adopted* you," I continue, my tone of voice pure Doris Day sweet reasonableness, "it's obvious isn't it, that by definition, *I'm your mother?*"

By now he gets it, that I'm joking, and starts laughing. The tone of the room has changed, and now he's all smiles. We quickly get into a long and engaging conversation about rice and the agricultural burning problem that I had written about.

Since he's a brilliant guy and a skilled debater, in any serious argument, I was destined to lose. But I had a way around that little issue. Whenever he started to make a point that I couldn't counter, I'd look at him impishly, coquettishly even, and announce, "Now don't you go get technical on your mother!"

I can't quite fathom why being irrational and off-the-wall and totally from a different planet seemed to appeal to him, (shades of Gay Vanner and "It's a *box*") but I'm pretty sure it did. We became fast friends and allies. He did a lot to help me and went out of his way, whenever he could, to make me look good, whether in the media or with American Agri-Women.

Actually, through him I learned what seemed like an amazing lesson in duplicity. A public relations guy, whom in order to protect the guilty, I won't name, was getting a fee of several hundred thousand dollars to help "protect" the rice growers from Leroy Greene.

The public relations guy was unaware that by this time, Leroy was my closest pal. (After all, I was Leroy's mother!)

The PR guy told the rice growers that Leroy Greene was planning a press conference in which he would attack the rice farmers and drum up support for legislation that would put them out of business. The legislation involved ending agricultural burning, which the rice farmers at that time needed to free their paddies from stem rot virus.

The PR guy told the rice growers that he'd need extra money to use his influence to get the press conference, which was scheduled for next week, stopped. The growers paid up because this was a question of survival. They thought.

But, er, well, not quite. I asked Leroy Greene if he had such a press conference planned. He answered that this was the first he had ever heard of it, and no, he wasn't planning a press conference. But nevertheless, the next week, the PR guy told the rice growers that their money had been well spent because he had personally prevented Leroy Greene from having the terrible press conference.

The rice growers had paid this PR con man to prevent a press conference that was never going to happen.

Sweet, huh?

Actually, Leroy made me look good to the rice farmers because he announced in the press that he was withdrawing the anti-burning legislation, and it was the "Rice Princess" who had persuaded him to do it. I did play a role because I was able to convince him that if he'd give us a year, we could clean up our own act. And we did.

This is changing the subject, but something that I loved about the California legislature back then: it was rough and tumble, but it wasn't toxic the way politics seems now. Leroy could joke with his colleagues on either side of the aisle and they with him. My favorite was, Leroy had sponsored some kind of legislation regarding prostitution, and it got a lot of attention. His Republican counterpart told the press, "Assemblyman Greene's prostitution bill? Why all the fuss? He should just pay it!"

### Maureen Reagan, President's Daughter and New BF

One show that had an impact on my future was a show I did on international trade with Maureen Reagan, President Reagan's daughter. She was interested in agricultural trade, among other things, so she was a totally appropriate guest for *Mitzi's Country Magazine*. I invited her on the show to talk about a magazine she was publishing on agricultural trade.

Having the president's daughter as a guest on my show was impressive to my colleagues at KXTV. A week before the taping, Secret Service people were all over the station, checking for possible security threats. It was highly intrusive, but also, from my point of view, utterly delightful. Everyone at the station was talking about how Mitzi had sufficient clout to have the president's daughter on her show.

Actually, it's not that I had any clout at all. I simply learned that Maureen Reagan lived in California and she was the producer of a print magazine involving international trade. I wrote her a letter inviting her to talk about it, and she accepted.

The day of the taping, the Secret Service was there in force, and before her arrival, a guy with a walkie talkie of some sort (this was before the days of cell phones), was announcing to other Secret Service men that she was fifteen minutes away, then ten minutes away, then four blocks away.

The station manager and a dozen others lined up outside the station to greet the president's daughter. I could see that they were fascinated as a caravan of limos pulled up to the station, and I went up to Maureen's car and greeted her. Out of anyone else's hearing, I told her, "Miss Reagan, you can't believe what this is doing to my standing in the station. Everyone is so impressed that you've been willing to be on my show."

She answered, again out of everyone's hearing, "Then let's put on a show for them! What are your children's names?"

I told her, and by the time we had moved close enough to the entrance of the station for the station manager and others to hear, she had her arm around me as if we were old, old friends, and she casually asked me, in everyone's hearing, how Jose and Carlos were doing! She spent the rest of the hour acting as if we had known and liked each other for years. She acted as if she was enjoying this little joke as much as I was.

This could have been around 1982 or so, but it was to have a big effect on my life three years later. I'll get to what happened in a moment.

**The Show Grows**

The show began to attract viewers. And more viewers. One of the things that I was really proud of was, it also got fan letters. Possibly the biggest status symbol I'll ever have occurred at KXTV. All the other shows had one box for their fan letters. I had so many fan letters that it took three boxes to fit them. A single show could yield hundreds of fan letters. People joked at the station about how it could happen that I got so many letters.

Within a year, the station moved the show from, I think 6:00 a.m. to 8:00 a.m. And they changed the name of it from *Focus on Farming* to *Mitzi's Country Magazine*. Further, the agricultural community loved it because every week, I'd showcase another California crop and I'd give agricultural leaders a chance to talk about how wonderful their products are.

In addition, I could give 4-H and Future Farmers of America kids a chance to be on TV and practice their communications skills. It was like, to use a baseball analogy, a farm league for the farm kids to learn the communications skills that their industry depended on.

The whole thing was a recipe for popularity.

## Becoming a Syndicated Newspaper Columnist

But it got better. For just a slight additional amount of work, I found that I could write an article for the local newspaper, based on the research I had put into producing that week's show.

Then it occurred to me that if I could get the newspaper articles syndicated, for the same amount of work, I could be making a lot more money. I went to the library and checked out a book, *Writer's Market*, that gave the addresses of syndicators.

This was before computers, so I laboriously typed out maybe thirty different query letters to syndicators and enclosed samples of my published work.

I didn't get a single reply.

Months later, after a board meeting for KVIE, the local public television station where I was vice president, I complained to my friend Dick White about how I hadn't gotten a single reply from all the query letters that I had sent. He said that his friend, the head of Capitol News, might be interested in my column, and he'd set up an appointment.

I met with Fred Kline a couple of days later, he liked my work, and suddenly I was a syndicated columnist with my column going to 200 California and west coast outlets.

## Becoming a Syndicated Radio Hostess

The research I did for the TV show and for the columns meant that with almost no additional work, almost from the top of my head, I had enough information for a radio broadcast. I got a job with the Coast to Coast Radio Network, which broadcast out of San Francisco, and once a week, I did a show, *Tips from Farmer Mitzi.*

I have several "favorite moments in life" memories, but among the top of these had to do with holding, simultaneously, jobs in radio, television, and newspaper. The favorite moment happened because I had not gotten around to telling my bosses about my multiple moonlighting jobs. One day at the California State Fair, where I was a director, all three of my bosses were present at a reception. I introduced them to each other, and each man seemed close to astonished to know that I was also working for the other two.

## TV Syndication? Not with That Icky Lisp!

Soon after this, it occurred to me that I could make a lot more money and have a lot more fun with my TV show with virtually no additional work. How? Getting the show syndicated. But how to get from here to there?

The first problem to be solved was that I had a disqualifying speech impediment. I had a lisp that you could not only hear, you could see it, especially on television. It was severe enough so that in the course of my life up until then, people had told me that before they got to know me, they assumed because of my lisp, that I was stupid.

The problem was, curing a lisp at age thirty-nine was not an easy thing. I went to three different speech therapists, and all three said that it couldn't be done. The third one, however, said that even though it couldn't be done, if I wanted to try, she would be happy to take my money.

Her office was an hour's drive away, in Sacramento, and I saw her three times a week for almost a year. I also practiced her exercises at least an hour a day, which wasn't hard to do because I'd practice the exercises when I was out jogging.

The first nine months were discouraging, as in really, really, really discouraging. There was no progress at all. I couldn't hear the difference between a correctly pronounced S and a lisped S. Next, the muscles in my tongue needed for curling in order to make a correct S had completely atrophied. They hadn't been used ever, so maybe atrophied is the wrong word. Trying to move muscles that weren't there was akin to asking you to pick up a pencil with your earlobe and draw with it: there were simply no muscles or nerve connections to even try with.

Think of it: if I asked you to pick up a pencil with your earlobe, how would you even start? You can't just will it to happen when the muscles and nerves aren't there.

I had nine months of absolutely zero progress. I'd ask all my friends what they did with their tongues and I'd try to imitate them, but there was nothing there to work with. But finally, nine months into it, I found that I could slightly move the tip of my tongue. It's almost impossible to improve on nothing, but once I had something to work with, progress followed rapidly. I began to hear the difference and gradually began forming non-lisped words. By the end of the year, I was pretty much lisp-free.

*Watching rice being augured from the combine into the bankout wagon during the harvest at the Sacramento farm. There's something unbelievably satisfying about growing and harvesting food.*

I can hardly express how much this did for my self-confidence. It took away one of my last problems with public speaking and it opened the door to the possibility of a bigger career in television.

Getting my show syndicated now became a focus. Part of the problem was, to get my show syndicated would mean finding a sponsor willing to sink a great deal of money into it. It would mean learning about the culture of business, as opposed to the culture that I had spent my adult life in, that is, academia. What would it take to persuade a national sponsor that they wanted and needed *moi*?

## TV Syndication? Only If You Can Sell It!

With my speech impediment behind me, the essence of my problem now, I calculated, was that I needed to learn how to sell my program. I therefore signed up for the fourteen-week *Dale Carnegie Salesmanship Class.*

I learned at least as much about the real world and how to operate in it from those fourteen weeks as I learned in four years at Harvard. The salesmanship course encourages you to think in terms of what your prospect wants, not what you want. Your job is to know your product and your prospect so thoroughly that you can honestly believe that what you have to offer will, in one way or another, make that person or organization's life better. If you don't believe that, you shouldn't be selling it.

Each week we learned some new psychological principal, or some way of overcoming fear of failure. A lot of the course had to do with developing more empathy and greater understanding of where your prospect is coming from. There was also a lot about being professional and developing a reputation for doing what you said you would do and delivering what you promised.

Part of the fourteen-week course was developing a sales plan. You were to learn as much about the market as possible, as much about your target company as possible, and as much about the individuals as possible. In addition, you should know enough about your product so that few people on the planet would know as much about it as you. Then most of all, you should be able to talk fluently about how what you had to offer would be valuable and desirable for your prospect. It should solve a problem or problems or in some way be a great asset to them. Surprisingly, if there were flaws or defects or disadvantages to your product, you should frankly mention them, but you should be equipped to say how these could be dealt with.

After spending time analyzing who would be my best prospect, as in which company would most benefit from my TV series, I thought a food company, such as a supermarket would be ideal. I made friends with a senior vice president at Safeway and secured an appointment to make my pitch.

However, the Dale Carnegie course recommends practicing your pitch before taking it to the most likely prospect. I thought DuPont Agricultural Chemicals might be good for my practice run, given that they sold agricultural chemicals to farmers. Using Dale Carnegie logic, I tried to figure out what my show could do for them.

My specialty was telling the urban public tips about how to select, store, and serve farm grown foods. DuPont wants to look good to the farmers who buy their agricultural chemicals and, I figured, a really good way to do this would be for DuPont to be seen helping the farmers sell their products. My show could do this.

For example, I could tell the urban public useful tips on storing bread. It goes stale more rapidly in the refrigerator than at room temperature, but that staling process is much, much slower in the freezer. I could show visuals of starch grains crystallizing at refrigerator temperatures, and how this didn't happen at room temperatures or freezer temperatures. Part of the show would include beautiful visuals of bread, and at the end of it, the goal was for people to appreciate bread and want to go out and buy some, and maybe try out the tips I had been sharing.

I suggested to DuPont that they sponsor my show, and then show clips from it at the National Association of Wheat Growers. The wheat growers would, I hoped, feel warmly toward DuPont for focusing on their product in a way that was good for their image and that might increase sales.

And by the way, DuPont would have the cost of producing my show, but it wouldn't have to pay the costs of buying advertising time. It would be barter. In return for providing stations with usable programming, the stations would be asked to give DuPont free advertising time.

That was the plan for my rehearsal pitch. I had a dandy way of getting to DuPont to try out the pitch. I learned that the vice president for Ag Chem, Dale Wolf, was visiting California from Delaware, and I simply invited him to be on my existing show at KXTV. My local farm show in Sacramento was really too small to be worthy of his attention, but he accepted my invitation anyway.

I got everyone in the station to make a huge fuss over him, as if he were visiting royalty; I absolutely wanted him to have a good experience on the show.

At the end of my on-air interview with him, I told him my idea for DuPont's increasing its customer goodwill. Dale Wolf said it was an interesting idea, and if I were ever in Wilmington, Delaware, I should come call on him.

Guess who happened to be in Wilmington two weeks later.

But before going, I learned every possible thing I could about Dale Wolf. I read about him, talked with people who knew him, and generally tried to learn as much about what made him tick as, if he had had one (which he didn't), his psychiatrist would know about him.

When I visited him in Wilmington, we talked and then he introduced me to maybe half a dozen of his subordinates to discuss the idea. They all seemed at least slightly interested, and I did have a story to tell that I had practiced and practiced as part of my continuing Dale Carnegie course. At the end of the day, Dale told me to put everything together in a written proposal and he would get back to me.

I went back to California and wrote a draft proposal. Then, I talked by phone with each of Dale's subordinate's, reading them portions of it and asking their help on how to improve it. That turned out to be a great move because they could tell me the buzz words that worked with DuPont and what things never to say, and what hot buttons needed to be pressed.

By the time I had talked with the last guy, I had changed virtually every word of my original draft. I mailed the brand new version to Dale Wolf, and nervously awaited his response. A couple of days later, he telephoned me with the good news that he liked my proposal. "But," he added "I'll need to show it to my people to see if they like it."

Since his people had written virtually every word of it, surprise, surprise, it turned out that they did like it. Suddenly my TV show was syndicated to seventy-six stations. The practice pitch had resulted in a sale and I never did talk with Safeway about it. Yay, Dale Carnegie!

Part of my contract with DuPont included speaking engagements at dozens of agricultural conventions. I adored this. It was marvelous being treated like a celebrity, and not just a celebrity, but someone who was helping them.

What a gig! Plus, one of the super bonuses of the whole thing was a friendship with Dale and his wife Clarice that lasts to this day. A quarter of a century later, Dale still calls me on my birthday.

### *The Farmer's Cookbook* Series

My four TV broadcasts a week, plus one radio show, plus the weekly newspaper columns actually didn't take that much time. That meant I could work on some other projects that attracted me. Most of the radio and television shows and the newspaper columns included recipes from the farmers who grew the foods I was talking about. When I put these together, including the stories and tips that went with them, I had a jim-dandy cookbook.

*The Farmer's Cookbook* series went through, I think, eight printings and somewhere in the 1980s, there was a review of cookbooks, and mine was listed as "a classic." I used to promote it regularly on the Jim Eason Show in San Francisco, and I'd generally sell $4,000 worth of books each time.

I also would sell the cookbooks at the end of speeches at, say, Business and Professional Women's Club lunches, or Chamber of Commerce, California Women for Agriculture, or whatever. I'd average a speech a week.

During this time, I joined the National Association of Farm Broadcasters, and out of nearly 1,000 members, I think there were only three women. After a couple of years I was voted regional director. This was in addition to being a vice chairman of the California State Fair, and vice president of the local public broadcasting station, KVIE.

## American Agri-Women

Since technically, I was still a rice farmer, I qualified for something else that I loved. I became active in women's agricultural politics. I have a great many reasons to be glad for this step but one of them is, without it, I wouldn't have met my beloved hero husband, Frank Perdue. More on how this happened later.

In 1980, I joined a group of other women who were connected with agriculture, California Women for Agriculture, and because I had a farm television show, a farm radio show, and a farm newspaper column, they appointed me director of communications. It was a great experience for me.

It was possibly the first time that I came to cherish, value, and love women in general. I don't think it had come into my consciousness before how much I cared about my fellow women and wanted to help them do well. It helped my transformation that we were all working toward a common goal, which was helping agriculture. Collectively, we felt that our way of life was threatened by political forces that were unaware of the harm they were doing to us. Our purpose was to educate, and our means was by letting opinion leaders and politicians know our side on controversial issues.

Because of my media work, I was in a position to help. By 1983, I was second vice president of American Agri-Women, and by 1985, I was first vice president of a 30,000-member farm women's organization.

## President Reagan, an Untold Story

Being vice president of American Agri-Women was a springboard that led to an adventure in international diplomacy. In 1985 Maureen Reagan included me in the US delegation to the United Nations Decade on Women that was meeting in Nairobi. The invitation was based largely on the interview I had had with her several years before, but it was also based on my title as first vice president, and soon-to-be president, of the oldest and largest US farm women's organization.

It was a fabulous experience. To be a member of the delegation meant dozens of hours of State Department briefings on the UN issues we would be discussing, plus we were to read what must have been 10 pounds of background material. I bet that we were one of the best briefed delegations there.

The day before we flew to Nairobi, President Reagan invited the delegation to lunch. I got to sit at the president's table, but I and my fellow delegates were so awed by being at the president's table that none of us could say a word. The first course went by with the president telling story after story, all of them enthralling and apropos.

It made me think of what I imagine President Lincoln must have been like: both men were famous for an endless supply of great stories. But what's wrong with this picture is, because he was talking, President Reagan hadn't consumed one calorie of food.

Halfway through the second course, I thought it was my patriotic duty to say something so that someone else would be talking and the president could eat something. Besides, as a television hostess, I was supposed to be good at keeping a conversation going. I mean, professionally, this is what I *did.*

I worked up my courage and tried my best conversational gambit. I told the whole table that I would like to ask them each a question, and I would tell them the point of it after they had all answered. (Meanwhile the president had started eating.)

I asked the group, one by one, to name their hero. The person could be famous or not famous, living or dead. Several of the women said their heroes were their mothers, others named famous politicians or scientists or philosophers. I had deliberately arranged to go around the table ending with the president, with the thought that this would give him the maximum amount of time to eat.

For the record, I said that mine was a cross between Mother Teresa and Princess Diana. (Today it would be Frank Perdue, with my sister Augusta a close runner-up.)

When it came time for the president to give us his answer, he paused, and then turned his head around and for the longest time gazed at the portrait of President Lincoln that was hanging behind our table. I think every one of us was expecting to hear him say that his hero was President Lincoln.

But he didn't. Instead he turned to face us and said, "The Man of Galilee."

The point of my question was supposed to be to tell everyone that psychologists say that you cannot name a hero whose qualities you don't, at least in some measure, share yourself.

But it seemed too presumptuous and improper for me to announce to the table that President Reagan had, at least in some degree, the qualities of Jesus Christ. It turned out that I didn't have to say anything because an animated discussion began on why people had chosen their heroes. People apparently didn't remember that I had said there was a point to my question. But in retrospect, I do believe that Reagan did have some of the sheer goodness and caring and compassion that The Man of Galilee embodied.

## The United Nations Decade on Women, and Courage Lessons from the Israelis

The next day we flew on Air Force One nonstop to Nairobi. The thirty or so members of Maureen Reagan's delegation had been chosen for linguistic ability and for areas of expertise. I had the easy languages, French and Spanish, but other members were fluent in many other languages. Our job was to fan out and talk with members of the other delegations, preferably in their languages and find out what issues they cared about.

The purpose of this was, we, from the United States, had one major goal for the conference, and that was to get the United Nations to rescind its wording that Zionism and racism were the same thing. We were willing to support the goals of many other countries if they would support us on this.

The Soviet Union had the opposite goal. Its members were trying to keep the wording in place. Valentina Tereshkova, the first female astronaut, was the leader of their delegation, and I think she and her delegation were less effective than Maureen's.

While we worked the large hall—it must have held more than 1,000 people—talking with as many women as possible, always in their languages, Tereshkova's delegation seemed always to be surrounding her and not fanning out. I wondered at the time if this might be related to a fear that they might defect, and therefore they couldn't be out wandering around.

I watched Tereshkova intently. She was tall, shapely, and had the posture and demeanor of a duchess. She also, from what I could observe, seemed to expect people to come to her, almost as if she were holding court. I kept thinking that the Americans were much more "of the people" than the Russians.

The day when the vote was to take place, the one about does Zionism equal racism, we didn't know if it would go our way. If it did not, Maureen had planned for us to walk out in protest, get on Air Force One (which her father had loaned us) and leave. We were to hold our heads high, look straight ahead, and even if people were jeering at us and even spitting at us, we were to behave with dignity.

There was so much at stake, for our delegation, for America, and most of all, for Israel.

I had made friends with some wonderful Israelis, and I kept thinking, "They endure this kind of tension continuously, while I, for whom it is an almost once in a lifetime experience, can hardly stand it."

I asked my Israeli friends if I could sit with them during the vote. I wanted to do it partly out of solidarity, but also partly because, as I told one particularly wise Israeli woman, "I need courage lessons!"

It was amazing, but even though it was Israel that was the brunt of this, the Israeli women ended up holding my hand and comforting and supporting me. I'll never forget the generosity of soul this showed. Looking back on it, it doesn't even make sense that they were soothing me; it so should have been the other way around. But then maybe what was really going on was, they've endured this before and knew the ropes, and they knew that this was new to me and I was completely ignorant of the coping skills that they had learned.

Ah, but then I'll never forget the rejoicing I was part of when the vote did go our way.

## How a Bottle of Coke Became Almost the Most Beautiful Thing I've Ever Seen

There was another part of that trip that I particularly cherish. As a representative of agriculture, I had been invited to visit a Masai village. I had gone to Northrup King ahead of time and asked the company to donate 1,000 packages of seeds that would grow well in that climate and latitude and that were foods that were part of the Masai diet. I liked seeds as a choice of gifts because they were easy to transport, and because there were pictures on the seed packages, no translation would be necessary.

In addition to getting the seeds, I also spent a couple of months learning polite phrases in Swahili. When I actually arrived in the village, I felt as if they were treating me like a visiting princess. I also enjoyed how hospitable they were.

I was led to a stage with maybe a dozen dignitaries on it, and the head man gave a welcoming talk in Swahili. Although there was a translator, I actually understood a good bit of it because he was using quite a few of the polite phrases I had already learned.

When it was my turn to respond, I gazed out over the 1,000 or so assembled villagers, and said, in Swahili, all the polite phrases I had learned. It was a speech of several minutes in which, speaking their language, I thanked them for their hospitality, told them how happy I was to be here, and ended with a polite phrase about "follow in the footsteps," which is a patriotic reference to something Jomo Kenyatta used to say. And then, in Swahili, I asked people to distribute the seed packages.

The talk in their language and the gifts brought down the house! They cheered and cheered and cheered, and I felt that I was having one of the best moments of my life. I felt I had been a good ambassadress for my country and that it had all been perfect.

Until.

Until I saw at the far end of the crowd which, by the way, extended about as far as I could see, that they were parting to let a procession of women who were carrying trays with foot-high gourds. I knew what was in the gourds. Milk.

I also know that the milk wasn't refrigerated because there was no electricity here, the temperature that afternoon was probably 90 degrees, and further, I knew that there were, at the time, a number of diseases that were endemic to the area. Ones that I particularly didn't want to contract, included tuberculosis and schistosomiasis.

I also knew, as my language instructors had told me, that it's an unpardonable sin to refuse refreshments.

What was I going to do? Refuse the refreshments and undo

everything wonderful that had just happened and make a bad impression for my country? Or drink the milk and get a life-threatening, incurable disease?

The procession of ladies carrying milk gourds was approaching closer and closer, and I couldn't figure out what to do. My mind was like a pinball rapidly bouncing between rubbers, first thinking I'd drink the milk and then deciding I couldn't, and then feeling that I had to drink it. Drink it! Don't drink it! You have to drink it!

In the middle of all this, my thoughts were suddenly interrupted by the world's most beautiful sight.

A bottle of Coke.

The Masai villagers had understood that I would be uneasy about drinking unpasteurized room temperature milk. I gratefully accepted the Coke, while everyone else drank the milk.

Later, on the same Decade on Women trip to Kenya, I found out that I probably would not have gotten sick from drinking the milk. A professor of dairy science from Egerton University told me that the Masai have devised an effective way of killing milk-borne pathogens. Milk has a pH value in which milk-borne pathogens flourish. An acidic environment kills them.

The Masai are able to create an acidic environment using a weak acid that is always at hand, so to speak. Both men and women have access to this acidic liquid, but it is a great deal more convenient for a man to add it to a milk gourd than it is for a woman to do so.

That's because it's easier for a man to aim the acidic liquid.

So, I wouldn't have gotten some terrible disease from drinking the room temperature milk, but I'm still grateful for the Coke.

## Augusta's Dream from Age Twenty Comes True, along with a Nightmare

During this trip to Kenya, something happened that possibly saved my sister Augusta's life. I heard from one of the advisors to the delegation that the position of United States ambassador to the United Nations in Geneva had just become available. Augusta's childhood dream had always been to be married to a United Nations ambassador, and on the wild chance that this might be right for my brother-in-law,

Joseph Petrone, I telephoned them in New Hampshire from Nairobi.

The Petrones followed up on this and secured the appointment. Before being sent overseas, however, the State Department required that both of them have complete physicals. Augusta had just had a complete physical three months before and had been fine. It seemed a waste to go through another physical, but they had no choice.

The physical revealed that Augusta had ovarian cancer and the tumor was already the size of a grapefruit. The type of cancer was a particularly aggressive one, and I heard that she had one chance in a thousand of survival, given that the tumor was so large and so aggressive. After all, it had grown from undetectable to grapefruit size in a mere three months.

Augusta's reaction to this makes me admire her more than any other person in the world, living or dead. I talked with her just before she went under the knife, for an operation that was unlikely to save her life.

She told me she wasn't afraid or unhappy: she was grateful.

*What?!*

She explained. She had had a happier, more fulfilled life than she had ever bargained for, and she simply had to be grateful for the time she had been given.

On the other hand, if she survived, even better! In other words, she couldn't lose!

When she woke up from the surgery, she didn't immediately know what they had discovered. She had tubes coming from seemingly everywhere and couldn't speak. The likelihood was that she would hear a death sentence if, as seemed virtually certain, the cancer had spread.

Under those circumstances, what was the first thing she did on coming to? She saw a nurse bending over her, and Augusta winked at the nurse.

"Why did you wink at the nurse," I asked.

"Because I thought the nurse might be worrying about me, and I wanted to reassure her."

I believe that my sister isn't my sister. I think she's really an angel, masquerading as a human. No ordinary mortal could be so selfless and so admirable.

## Presidency of American Agri-Women

In 1985 I had been first vice president of American Agri-Women, and by 1987, I became president of the organization which by then represented 35,000 women.

I viewed my role as president as being one of nurturing other women to develop the skills and abilities which would not only help them serve agriculture, but that also would help them be all they could in any area. At our various conventions, I made sure to include sessions on public speaking, lobbying, time management, parliamentary procedure, how to do well during television or radio or newspaper interviews, and so on.

When it came time for the thirty-five or so chapters to give their reports, I'd be encouraging to those who were terrified of public speaking, and I even followed something of the format used by Robbie Robinson during her BPW speaking classes: I'd encourage the entire audience to applaud loudly for every talk given.

I'd also say something encouraging about whatever strengths the speaker had shown. If a speaker was really scared, I might share with her (and the audience) that I had once been too scared to use the telephone, and that one of the ways to overcome fear was just to plunge in and do it, especially when you know you have a sympathetic audience that's pulling for you.

One of the little tricks I'd do is, I'd find out ahead of time which speakers were having the most trouble with the idea of getting up in front of a group to give their report. I'd arrange with them to go first, so they could get it over with and enjoy the other reports.

I had such a good time with all of this! It suited my personality so perfectly!

I also felt that I became tremendously close to a large number of people. I think many of them sensed that I adored them, and I felt the appreciation coming back to me. I'll always be grateful to American Agri-Women for the privilege they gave me of being their leader for two years.

They did award me the Leaven Award, which is their highest award, and which they had never given to an AAW president before. It meant the world to me.

One of the things that AAW did during my term as president was, we encouraged every member to get involved in political campaigns. Women in agriculture didn't often have an abundance of money to contribute to a campaign, but we could give time, whether ringing doorbells or hosting events for the candidate, or writing letters or any of dozens of other volunteer activities.

The goal was to have our members have at least some clout with the legislators at all levels and from both parties. We felt that this was a shortcut for people without much money to have some say in legislation that affected our survival.

Since I was encouraging everyone else to get involved with politics, it was clear to me that I had an obligation to do so also. I decided to aim for the top and volunteered to work on a presidential campaign. That meant moving to Washington for a couple of weeks in late winter of 1988.

The problem with this effort was that by the end of the two weeks, I knew that my candidate was going to wash up in the primaries, and although I loved and admired him, I wasn't entirely sorry. The inefficiencies of his staff horrified me. I thought if this was a sample of his administrative ability, the country would suffer. I actually remember joking with someone from a competing campaign staff that if either of our candidates won, we were so inefficient that all the Russians would need to conquer the country would be boots.

I was feeling down, that I had invested the vacation time and the money to spend all this time in Washington for a candidate that I no longer wanted to win. Still my last day visiting Washington, my friend Herman Pirchner invited me to a couple of parties.

# Chapter Six:

# *1988–2005, Salisbury, Maryland*

### Frank and I Get Engaged

The first party was fun, but uneventful until roughly ten minutes before we were to leave for the next event. Fifty or so guests in their festive cocktail attire were milling around, sipping their drinks, and then suddenly something occurred that made me think of the Parting of the Waters of the Red Sea. It was the guests, moving to the sides of the room to make way for the VIP guest of the evening who had just arrived.

"Who's that?" I whispered to Herman.

Behind his cupped hand, Herman whispered in my ear, "That's Frank Perdue, the Chicken King!"

The Waters of the Red Sea may have figuratively parted as Frank came in, but seconds later, they flowed back around him and he was surrounded by a circle of people five deep.

I didn't entirely know what to make of what I was watching. Why were people crowding around him like this?

Perdue ads didn't reach California, so I had no idea that this man was so famous or wealthy. However, I had heard the name, Frank Perdue, because a soon-to-be ex-friend had recommended that Frank use the same lawyer I had used for my divorce.

In my mind, I flashed through the little I knew about Frank Perdue and my lawyer, Warren Ettinger. The only connection I could come up with was a revealing one. Perdue was divorcing, and Ettinger was both a divorce lawyer and a criminal lawyer. The obviously famous person I was observing had considered using a divorce lawyer with an unusual combination of skills.

We probably had something in common, I diagnosed: seriously unpleasant divorces.

Frank was busy shaking hands with the people surrounding him. I watched as he looked each person in the eye, and seemed for an instant to be giving him or her his entire attention. Then, with a politician's skill, he eased on to the next. It was a bravura performance of working the room. I was dazzled.

In general, I avoid going up to celebrities, and that's because there's usually nothing to say. You just shake their hand and move on. But in this case, we had something in common, and besides, I was starting to find him attractive. It occurred to me, for perhaps the first and only time in my life, that I would very much enjoy shaking a stranger's hand, that touching him would be—enjoyable.

As I've said, Frank was working the room, shaking hands with people, and when he got to me, he looked at me with his "You're the only person in the world who's important to me at this moment" look and firmly shook my hand.

I was finding him more attractive by the second. "Mr. Perdue," I said, "you and I have something in common. We almost used the same divorce lawyer."

To my dismay, the "You're the only person in the world" look faded into bafflement. He tilted his head slightly, his expression cordial—kind even—but there was no flicker of recognition of what I was talking about.

I lowered my head and started to turn away, feeling both foolish and embarrassed.

But just as I was turning away, Frank reached for my shoulder and said, "Oh, yes, I remember…you're the woman from California who used Warren Ettinger!"

Frank told me later how he had liked how shy and modest and non-pushy I was.

He stopped working the room and we stood there, talking with each other. Since what we had in common was almost having used the same divorce lawyer, the subject was, naturally enough, divorce. We each began enthusiastically agreeing that marriage was an institution designed to make people miserable, and neither of us would ever consider the thought of the notion of the possibility of getting involved in something so horrible ever again. (For the record, I learned later that, in his case, this attitude was limited to his relationship with his second wife. He had a lifelong respect and fondness and admiration for his first wife.)

Although the topic was a serious one, the tone was one of banter, as in, who could top whom for saying how awful marriage was. I was thinking, "He's so fun to talk with! I feel so comfortable with him!"

Strangely, a few minutes into the conversation, the tone of it changed. Although moments ago, we had been gleefully agreeing that even the thought of remarriage was too dreadful to contemplate, we were now agreeing that this attitude was sad because in actuality it meant growing old alone. However, as we now further agreed, that would be our fate because we had both just come out of marriages that hadn't worked, and neither of us felt we could ever trust anyone else again.

All of a sudden, Frank looked down at me just as I was gazing up at his handsome, quirky, character-filled face, and he said, "I believe I could trust you."

"And I believe I could trust you!" I blurted out.

Looking back on it, saying this after such a short time astonishes me. I have always felt that "I trust you" is more significant than "I love you." How could both of us have dared say this to each other after only five minutes? And how amazing that it would have the same meaning for both of us.

Both of us understood that by having said we were ready to trust each other, that we were also saying that we intended to spend our lives together.

The conversation just naturally flowed to a discussion of what our marriage would be like, including how it would be supportive and not competitive and how we would each rejoice in each other's successes and we would be there for each other during setbacks. We were talking as comfortably and as trustingly as if we had known each other for years.

The conversation was magical, but brief. Reality intruded because Herman Pirchner was glaring at me, signaling by glancing toward the door that it was time to leave.

I knew that my conversation with Frank was going to be life-changing, but it suited me perfectly to leave at the moment. Something in me needs to be chased, and being just a little elusive was—I can't help it—instinctive.

I returned to California maybe five days later, having stopped on the way to visit and address various state chapters of American Agri-Women. As president, I had been invited to address a series of their state conventions.

Meanwhile, I was thinking about Frank non-stop and to my utter delight when I got home, there were half a dozen pink "while you were out" phone messages all lined up on my desk. They were from Frank. In the messages, he asked me to call him. However, I have a lifetime aversion to calling men (even in 2010 as I write this), so I waited for him to call again.

This aversion, by the way, was not from lack of wanting to speak with him. I desperately wanted to talk with him. It's just that for some reason, possibly the desire to be chased, I couldn't do it.

When he called again, almost his first words were, "I meant what I said when we met. I have never been more serious in my life."

I answered, "And I have never been more serious in my life."

How strange, that Frank and I were seriously agreeing to marry after having known each other in person for only ten minutes. I think of myself as a thorough-going skeptic, with a nuts-and-bolts approach to life, and a terror of being gullible.

But in this case, I somehow simply "knew" that Frank and I were going to spend our lives together. And incredibly, he felt the same way. Given that both of us had had unhappy marriages before and expected never to remarry, and given that for both of us, each having large estates, the complications of ever enduring another divorce were too horrible to contemplate, how did it happen that two such people could almost instantly know that we wanted to spend our lives together?

Well, it happened.

My rational side states, "Coincidence." My very-undeveloped mystical side wonders if I had known him in a previous life. It reminds me of my first date with my first husband, Francisco—I remember thinking as I looked at him, "Oh, yes, I remember, this is the man I'm going to marry. He's the father of my children."

What is a thorough-going skeptic to make of this?

I don't know.

Frank's and my first phone conversation was the beginning of a continuous series of nightly phone conversations. They often lasted an hour or more and during them I practiced a degree of honesty that I haven't had with anyone before or since. I was under the influence at that time of a book called People of the Lie by Scott Peck.

Peck's theory was that being anything less than honest was pointless. In normal life, I am not able to live up to that, but with Frank, I determined, come what may, to be as honest as a human being can be. I would do it without shading things, telling him bad things about myself, or disagreeing with things that he said. I believe he was pretty much the same way with me.

I wish I could regain that degree of honesty, but normal life with most people just doesn't seem to accommodate this. In normal life, it's too easy to say the polite thing or the gracious thing or to avoid hurting people's feelings, or to withhold information that could create distance. I told Frank things that I had vowed never to tell another human being, and no matter what, he just seemed to accept and understand. I had the feeling he was totally on my side.

After a month of these conversations, I came to see him, traveling from Davis, California, to Dulles Airport, where he met me in the company plane and we flew to Salisbury, Maryland. I remember looking at his face as we walked from the United terminal to wherever the company plane was waiting, and as I looked, I was thinking, "This is a face I can love."

The weekend we spent together was in some ways heavenly. I found him more compatible and attractive than any man I had ever met. In truth, he was and is the only person with whom I ever could feel complete respect and trust.

When we had known each other five hours, he gave me the Atocha emerald, one of the largest virtually perfect emeralds that exist. He owned it because he was one of the backers of the treasure hunter, Mel Fisher, who found the sunken treasure ship Atocha, which sank off the Florida Keys in 1622. The emerald was part of the treasure recovered from the Atocha.

It's my engagement ring. How amazing that he would give it to me, as an engagement ring, after only knowing me such a short time.

Part of the weekend involved a trip to New York, traveling there on a private plane. "What would you most like to do in New York," he had asked me during one of the nightly phone conversations we had been having the previous month.

"What I'd like to do more than anything is something I shouldn't ask because it can't be done," I answered.

As I was saying this, I was visualizing Time magazine with its cover story on the just-opened play, Phantom of the Opera. The article said the play was so popular anyone wanting tickets would have to wait years to get them.

"Try me," he answered.

"No, it's really impossible."

"Just say it."

"My dream for New York is to see Phantom of the Opera."

Not only did he take me to Phantom, we had the director's seats. Could anything be more romantic than seeing this play in the company of a brilliant man who had been able to get the director's seats? Er, while wearing the Atocha emerald as an engagement ring?

The weekend was the most romantic time possible, but alas, Shakespeare was right, the Course of True Love Never Does Run Smooth, and rather quickly there was a part that didn't go well.

## The Engagement Gets Broken

As I've hinted, I had already been in one unhappy marriage, and I was still terrified of making another mistake. While I was traveling back to California, I had to switch planes at the Denver Airport, and while there I telephoned the woman who had suggested to Frank that we share the same lawyer. I thought she'd enjoy knowing that she had had such an impact on both our lives.

Er, wrong!

Lorraine LeWine (which is not her real name) was aghast when she heard that Frank and I were engaged. "I've known him for years," I heard her angry voice say over the phone, "and he's a complete monster. You've had one unhappy marriage, and you don't need another!"

She went on to tell me that his specialty was making women fall in love with him, proposing marriage, and then dumping them. "Typically," she told me, "they end up needing counseling for years! Listen to me, your friend, and stay away from him! He is so evil that his soul is damned!"

I held the phone away from me for a second, staring at in horror and disbelief. Thoughts flooded through my mind about the mistake I had made in my first marriage, and whether I could endure making a worse mistake?

I put the phone against my ear again, and as the loudspeaker at the airport crackled in the background, I heard the woman cataloguing the horrors of what an evil man Frank was. His children hated him, he liked driving women to suicide, he was narcissistic and cruel. Generally she was listing off a catalogue of everything that I would find repellant in a man.

I had so little confidence in my own judgment, given how misguided I had been with my first marriage, that I listened to her. After all, she had been a good friend, we had gone on a religious retreat together, and I thought I knew her well. I couldn't conceive that she would lie to me. My mind couldn't process the notion that such a devoutly religious person who seemed to have my best interests at heart, could say anything but the truth.

The flight from Denver to Sacramento was agony. Every cell in my body was screaming with pain. I couldn't endure another bad marriage, and yet I had never met anyone ever who attracted me so much in every way. I loved his voice, his touch, his ideas, his drive, his brilliance, and most of all, I guess, I just loved being near him. And yet there was no way I could continue with the heartless ghastly monster that Lorraine was portraying.

As soon as I got home, I started figuring out how to return my engagement ring. I didn't want to put it in the mail because if it didn't get delivered, I would owe him a major fortune. I don't know for sure what the Atocha emerald would cost to replace, but I was guessing that one of the world's largest most perfect emeralds was probably worth at least double what I had paid for my house.

I asked my friend Richard White, regional director of the FBI, how to return an expensive ring. "The one thing not to do," he advised, "is send it insured with the US Postal Service. That's like a beacon signaling mail thieves that 'Here's something worth stealing!'"

Instead, he recommended sending it by FedEx, uninsured, in a large box. "FedEx has a perfect record of tracking packages," he told me, adding, "As an added precaution, you should pack a book along with the ring. A book-size package won't attract attention the way a ring-size package might."

With a breaking heart, I did just that. I was still in love with Frank, and certain that I could never love someone so much again (and as of now, haven't and don't expect to), but I couldn't handle another bad marriage. I wrote Frank a letter, accompanying the returned ring, telling him that I wouldn't see him again, and that the fault was all mine.

When he got the package with the ring and the letter, he began calling me, but I wouldn't pick up the phone. He sent me FedEx letter after FedEx letter, which I sent back as if unopened.

Actually, of course I did open them. The letters inside would melt stones. Frank writes brilliantly and I yearned to get back together with him, but my friend's words kept echoing in my mind; that I had had one terrible marriage and that this would be worse, and I shouldn't be conned by him.

For several months, I was in constant pain. There was a thought which kept echoing in my head: "I'll never marry unless I love someone as much as I loved him, and since I can never love someone so much again, that means I'll never marry again."

I had plenty to keep me busy during this time. I was the hostess and producer of a weekly television show on the Sacramento CBS affiliate, KXTV, I had a weekly syndicated column that I wrote for Capitol News, I was president of the oldest and largest farm women's organization, and I managed close to a thousand acres of rice farms and vineyards in California. Plus (and most important) my two sons, Jose and Carlos, were teenagers. Keeping busy should have been an answer, but it wasn't.

This is jumping ahead a little, but I later learned that Frank was going through something similar. For both of us, career success loses much of its meaning if you don't have someone (to use Frank's words) "to bring it home to."

It was at this point that my younger son Carlos did one of the sweetest things possible. We were driving near the Safeway in Davis, and he could tell that I was unhappy. "Where does my little mommy hurt?" he asked.

How sweet to hear the same kind of words of comfort that I had used when he was a child: "Where does my little Carlos hurt?"

## If You Enjoy Paranoia, Read This!

During this time, as far as I was concerned, Frank and I had broken up, but I still loved him and cared about him. A girlfriend of mine, Ann Thompson, told me she had access to a lot of information about Frank. Since Lorraine had told me that Frank was a totally bad man, I wanted to know more about the man I wouldn't see but was still in love with.

It turns out that Ann, as the highest ranking female executive at a labor union that was targeting Perdue Farms, had access to the union's research library. The union had dossiers about all businessmen with whom they might have dealings. She led me into a room at the union's headquarters that looked as large and professional and business-like as I'd expect to see at the Library of Congress.

The librarian there took us to one of the many hundreds of file drawers and pulled out the drawer with information about Frank Perdue. I'm guessing that it was at least three feet long and it was crammed with files and documents on Frank Perdue.

They had an astonishing amount of personal information on him. I started pawing through the files and to my astonishment found that I could read files on Frank's:

- Personal foibles
- Female companions
- Political attitudes
- Political contributions
- Friends
- Relations with competitors
- Health status
- Relationships with each of his children

There was even a report on him that I think was more than 100 pages long that I learned was written by a woman the union had paid to get close to Frank. She wrote a complete report of where they went, what they talked about, what Frank drank, what he ate, what his political views were, what he thought of different people, and what he said when they were flirting.

Years later, when I told Frank about this, he was astonished to learn that a woman whom he had dated had developed and exploited their relationship for ulterior reasons.

Note to all businessmen: if you ever have feelings of paranoia, and that you're a target, you could be right.

## We Get Re-Engaged

I told you that I had sent the Atocha emerald back to Frank. A couple of months later, in June I finally answered one of his letters, but not with any intention of getting back together. I told him that I would always take an interest in my ex-fiancé's well-being and wished him well. I also mentioned that I'd be in Washington, DC, for a meeting of American Agri-Women, the organization which I was currently president of.

Looking back on it, I'm puzzled that if I really intended not to get back together with him, why did I tell him I'd be in Washington? I guess subconsciously, I did want to get back together.

I attended the American Agri-Women meeting, with a broken heart. During one of the lunches, I sat with some people from USDA. The topic got onto romance. Frank was still so much on my mind that I blurted out that I was in love with someone, but it hadn't worked out, and I didn't think I could ever love anyone else.

At this moment, the door to the meeting of several 100 people burst open, and in strides Frank. I saw him heading toward the podium and rushed up to him. To avoid a scene, I whispered to him that we should talk outside.

"I know the reason you haven't wanted to see me," he said the moment we were outside the banquet room. "I can prove that what your friend has been saying about me isn't true."

"I've had one bad marriage," I answered, "and I can't handle another one. I believe her and I don't believe you."

"She told you my children hate me. Let's visit them and you can see for yourself."

Fortunately, my part of the American Agri-Women meeting was over, and we flew in a private plane to meet all his four children, making stops in Portland, Maine, then Richmond, Virginia, and finally, Salisbury, Maryland.

To my astonishment, it was clear that his children adored him. The more I talked with each of them, the more I realized that they idolized him, and wanted nothing more than to see him happy.

What a contrast with what Lorraine had said! "She's lied about his children," I reasoned, "and that means everything else she said is in doubt!"

It was the most wonderful revelation! For months all the colors seemed to have gone out of my life, but now, when I looked at a tree, the leaves were so green! The crimson and white stripes on my dress were so lively; the blue of the sky such an incredibly deep luscious azure!

It was like coming back to life!

Frank gave me back my engagement ring and the wedding was on again!

Now I had to tell my kids. I phoned them both, slightly afraid of what they would say about my marrying a man I had only known in person a few hours. Both said that their only concern was my happiness, and if he made me happy, they were all for it.

I returned briefly to Davis, California, to wind up my affairs in California. That meant quitting my job at KXTV and at Capitol News, arranging to be away from my farming operations, and selling my house. The most poignant part of all this was saying good-bye to Fred Kline, my boss at Capitol News.

My relationship with Fred was more than professional. I think he looked on me as a daughter. He asked me to have lunch with him before leaving, and I was preparing to be scolded for burning all my bridges in order to take up with a man I had known in person for roughly thirty-six hours.

As we sat at Fred's favorite restaurant, eating its signature avocado, nuts, and sprouts salad, Fred told me, "I'm happy that you're doing this. I understand."

I was dumbfounded. As I said, I was prepared to be scolded.

"When Verna and I met forty years ago," he continued, "we also knew immediately. In the time since that day, we've never spent a night apart. Go for it!"

## A Series of My Favorite Moments in Life

Frank and I were still talking by phone for an hour or two every night. When discussing the wedding date, I wanted the date to be August 8th, 1988, since it would be so easy to remember 8/8/88, but we settled on the date July 31, 1988.

However, since we were to be married in an Episcopalian service, and since the Episcopalians have a six-week prenuptial counseling period, that meant that if we were to make the July 31st date, we'd have to start the clock ticking almost immediately. By phone, we agreed to meet in New York as soon as I had wound up everything in Davis.

The reason to meet in New York was because that's where Reverend Draesel had his church. We met in his chancery, and this was now the beginning of the third time I had seen Frank Perdue in my life.

Reverend Draesel was delighted with our news and, congratulating us, asked, "How long have you known each other?"

"Do you mean in person?" I inquired.

"Well, yes!"

I looked at the watch on my wrist, and holding my wrist first a little closer and then farther away so I could read my watch, I answered, "Thirty-six hours."

This was not an answer Rev. Draesel was expecting. After hearing it, he was unwilling to agree to perform the ceremony. He said he would need to interview each of us separately.

It took roughly an hour each. During my interview, he asked me to describe my father.

"My father was a brilliant man," I told him. "Underneath he was a very shy man and introverted, but somehow, almost through force of will he learned to be sociable and learned how to say the right things. He had tremendous focus, fabulous drive, and an ability to see opportunities where others saw none."

Warming to my subject, I went on to tell Rev. Draesel that my father, as the co-founder of the Sheraton Hotel chain, was also a high-achieving and successful man who was also a profoundly good and moral man. I said he wasn't good at expressing affection and that while I knew he loved us kids, his relationship with us was reticent more than demonstrative."

"All in all," I finished, "I was enormously proud to have him as a father. I was lucky beyond belief."

At the end of this, Rev. Draesel asked if I realized that in describing my father's characteristics, I had just described Frank. He also said, after interviewing Frank, that we were ready to proceed with the marriage.

My twenty-fifth Harvard reunion happened almost immediately after this, and Frank accompanied me for part of it. I particularly gloried in this reunion, partly because I have a ferocious love for Harvard, but even more because I was chosen to be the class reunion speaker.

I had a speech prepared, but I asked the 500 or so people in the hall for permission to make some comments in response to the experiences we had at the reunion, and then extemporaneously talked for maybe five minutes. My remarks were about things that we were all experiencing, including insecurities and wounds that we had as second class citizens at Harvard, and what we did with those wounds to make us stronger and better and more understanding. It was, I think, a stem-winder of a speech, and at the end, people rose to their feet cheering and cheering. It was a moment to cherish for a lifetime.

Something else happened that weekend that was one of my favorite (er, out of many) moments in life: there was a concert at Symphony Hall, and at this event, Frank met my son Carlos for the first time. Carlos was only sixteen years old but, even so, Frank felt that he needed to ask for my hand from a male member of the family.

Because Frank was such a celebrity, there was a circle of perhaps fifty people surrounding Frank, me, and Carlos. I introduced my two guys. Then Frank said formally, as a circle of fifty strangers watched, "I'd like to ask for your mother's hand in marriage."

Carlos answered, in front of the crowd of gaping spectators, and loud enough for all of them to hear, "Sure, take her! She's yours! But it will cost you!"

Both Frank and the surrounding crowd did one giant double-take. Some even stepped backward. This wasn't part of the expected script!

"The cost is," Carlos continued, allowing a pause of a couple of beats, while the crowd leaned forward, "a Ferrari Testarossa or a pepperoni pizza, whichever you think she's worth!"

Frank roared over that, and so did the crowd.

Actually, it was a perfect introduction to my kids. One of Frank's characteristics is an unending sense of humor, and he and Carlos were on absolutely the same wavelength. Frank ended up getting along perfectly with both Carlos and Jose, the entire time we had together. He respected and enjoyed them, and it was mutual: both kids told me year after year that he was the guy they admired most in the world.

Carlos also proved to be most entertaining as the wedding approached. The night before our wedding, at the rehearsal dinner, there were many dozens of flattering toasts. But then sixteen-year-old Carlos gets up and says something along the lines of:

"Everyone has been saying wonderful things about Frank and Mitzi, but I'm here to set the record straight. Frank asked for my Mom's hand in marriage and I told him 'Sure, take her,' but that there was a price: either a Ferrari Testarossa or a pepperoni pizza. Since Frank has delivered on neither, the marriage can't go forward!"

The guests rose to their feat cheering over this toast. It was exactly the sort of humor both sides of our families would enjoy.

Continuing with the joke, several months later Frank actually gave Carlos a Ferrari. As Carlos describes it, "Sometime later, a Ferrari Testarossa arrived at my dorm at Berkeley. It was beautiful, red, and came with a phone. It was also twelve inches long and functioned only as a phone. What a guy!"

### Blackmail, False Witness, and the Threat of Automatic Weapons

However, I've got to say that not everything that was going on at this point was laughable. As I mentioned earlier, Lorraine DeWine had tried to keep Frank and me apart and alas she didn't disappear from the picture. Having failed to persuade me that Frank was a monster, she turned into her own brand of monster. I started thinking of her as the Homing Vampire because she had unnatural skill in selecting targets where she could do the most harm.

She sent FedEx packages to the Perdue Farms Management Committee and to the board of directors as well, telling them, among other things, that I was a fake, that I hadn't gone to Harvard, that my father hadn't started Sheraton, that I was poor and a fortune hunter, that my mother was crazy, that I loved lawsuits and would make a fool of Frank in court, and that I liked to sleep with guys much younger than me (my personal opinion of that thought: yuck!) and had told her, "You should try it!" She painted me pretty much as a fortune-hunting, trouble-making, promiscuous, sex-crazed, cradle-robbing opportunist and fake.

Nice, huh?

What must this have looked like to Frank's friends and associates, given that he had just come out of a marriage that hadn't worked? They knew nothing about me, but they did know that Frank had made a mistake before and was going into a new marriage almost immediately after ending the old one.

I can't imagine how Frank had the courage and conviction to go ahead with our marriage, given that people who cared about him were telling him to go slow, and that he didn't have to marry me. Nevertheless, he said he wasn't going to listen to my friends or his friends, and the marriage would proceed.

At this point, the Homing Vampire changed targets. She said she was going to sue him for millions of dollars by alleging that he had given her a dreadful social disease (which I know he couldn't have given her because we were married seventeen years and I would know if he had such a thing, and he didn't).

She knew that, if there's a lawsuit, you can allege anything (and what a vile thing to accuse someone of!) and evade the libel laws. Further, as she told Frank, she had many friends in the newspaper industry and could guarantee that she could get them to publicize the case.

This was becoming the stuff of nightmares. If Lorraine sued him for the alleged terrible social disease, I worried that the suit could be in the papers everywhere. It could have been more than just embarrassing; it could have harmed the brand, which in turn could affect the livelihoods of 20,000 employees.

I told Frank that if he wanted to postpone the wedding, I would understand.

"We're not going to postpone it," he answered, "and further, I have no interest in giving in to blackmail!"

We're now about a week before the wedding is to take place. Having failed to move Frank with the threat of her bogus lawsuit, the Homing Vampire changed tack and said she would call off the dogs if Frank gave her a mere million dollars. Oh, and if that wasn't enough torment for us, she began threatening to disrupt the wedding.

We're now two days before the wedding, and I remember the shower, given by my friend Esther Coopersmith that afternoon. It was a lingerie shower, and my wonderful friends outdid themselves with fabulous, naughty or sexy or ultra feminine underthings.

However, the experience was surreal. None of the guests at the shower knew that I didn't know whether the wedding would take place or not. When I'm under stress (and this was among the most stressful things I've been through), I repeat to myself that I must act with grace and dignity. Repeating "Grace and dignity" over and over again helped keep me from a white-hot, hand-wringing, garment-rending, shrieking freak-out.

The whole situation was so fraught with the possibility of a very public scandal that I felt I couldn't confide what was going on and, further, I didn't want to ruin for everyone else, especially my hostess, what was actually a lovely shower.

I smiled and was appreciative as I opened a heavenly fake nurse's costume and held it up for everyone to see. Or I'd open and pretend to model an exquisitely lacy garter belt or a black lace bustier, or a lacy white nightgown with feathers on it.

Although I was smiling and enthusiastic, on the inside, because of the blackmail and the threats of a violent disruption of the wedding, I felt as if I were going through open heart surgery without anesthesia. "Grace and dignity, dignity and grace," I kept repeating to myself.

I don't think my hostess or any of the guests had any idea that things were in such turmoil for me. I've since wondered if I should have told them, and maybe today I would have, but back then, I was terrified of having any of this become public. And then one other thing, in spite of what I was going through—part of me did enjoy the shower and I did feel supported by the warmth and caring of my friends.

That wasn't the end. The morning of the wedding, I remember, as a hair dresser was fussing with my hair, I was taking a phone call from the security company assigned to cover the wedding.

"Do you think," the voice on the phone inquired, "that the person who has threatened to disrupt the wedding is likely to have accomplices? Is she likely to have automatic weapons?"

The question dumbfounded me. It's my wedding day, and I'm trying to figure out if my ex-close friend had accomplices who would use automatic weapons to disrupt our wedding?

"I'm not sure," I answered. "When I thought I knew her well, I would have thought she'd have no idea how to get or use an automatic weapon. But now I'm not sure of anything."

"In that case," the calm and authoritative voice on the phone continued, "we'll need to have a team that can handle several people with automatic weapons. But don't worry; we know how to do this."

The hair dresser went back to arranging my curls, and I went back to telling myself, "Grace and dignity! Dignity and grace!"

The ceremony itself was, I think, unusual. Because of the threats of disruption including possible violence, we had two ministers performing the service.

The plan, which we actually rehearsed with the two ministers, was that if there were a disruption of the violent sort, the ministers would simply jump to the part of the ceremony in which we are each asked (speaking rapidly) if we take this man (or this woman) to be our lawfully wedded husband (or wife), and after we had each rapidly said, "I do", then the minister would quickly say, "I now pronounce you man and wife."

It would be a done deal. Everything else about the marriage ceremony is decoration and the only legally important part of it is the "I do's" and the "I now pronounce you man and wife."

On the other hand, if the disruption came from someone speaking up during the part of the ceremony about whether anyone knew a reason for this marriage not to take place, and "speak now or forever hold your peace," one of the ministers would walk over to Lorraine and usher her into the chancel to explain her reasons. Then the other minister would follow the other plan of jumping to the essential part of the ceremony and making it a done deal before she got out of the chancel.

During the actual ceremony, when we got through the "speak now or forever hold your peace," and nothing happened, I felt I could breathe again.

The reception was at a house I briefly owned on Kalorama Avenue in Washington, DC. My owning the house was an odd story in itself.

The last couple of years of my life in Davis, I was spending so much time in Washington as president of American Agri-Women that it sort of made sense to buy a place rather than have the money just go up in smoke on hotel bills. I found a place that I liked in the Kaloramo neighborhood, and as part of the bargaining over price, I offered the owner, Mr. Spence, a low price but in return, he could live in the place for up to three months while he was looking for another home. The problem with all this was, by the time I took possession of the property, I had become engaged to Frank Perdue and never lived in it.

The only use I ever got out of it was that's where the wedding reception was held. But that's not the end of the story.

### A Male Prostitution Ring in My House, a Month of Front Page Headlines, plus the Blackmailer Isn't Satisfied

Within days of Frank's and my marrying, Spence began turning up on the front page of the local newspapers. He was front page material, especially of the Washington Times, for almost a month.

He had been running a gay prostitution ring out of the house that I had just bought. Further, he was blackmailing all sorts of politicians and the place became known as "the Scandal House." He ended up committing suicide, dramatically dressing himself in a top hat and tails and, I think, taking pills, while barricading himself in the Ritz Hotel in Boston.

The suicide was understandable, given the legal troubles he was in, but also, given the fact that he was already dying of AIDS.

My terror during all this publicity was that the press would discover that the true owner of the Scandal House was Mrs. Frank Perdue. I barely had met Mr. Spence, but guilt by ownership if not by association could have added spice to the tale.

Since the Homing Vampire was already doing everything she could to blacken my name, I was beside myself with worry that I might unwittingly have brought scandal to my new name. It would have been so easy for a scandal-mongering reporter to make it look as if Mrs. Frank Perdue hung out with Spence. Why else would I buy his house?

What a way to become a member of my new family, bringing with me a feeding frenzy of press because of having had (however unknowingly) a connection with the blackmailing owner of a gay prostitution ring. It was a great big steaming pile of...uh, well, er problems.

However, as happened many times in my life, something that could have been horrible didn't happen. The press never inquired about who now owned the Scandal House.

That bullet was dodged, but things were not smooth sailing yet.

Lorraine's efforts at disruption hadn't ended. When Frank and I came back from our Positano honeymoon, she called Frank and asked to meet him when he was next in New York.

Frank asked what I thought about this and my thinking, which was oh-so-wrong, was that Lorraine was ashamed of how she had acted and wanted to apologize and make up for it. I told him I was fine with his meeting with her. I thought it could give her a chance to put her unfortunate behavior behind her and get on with her life.

When Frank met her at the restaurant of the hotel where she was staying, Lorraine told him that she needed to speak with him with no audience and that it would have to be in her room. Frank agreed to this, but once in her room, Lorraine unfurled a set of papers which she had had her lawyer draw up for Frank to sign in order to begin annulment proceedings!

*Mr. and Mrs. Frank Perdue at St. Margaret's Church in Washington, DC*

Frank of course walked out.

Lorraine has been a puzzle to me ever since. She and I had once been friends, and we had even gone on a religious retreat together. She is ostentatiously Christian yet this Christian woman bore false witness against me, blackmailed Frank, and likely had adultery in mind when she asked Frank to her bedroom to sign the annulment papers.

I don't know what went on in her mind, but looking back on it, the guess that most seems to fit the facts is: the reason she was eager to find a divorce lawyer for Frank, and the reason she put so much effort into trying to disrupt our relationship, is that she may have had designs on him for herself.

But back to my marriage to Frank.

## After That, We Settle Down Comfortably

I look back on our marriage with amazement. When we married, we had known each other in person only a couple of days more than six weeks. Yet there was no adjustment period. I felt I had known him forever, and it was astonishingly easy to integrate into his life, especially after all the drama that we had just endured.

Actually, it shouldn't have been so easy, given how different our backgrounds and personalities were. I was a social register international debutante, Harvard-educated, and had spent a good bit of my life hanging out with the snobbier sort of academics. His background was farming, he left college before his junior year, and his view of society people was mixed at best. I am strongly extroverted, and he was basically shy. I am introspection incarnate, and he was virtually never given to introspection. I am an attention-seeking show-off while I think he was immune to the joys and pleasures of adulation. He was tough to the core, and I've often felt that I have the backbone of an over-cooked noodle.

Knowing this, who could have predicted how exquisitely happy we would be? Frank certainly and without competition gave me the happiest years of my life. I hope (actually, I believe) that it was the same for him.

There were a number of reasons why it worked, at least from my point of view. One of the first things that comes to mind is, he was utterly fair. If I had a grievance, it made no sense to argue about it because he would listen to my side with what felt like celestial impartiality and would often accede to my side even when it was strongly against his self-interest. I certainly didn't always get my way, but I always felt I had been heard and heard fairly and even generously.

Further, he put enormous store in solving issues immediately. Something that happened quite a few times would be, he'd be leaving in the morning for work, and he'd sense that something was bothering me. He wouldn't leave until we settled it, even if that meant he'd be late for an important meeting or even a board meeting.

That, of course, put tremendous pressure on me to do my part in resolving whatever it was as rapidly as possible because I didn't want to cause him to be late. For a man who put extreme value on being prompt, his willingness to put our relationship first had a huge impact on me, and I didn't want to abuse that generosity.

Another factor in our marriage working, again from my point of view, was that I had infinite respect for him. To this day, I still think he may be the most totally good person I'll ever meet. I can think of a hundred occasions where he put the good of others above his own good.

For example, on weekends, when most people might be watching TV or playing golf or whatever, he, with me accompanying him, would be calling on people in the hospital or visiting retirees in their homes. He knew that his presence could cheer them and make them feel valued, and he did it. I went, not because I'm nice, but because I loved being near him and delighted in watching him in action.

We also attended a phenomenal number of funerals. My attitude toward funerals in most cases used to be, you go out of grim duty, because it's an important social obligation and you have to do it. His, in contrast, was a sincere desire to be there for people. There was a generosity of spirit to him that I could never match. I'm not entirely devoid of it, and I dearly hope I have improved over the years, but I have witnessed that I don't have it at all to the extent that came naturally to him. I passionately admired this generosity of spirit.

He was remarkably even-tempered. In seventeen years, I believe there was only one time that he was mad at me.

That one time was when he felt I hadn't treated a chicken right. I do magic tricks and I had once pulled a baby chick out of a hat as entertainment during one of our parties. After the party was over, Frank told me in the strongest possible tone of voice, "Never do that again!" I was not to do that ever again because, as he explained to me, a chicken is a flocking animal, and removing a chick from its flock and putting it in a black bag as part of the magic trick meant that its social and psychological needs weren't being met.

Trust me, I never did do that again.

## The Perdue Approach to Social Affairs

Frank and I were quite different people, but it all seemed to work wonderfully. I think it somehow delighted him that I was utterly different from his work environment.

Professionally, he was the uber alpha male with a lot of authority and power. With me, it was whimsical, nutty, illogical, and I hope fun.

As an example, here's what happened within days of our getting back from our honeymoon. We were walking on the beach in Watch Hill, Rhode Island, on a mild mid-August afternoon, with the beach almost empty, and us walking barefoot, carrying our shoes in our hands.

In the middle of these relaxed moments, completely out of the blue, I looked up at him and announced, "Franklin, we should entertain everyone who works for the company."

He looked at me as if I had set down from a different planet. "That's a totally impractical idea," he responded.

"I think we should start in late September," I continued.

"Absolutely not," he answered, adding, "Don't even think of doing something like that so soon!"

"Shall we start with, hmmm, let's say, 100 people," I asked.

"That's an impossibly large number. No!"

"I think we should begin with the secretaries," I continued, apparently oblivious to the firm "No!" that I had just heard. "Uh, yes, the secretaries," I continued. "They're everywhere in the organization, so they can spread the word that our parties are fun and not scary!"

And so it went, for several more rounds, with every step of the way, his saying "no" and my simply barreling on as if I was simply unable to process the notion of "no."

Surely this was different from what he experienced in the work environment! But he kept going along with it. If he had said "no" in a tone that told me he meant it, I would have backed off, but instead his "no's" were more in the nature of "You've got to be kidding." Actually, it would be more accurate to describe the tone as "Tell me again the name of the galaxy you came from?"

Anyway, in September, we inaugurated a series of almost weekly parties, 100 guests at a time, that continued for most of our marriage, except when we were traveling or when he eventually became too ill. Oh, and by the way, we did begin with the secretaries.

Frank loved the parties. At the end of each party, he would speak briefly, thanking our guests (his employees) and telling them that he knew the company would never have been what it was today without them. Then he'd answer questions, so a truck driver or a sanitation man could ask the founder about whatever interested him or her.

We invited people in groups who knew each other, on the theory that for at least some people, it would be intimidating to be invited to the home of the head of the company. We figured that if guests came with people they knew, they'd be more comfortable.

Another factor in all this was, we wanted to make sure that people didn't spend scarce money on new clothes for the event, so each invitation invited people to come dressed for their sport. The sports we offered at our Woodland Road house included volleyball, horseshoes, ping pong, basketball, tennis, badminton, and pool.

All of the "catering" was done in-house by Cindy and Greg Downes, who worked for us anyway, and the Salisbury Perdue Plant's cafeteria. It was relatively inexpensive, and I had the kitchen fitted out as if it were a professional catering kitchen, complete with warming ovens, warming trays, and plates and utensils for probably 150 people. I think the chef at the Perdue cafeteria loved me because, as he told me, cooking for my parties meant he could try out all sorts of fancy cooking that wouldn't fit in a cafeteria menu.

It's hard to assess the success of this effort, but I had many clues. Several times, when Frank and I attended funerals of deceased employees (called "associates" in Perdue-speak), the next of kin told me that the most exciting thing that happened in the deceased's life was being invited to Frank Perdue's home for dinner.

I'd also hear from, for example, human resources people at Perdue, that this effort was phenomenal for creating good will, and that no other Fortune 500-size company had the head of it entertain everyone in his or her home. The whole thing had the look and feel of a spectacular success.

In fact, Frank enjoyed it so much that we soon branched out to include the farmers who grew chickens or grain for Perdue, and we even began inviting the suppliers, such as the local businessmen or women who supplied wood chips or propane or whatever.

It's incongruous but Frank, who was basically a shy man, absolutely adored having the house full of people. He used to tell me that he loved seeing the house come alive, filled with animated guests having fun.

He was a gracious host and occasionally would even serve his guests from the buffet line. He was good at going around and shaking everyone's hand and, for the moment, giving each person his whole attention and making the person feel important. In fact, that was one of Frank's gifts, being able to talk with anyone at their level, whether a worker from the line or the president of the United States. I've seen him relate to both with equal ease, grace, and sincerity.

I have a favorite memory of these parties. One evening, I noticed an African-American couple off on the sidelines, not mingling or participating in the bustle and fun of that night's party. I went up to them, trying to discover what was wrong.

"My wife works for Perdue sanitation," the guy told me, "but I don't. I work for the city department of sanitation. If I try to tell the guys who work with me I had dinner at Frank Perdue's house, they'll never believe me."

I knew that everyone in the wife's department would believe her because this was the night we were having the sanitation workers here at our home. But what to do about the guy, who had no witnesses?

My Polaroid to the rescue! I grabbed it from my office, which was next door to the living room where that party was taking place, and then looked for Frank. Predictably, he was in the center of a large crowd of people, shaking hands and making each person feel important. I interrupted the scene and in a low voice, explained the sanitation guy's problem.

Frank instantly understood, and grinning, left the twenty or so people who had been surrounding him and walked to the corner of the room where the couple was. He shook hands with the guy, and then put his arm around him as if they were old buddies. I snapped a Polaroid picture of the two, and then a minute later, Frank was autographing the photograph with the Sharpie pen he always carried in his shirt pocket.

I watched Frank write, "To Mike, it was great having dinner with you last night, Frank."

The couple beamed.

I'm not sure how many people we entertained during those years, but it has to be in the five figures. It really was a lot of entertaining because in addition to that, we entertained his business associates, we entertained buyers, we put on events for many different charities, or we'd have book parties for local authors.

Frank particularly loved the annual parties we gave for United Way's largest donors. He was genuinely thrilled that each year we'd surpass the previous year's record and he loved it that the company was United Way's largest donor. Kathleen Momme, the head of our local United Way, told me that being able to offer dinner at Frank's house as a perk for giving $500 or more vastly increased the number of Anchor Society donations.

Another annual event that he loved was the party for Perdue Scholars. He loved being around them and interacting with them, and especially, answering their questions.

**"I'm Not Going to Change Anything in the House. I Love It Just as It Is."**

*This was our Thanksgiving turkey*

Something else that was going on during this period was constant redecorating. When I first moved in, I had told Frank that I loved the house just as it was and didn't want to change a thing. However, there was an exception: the light in his closet was too dim.

"Frank, it's the only thing in the whole house that I want to change, but I need to put in a brighter lightbulb. When I'm packing for you, in this light I can't tell whether I'm choosing blue socks or black."

The brighter light, however, revealed some chips in the paint in the closet. Oh dear.

"Frank, we can't have chipped paint. We need to repaint the closet!"

However, once the closet was repainted, it was totally clear that we had to paint the bedroom so it would go with the brighter paint from the closet, and using that logic, pretty soon every room in the house was repainted.

Unfortunately, the new bright cheery walls revealed that the thirty-year-old carpets were faded and worn and would need replacing. But then the contrast between the lovely fresh, sea-foam green carpets and the old faded drapes meant that of course the drapes needed to be replaced. In the end, virtually nothing was left unchanged.

Usually I would make these kinds of changes when Frank was away on business for several days. It was a case of "While the cat's away, the mice will play!" My favorite instance, and also the first time I did this, was when with Napoleonic precision during one of Frank's four-day trips, I arranged for the entire very-large living room to be totally transformed in every detail. I changed the carpets, the drapery, the lamps, some of the furniture, the display cabinets, and so on.

He came back, marched to the entrance of the living room, and stood there, arms crossed over his chest, glowering. I, of course, was scared out of my mind. What if I had gone too far?

And then he said, "My God, this is beautiful!"

He loved having his house looking its best. I remember once when he was talking about the advantages of being married, that having his house look nice was way up on the list.

But of course, as a businessman, he wanted to know what the changes I had just made cost. I told him fifty cents.

"No, but tell me what it really costs!"

"Fifty cents, Frank, that's what it cost!"

Later on, I changed the entrance doorway to one that had partially glazed glass and looked less like a fortress. The job was to be done by mid-afternoon, but he came home early that day and saw the workmen putting on the finishing touches before leaving.

He liked what they had done but, as usual, he wanted to know what it cost. Here was his chance to find out because he could ask the workmen himself!

"Say, can you tell me what this new door cost?"

"Yes, Mr. Perdue. It cost fifty cents."

As a precaution, I had told the workers that if Frank ever asked, they were to tell him the fifty-cent answer.

I wonder how this sounds to you, Dear Reader. Frank and I had an endlessly joking and teasing and quipping kind of relationship and I think he adored it. If ever there had been a whiff of "I Really Want To Know," I would have caved in an instant. But I think he enjoyed having something a little bit wild and off the wall and unpredictable in his life. I like to think he felt younger with me around.

The redecoration was kind of our shtick. There was an understanding and rules to it, and since he seemed to love the end result, it was highly enjoyable on all counts.

## "To Love a Man Is to Facilitate His Life"

I also dreamed up some other things designed to please him. One of my mottos is, *"Aimer un homme c'est lui faciliter la vie."* I knew that one of his highest goals was to be close to his family and to have the family be close, so I tried many things that I hoped would support this. I created a yearly family album, and each year for Christmas I'd present each family member with a twenty-or-so page album of photographs of the previous year's vacation. I'd have captions for each photo and I tried to make sure that every family member appeared in the book.

As part of the *Family Album*, I'd also ask everyone the *Family Question*. This would change each year, but the answers would always be revealing. The first year, I asked everyone who their hero was. In subsequent years I'd ask things like, what was the best advice your parents gave you, or what's your favorite movie, what's your earliest memory, or if you had two extra hours every day how would you spend them?

Because everyone got to read everyone else's answers in the Family Album, it was a way of having us get to know each other better and creating family glue.

I also wrote the *Perdue Chicken Cookbook*, which I hoped would be good for the company, plus the *Perdues' News*, about which I'll write more later.

### Undeserved (but Highly Enjoyed) Reputation as a Linguist

We also did a fair amount of travel. Whenever we'd travel abroad, I'd usually know about it several months ahead of time, so if we were traveling to Russia or Japan or China, or wherever, I'd spend those couple of months taking weekly language lessons from a native of whichever country we'd be visiting. Salisbury University has a strong international aspect and seeks international students, so finding a native speaker from almost any country was easy.

By the end of, say, eight weeks of learning four or five polite phrases each week, I could say a lot of nice things to the people we were visiting and I could say these phrases in their language.

*This is me at our condo at the Pyramid in Ocean City, Maryland. We entertained thousands of people there, usually for donor recognition events for charities. It would be a perk for donors to be entertained at Frank Perdue's home.*

I'd learn phrases such as, "Your hospitality is wonderful!" or "The food is delicious!" or "We are so happy to be in Beijing!" During our trips, I'd use these phrases and similar ones continuously.

Our trips invariably ended with our hosts giving us a farewell banquet. Typically this might include fifty American ex-pats, and fifty local businessmen. At the end of the banquet, our host would give a toast to us.

Then it would be Frank's turn to respond. However, Frank didn't enjoy public speaking, so I who adore it, would be our spokesperson. I'd look at the interpreter and, all innocence, ask "Would you please translate for me?"

On the face of it, this is an absurd question because what else is an interpreter there for?

However, I had a reason for it, and it was to create a certain shock value because, as the translator would soon discover, the translating I wanted wasn't English to the host language, it was the host language into English.

I'd launch into a three or four minute toast in Shanghainese or whatever the local language was. I did this by putting together all the polite phrases I had learned previously, but I'd always add one or two new sentences that I had learned that day and that were topical for that day.

In Shanghai, my talk went something like, "We are so happy to be in Shanghai! Your hospitality has been wonderful! We are so impressed by the beauty of the city, and we loved the beautiful array of orchids we saw along the road we drove here. I've just learned that the road is new, and it's so beautiful!" And so on.

Between breaks, the translator is translating all of this into English. That meant the Americans present would know that I really was speaking Shanghainese.

From my point of view, the best was yet to come. When I finished, there would be applause, and then often someone would ask a question in the native language.

Sometimes it would be simple enough so that I would understand it and could answer it using one of my stock phrases. But most often, I couldn't make head nor tail of it and would use my final phrase, in the native language: "Thank you for your question, but I must admit that I don't know any more words than the ones I've just used."

For some reason (for some delightful reason), this would bring down the house. The native speakers would totally laugh over my admission that I didn't know how to say anything else.

But meanwhile, to the English-speaking people, it looked (as some of them told me) that I was so fluent that I could not only answer an unscripted question but I could also tell an uproariously funny joke at the same time, all in the native language.

I'd respond to these compliments with perfect honesty that no, I wasn't fluent, I only knew a few phrases. And then they'd tell me I was being too modest. So, I'd get credit for modesty on top of everything else!

I actually heard at a meeting of the National Broiler Council that there were people who believed that I was fluent in seventeen different languages.

Speaking of overseas travel, I have a favorite moment of Frank's teasing me. I have mentioned several times, haven't I, that we were endlessly teasing each other? We were in Shanghai once, and some buyers who were important to us had invited us to a splendid restaurant for a many course meal.

The restaurant where we were eating lunch had an amazing feature, a fifteen foot long fish tank. In it were swimming large fish, I'm guessing about two feet long. The idea was, your host got to pick which fish you would all dine on, and the fish would be so fresh that it was swimming in the tank one minute, and then filleted and served the next. Served raw, I might add.

The prize part of the fish at this restaurant was the eye. Frank, as guest of honor, was offered a very, very fresh fish eyeball. It was about the size and shape of a large grape.

Frank took the plate with the fish eyeball, stood up, and holding the plate aloft in a theatrical gesture, a wicked twinkle in his eye, addressed our thirty or so hosts.

"I recognize the great honor you have given me," he announced. "However, I love my wife so much and she means so much to me, that I would like to give this magnificent honor to her!" And then he lowers the plate and thrusts it, with it's unwelcome cargo of raw eyeball, into my hands.

I, of course, had to eat the thing. But before I did, I shot a glance at the other people in the room, all guys, and realized that they absolutely got what was going on. They all had little half-suppressed grins.

Using chopsticks, which in itself wasn't all that easy. I plopped the eyeball into my mouth. I would dearly have liked to swallow it whole so as not to have to chew it, but the thing was too large.

Can you imagine having to crunch down on a raw fish eyeball?

Actually, it wasn't bad. It was salty, and in texture, size, and shape, reminded me of a very large grape. Because it was so fresh, it tasted only slightly fishy.

As I said, it wasn't bad. It was almost fun, in part because for the moment it was like being a kid again, doing something on a dare, as in, "Hey, Mikey, I bet you wouldn't dare eat that worm!"

We both laughed about it later, Frank especially, because he knew he had really gotten me on that one. And by the way, it wouldn't have been funny except that Frank knew me well enough to know that while I don't really relish eating the eyeball of a recently-alive fish, it's not the end of the world either.

Humor was a big part of our relationship. I have often thought that laughter is both a symptom and a cause of a happy relationship. It was certainly a hallmark of ours. In our case, when we were alone, I almost always had a smile on my face, knowing that soon enough there would be some quirky, new, off-the-wall thing he'd say or do that would make me giggle, or laugh, or collapse on the floor, holding my sides with laughter.

For instance, one day we had been with some supermarket friends in Boston and had had dinner with several of them on a Saturday night. The next morning Frank woke up before me and was busy at the desk in our hotel room, reading marketing reports or whatever. I was still half asleep when I heard his voice announcing to me with great seriousness, "Today is the Lord's Day."

"Um yes, it's Sunday," I mumbled groggily.

"And because it's the Lord's Day," he continued, with growing forcefulness, "it's okay to take the hotel's shampoos and soaps and conditioners, but *I forbid you to steal the curtains!*"

It took me a moment to grasp the complete, astonishing absurdity of this and then of course I was convulsing with laughter. Who but my dear husband could even think of something so literally off-the-wall as the thought that you shouldn't steal the hotel's curtains because it was Sunday?

I mean there are layers and layers of ridiculousness to this idea. I think Frank Perdue is the only person who could ever put such unconnected ideas together and make them funny. I still laugh over it.

## My Day Working on the Line in a Chicken Plant

Early in our marriage, I got a minor reputation for something I did that was work-related. It was something that was described on the radio and in many newspapers and it began when one day when I was having lunch at the cafeteria at the Accomac, Virginia, processing plant. I happened to sit beside an African-American woman who worked on the line. We got to talking about our lives.

Because she was asking me lots of questions about my life, I dared ask her questions about what her job working in the processing plant was like. She said she loved it and looked forward to each day. I put what I'm about to say in a more tactful and indirect way than I'm writing it here, but in a roundabout way, I expressed the notion that I would have thought that just maybe the work could get…boring?

"Not at all," she assured me. "Each day is different and each day is great!"

I told her I couldn't even imagine that, working on the line, each day would be different. She answered that she couldn't explain it; the only way to convince me would be for me to come and work on the line and see for myself.

"If you can arrange it," I told her, "I'll do it!"

As a result, a couple of days later, it happened that Mrs. Frank Perdue was "working" in a Perdue processing plant, putting plucked chickens in the shackles, or to be more accurate, trying to put plucked chickens in the shackles that were going by overhead.

I was standing beside my lunch companion, getting at least a glimpse of what her life on the line was like. Contrary to everything I expected or even imagined, it was fun!

What was good about it, and what I wouldn't have guessed, was there was an unending stream of banter. People where I was working (I guess it would be more accurate to say "working" with scare quotes around the word) talked about their love lives, their dates, their kids, the TV shows they had seen the night before, what different celebrities were doing, and then also, there was a great abundance of teasing.

In this case, I was the butt of all the teasing, but the teasing was good-natured. What I was getting teased for, and with good reason, was that I couldn't get the chickens' feet in the shackles before the conveyor belt moved on. For every one I missed, someone down the line had to catch it and hang it for me. I think it took me half an hour before I could get even one foot in a shackle and I don't recall that I ever did get two in.

The words "Getting the hang of it" will forever more have new meaning for me.

The guy standing beside me, to show off, began hanging two at a time, one in each hand. For me, who couldn't get one foot in, watching someone else do four feet at a time, the performance was awesome. I concluded that getting this particular job right was a skill in the same way a typist develops a skill for doing things rapidly that simply couldn't be done without hours of practice.

Basically, my day "working" in the processing plant was a blast, although it's clear that I was worth exactly what they paid me. When it was over, we all hugged each other and many dozens of people at the plant wanted photographs with me. Oh, and I did tell my lunch companion that she was right, it wasn't boring and it had indeed been fun.

Shortly after that, I met a radio host who was broadcast nationally. He was pontificating about how separate management and workers are in America, so I told him about working on the line for a day and how much I had enjoyed the people I met as well as the whole experience, and how I had an increased awareness of the skill it takes to do their jobs. He mentioned this on his show and it also ended up in a lot of newspaper columns, I'm not quite sure how.

### Another Chicken Plant Encounter, Made in Heaven for Your Basic Boston Debutante

Along those lines, I had another, for me, highly enjoyable experience in one of the plants. I was going through a buffet line, again at the Accomac plant, and a tall African-American guy told me loudly, so his companions could hear, "You rich, why don't you give me all your money!"

By now there are twenty or so people around us watching and listening, and there's at least a minor amount of drama involved: this is the wife of the founder whom he's showing attitude to, and the possible outcomes could be really interesting.

Is she going to get him in trouble?

Is she going to call for help?

Is she going to be really, really upset?

Is she going to be embarrassed and flee?

Maybe she'll cry?

I'm pretty sure everyone is wondering how this confrontation is going to end.

Ah, but we Boston debutante hotel heiresses know exactly what to do in this kind of situation, right? I mean, as we practiced our bows and curtseys, we surely had training in how to handle a situation like this!

I grin at him cheerily and say, "Yes, that's a great plan! I like it!"

And then I flash my best, most enthusiastic smile!

He's looking taken-aback, as I continue, now with mock seriousness. "It does, however, need just one small adjustment and then it will be perfect."

I now practice what in public speaking we call, "the dramatic pause," and I do it for just long enough to notice that everyone of the by now forty or so people who are gathered around seems to be leaning forward, and I think some are even holding their breath.

"The way it really needs to work is," I explain to the guy is, "is instead of me giving you all my money, it would be really nice if you would give me all your money!"

Everyone including the guy laughed, and he ended up telling me, "You all right!"

## Watching Frank in Action

While I'm remembering plant experiences, I have to talk about what it was like going through a plant with Frank. In the Salisbury plant, he knew an incredible number of the associates. We'd go through and he'd introduce them to me by name, and often he'd know some off-beat fact about them, such as how many years a guy had worked there with no sick days, or how many children a woman had. I loved the infinite respect he showed to each person. There wasn't the faintest trace of distance or lording it over them. It was more like, we're all a team and we each have our role, and I very much respect your role.

I also adored going to poultry equipment shows with him. I like machines anyway, but going with Frank was like going with the world's greatest professor. Whatever machine, even when there were hundreds, Frank could talk about it with the manufacturer in staggering detail.

I remember marveling, as we went from exhibit to exhibit, and talked with guy after guy, that Frank had a truly amazing knowledge about every single machine. He knew what it did, what its weaknesses were, what its tolerances were, what the competition was doing, often who had developed it, and on and on. And when he didn't know, he'd ask and ask and ask and ask. He was a true informavore.

This isn't the only time I'll mention this, but Frank was the smartest guy I ever knew. He wasn't academically brilliant, although I bet he did have a very high IQ. (I base that thought on how I saw him perform on some math tests at Massachusetts General Hospital, a time when the examiner said that even after Frank was severely impaired with Parkinson's, he was performing on an Olympic level. The doctor said he would give several years of his life to see what Frank had been like before the Parkinson's.)

What made him the smartest guy I'll ever come across is that he had the most wonderful practical intelligence of how to operate in the real world and how to get things done, including a beyond-brilliant understanding of what motivates people, or what power levers were available, or what opportunities were there but invisible to others. He knew how to be a father, a husband, a community man, a corporate citizen, and a one-in-a-million businessman. I've met guys who may have had higher IQs ("may" is the operative word), but none who was such an unimaginable success in so many areas. He was smart enough, or maybe just innately good enough, to understand how to treat others and how to win their allegiance.

I had been used to hanging out with academics in my previous life, but in comparison to Frank, they all seemed like informavore amateurs. Frank had an encyclopedic memory, avid curiosity, and the ability to put his pieces of knowledge into patterns that ended up changing the lives of millions of people. What an incredible privilege for me to have spent time with such a man!

Something else that I couldn't help notice about Frank, in addition to his knowing so much—he was pretty close to indifferent to flattery. Because he was so gifted and so successful, plenty of it came his way, but the fact is, while he'd politely endure flattery, it seldom made him puff up with pleasure. He used to say, "Tell me what's wrong, because maybe I can do something about it. Telling me what's right doesn't get me anywhere."

Ah, the contrasts in our personalities! I *feed* off of flattery. Er, that is, I feed off of it if it's at least faintly plausible. But then my plausibility threshold is accommodatingly low.

Something else: as far as I could tell, he made business decisions based on facts and calculations, and not on who was or wasn't nice to him. I remember once watching him sign a contract for construction with someone who I knew (and he knew) spoke badly of him. Frank's answer to my questioning why he would deal with this guy was to restate a principal I heard him use several times, "Don't let your money get mad." And then he went on to say that, "The guy does a good job for a fair price."

## Frank as a Romantic

I was impressed that Frank, as a captain of industry and a tough man, had a romantic side to him. He'd always send me two dozen red roses at Valentine's Day, and something that really impressed, touched, and delighted me, he'd include with the roses some wonderful little love message, usually in French.

I have a favorite memory about this side of Frank. He was a passionate tennis fan and we'd go to Wimbledon each year for the matches. One year, as we walked to the tube (the subway), which was about a fifteen minute walk from our hotel, on our way to get to where the matches were being played, we passed a store window with the most enchanting china pattern. It was gold and green, and had beautiful birds painted on it.

In my mind, I could see it on our dining room table during a dinner party along with gorgeous white linens, and tall white tapers and candelabra. The plates were so beautiful that I yearned for them, so of course I began hinting that they'd be nice to have. Each time we walked by them, which was maybe six times because we were there a week, I'd hint and hint for all I was worth.

"Aren't those just beautiful?" I'd say, tugging at his jacket sleeve and pointing at the plates. Or another day, "Oh look, they're still there… wouldn't they look beautiful in our home?"

Nothing seemed to register.

We were to leave on a Sunday morning. I knew the shop closed at 6:00 p.m. on Saturday evening. I watched with a heavy heart as the second hand passed the twelve on my watch, indicating that it was 6:00 p.m. and the store was now closed. No more chance of getting the lovely china.

A half an hour or so later, Frank suggested we go out for dinner. We got in a cab, and pretty soon the cab pulled up at a restaurant that was just next door to the shop with the china. I felt a twinge of minor sadness, to be so near the china that I thought was so beautiful with no possibility, now that it was after closing time, of ever buying it.

But then, as I looked in the window of the darkened store, I saw that there was a candelabra with five lit candles, and they were shining from the store's display area. As my eyes focused in on the scene, I could make out that someone was standing next to the candles, holding a tray with a champagne bottle and three crystal champagne flutes.

Frank said casually, "Oh look, the store you liked is still open. Want to go in?"

His voice was casual, but he was beaming like a little boy. We went inside, and I learned that Frank had arranged for the store to be open and the champagne to be ready for us. As we sipped champagne, he invited me to buy any china I liked.

I fingered the china I had liked so much and learned that it was Lynn Chase Winter Birds. The store manager had laid out a place setting for me on an antique mahogany table. Up close, I could see details that I had missed as we were walking by the store window, and it was even more beautiful than I had thought. I held one in both hands, inspecting the deep forest green edge, trimmed in 24-karat gold. The wild birds would have done honor to Audubon. Each plate included paintings of pheasants and ducks and half a dozen other birds that I couldn't immediately identify.

However, once I was holding a plate in my hand, it was easy to turn it over and discover the price. I did a double-take. Each place setting was roughly three times more than I had ever spent on china.

Frank, oblivious to my shock, asked me how many place settings I'd like. In view of the price, I thought I should be modest in my request. "Four would be *wonderful*," I said.

Frank turned to the store manager and said, "The lady would like twelve. Please ship them to this address."

Could anyone be more romantic?

## Frank as Family Man

Frank was passionate about his business, but his family was also preeminently important to him. He wanted to make sure that his children and grandchildren learned the values that would give them the best chance at a happy and fulfilled life. However, as a shy person, it didn't fit his personality to stand up and lecture at them at a family meeting.

To bridge the gap between his wanting to communicate values to them and his not feeling that lecturing at them would be either congenial to him or enjoyable to them, we instituted a family newsletter.

It began with my interviewing him, writing it up, and sending the results in the form of *Perdues' News*. He'd give his opinions on such things as:

1. Spending money **(You're stewards, and while it's okay to spend the income, don't spend the capital.)**

2. Investment opportunities *(It's guaranteed that people are going to come to you with fabulous-sounding investment opportunities where you just absolutely can't lose. Except you can and probably will. When you get such an offer, immediately show it to a trusted advisor, someone with a financial background, and get their opinion. Also, the more urgent the person making the offer says the offer is, the more suspect it is.)*

3. Prenups *(Get one. If the person is unwilling to sign one, they are after you for the wrong reasons. Getting one puts aside the doubts about their motives, and in addition, as members of a family company, it's wrong to have the jobs of many people put at risk from having a divorce in which the spouse has a claim to the stock.)*

The newsletter started with information from Frank, but we also thought that for the sake of family cohesion, it would be good to include information about other family members. I began interviewing family members from Frank's generation. Every couple of months there would be a four-page issue on, for example, Madeline, Frank's first wife or one of the aunts or other relatives. I'd interview relatives (they were all Madeline's relatives) about their childhoods, parents, what Frank was like when he was young, and so on.

Actually, my relationship with Madeline is a source of pride. When Frank and I married, they hadn't been close since they had divorced a decade earlier. Their arrangement with their children had been that the children spent Christmas with him and Thanksgiving with her. That meant that Frank and I spent our first Thanksgiving alone, and it sucked. To me, Thanksgiving is about family, and being separated from the family felt lonely and barren.

I wanted to change the arrangement, and that meant making friends with Madeline. I had an opportunity to signal that I wanted to be friends when I wrote a 100-page biography of Frank to celebrate his fiftieth year with the company. As part of the biography, I described his marriage to Madeline, including his view of their courtship and how he admired many things about her. The fact is, I had never heard him say anything about Madeline that was anything less than admiring and respectful. I put as much of what he said about her in the book as I could fit without taking too big a side step from the narrative about him.

I don't remember ever discussing the book, *Building on a Solid Foundation*, with Madeline, but it had to have pleased her, to see Frank publicly valuing and praising her.

Before the celebration of Frank's fifty years with the company, I phoned Madeline and invited her to it. Hearing from me was, to use an Eastern Shore term, a shock to her system. We only spoke a few minutes and I could sense she was hesitant about seeing Frank again. I told her that there was no pressure, but I knew from Frank that she had played an important role in the growth of the company and that I hoped she'd enjoy being recognized at the fiftieth anniversary.

She did come to the celebration, and while I had many reasons to enjoy the event, possibly the biggest was it was the beginning of my friendship with Madeline. That was a long-term reason to enjoy the celebration, but a short-term reason was seeing how taken aback people seemed that Madeline and I were there together.

It turns out that she enjoyed that aspect also. At least I know for certain that she enjoyed the principal of knowing that our actions were the center of gossip. For example, for years, the three of us (Frank, Madeline, and I) used to attend baseball games together and we used to laugh about how much gossip that must create.

One evening, I had a migraine and the thought of the night lights at the stadium was more than I thought I could survive, so I pleaded with Madeline and Frank to go without me. They agreed to this, and as they were about to leave the house for the stadium, Madeline and I gave each other a big high five, saying "Let the gossip begin!"

I think it meant a lot to Frank that he and Madeline were friends once more, given that they had been married for thirty-seven years. After they became friends again, he'd often tell me how much he appreciated Madeline, especially after his unsuccessful second marriage. He valued

Madeline's common sense and hard work and what she had contributed to the company at its beginning and that she was a good mother and that she was frugal, and most of all, that she was an admirable person.

When Frank had open-heart surgery sometime around, maybe 2000, the night before the operation, we talked about how there was a 3 percent chance of his dying on the operating table. I told him that if this happened, he'd never have a chance to tell Madeline how important she was to him. I said it was a shame that he had told me and not her.

He agreed and said he'd like to write her a letter telling her. I got him the stationery he needed and then, after he wrote the letter, I got a stamp and mailed it for him. I don't know what he said, but Madeline told me later that his letter had meant the world to her.

This is jumping ahead of the story, but Madeline and I became close enough so that at Frank's funeral, we sat beside each other, and at the interment, we held hands. Today, my family and hers are close enough that at family weddings in Salisbury, Madeline has my son Jose stay at her house with her. How many blended families are close enough that the first wife invites the son of the third wife to stay with her (the first wife) during a family wedding? Oh, and my son Carlos and his wife Gea regularly call on Madeline, since they live within half a mile of each other.

**I Had a Co-Wife**

Although Madeline had been Frank's legal wife for thirty-seven years, there's another woman in this story. I was so close to Frank's secretary of thirty-two years, Elaine Barnes, that we to this day refer to each other as co-wives. We might as well have been Mormons because, as far as I was concerned, it was like having a three-way marriage, minus certain technicalities. We both loved Frank and I think we each had endless affection and concern for each other. I think we each recognized that the other was indispensable and irreplaceable in the great enterprise of Keeping Frank Afloat.

I think my relationship with Elaine worked so well, at least from my point of view, because we each loved him and understood that the man we loved would be less happy and less successful if he didn't have both of us. (Have I mentioned that my definition of love is when the other person's happiness is as important to you as your own?)

Elaine had so many gifts. One that I remember with glee is, she could change voices. She and I would be at the office at Perdue headquarters on Old Ocean City Road, talking and giggling about some gossipy girly thing, and then she'd have to answer the phone. This woman who a moment ago had sounded girly and fun, suddenly had the impressive voice of the executive assistant of a Fortune 500-size company. She was all professionalism; crisp, authoritative, knowledgeable, and unrecognizably different from how she had sounded seconds before.

She also just about never made the human mistakes that the rest of us are forever making. Once in every few years, she would make a mistake, but I always suspected that she did this to throw her friends off guard so we'd think she was human. I wasn't taken in.

She and Cindy Downes and I were like a wonderfully tuned, perfectly synchronized team. Between the three of us, we metaphorically speaking, tended his base camp, so he was free to scale the Mount Everest of his business accomplishments. It had to be nice for Frank that he virtually never had to give a thought to many of the nitty gritty things that could slow a man down, such as women in his life not getting along. I don't think Cindy or Elaine or I ever had a cross word for each other.

## Cindy and Greg Downes, and Tammy Cawood

Cindy and Elaine are quite different people, but they have in common the following: they are utterly reliable and if they say something will get done, you can take it to the bank; They solve problems. They're punctual. They have enormous insight. They're complete team players. They're wise. They have a wicked and improper sense of humor. They're good at prioritizing. Being around them is highly enjoyable.

I know Cindy better than Elaine, partly because, after working together for almost twenty years, most of it in the same office, it's almost like having a conjoined twin. I used to tell Cindy that her job description included legal aid, editor, accountant, mother confessor, psychiatrist, researcher, additional mother for Jose and Carlos, travel agent, bookkeeper, real estate agent, and generally, the person who can do everything.

One of the sadnesses in my relationship with Cindy is, she also became widowed. She lost her best friend, and I lost someone whom I also loved, her husband Greg Downes. He was another amazing person. He had the best sense of humor and it made me smile just to have him in the room. He bore his last illness with bravery and grace, and his relationship to his church is an inspiration to all.

One other person who was part of our Merry Band was and partly still is Tammy Cawood. Tammy's many jobs include groundskeeping, driving, decorating, helping make the house run smoothly, and forever advising me on makeup and fashion. We had a long-standing joke that I was her Barbie because she liked to have a hand in choosing what I wore and often helped with my makeup and hair. Since I admire taste and fashion, and am not innately good at it myself, I was always ready to take all the help I could get.

Tammy is an artist, and she played a large role in my decorated egg business. All the eggs that I'd put on display were made by me, but in cases when I'd get more orders than I could handle, Tammy would help.

## A Mystery Relationship

While I'm jumping around in my story, I suppose this is as good a time as any to talk about still another important relationship in my life. It's one that is entirely by phone, and it's only one or two phone calls per year, but it's responsible for a lot of the fact that I'm a happy person today and was spared all sorts of Terrible Mistakes.

The relationship is to this day a puzzle to me because I cannot even begin to fathom why it exists or how I got so lucky. In addition to puzzlement, which is 2 percent, I feel simply extraordinary, gasping for breath, genuflecting, murmuring "We are not worthy, we are not worthy" gratitude.

The guy is Dr. Zahour Yussef, the father of one of Jose's roommate's at Harvard. He's a psychiatrist who lives in Michigan, and every once in awhile, he'll call me to ask how I'm doing. I've never been his patient and I have no financial relationship with him. (In fact, under most circumstances, I'm a terrible candidate for counseling: I have a deep and sincere desire to tell other people how to lead their lives and minimal interest in having anyone tell me how to lead mine.)

I'm not superstitious, but it is simply uncanny how often Dr. Yussef calls when I'm struggling with something. I'll tell him about it, and in the course of half an hour or an hour, he'll say things I've never thought of, and suggest ways of dealing with whatever it is. In every case, he nails whatever the problem is, and gives me an exact recipe for dealing with it, no matter how complicated or difficult.

Often the advice helps not only in the immediate case, but it's something that can be generalized to the rest of my life. For example, once when my two kids had a quarrel, which I found devastating because a united family means everything to me, Zahour pointed out that to understand it, I shouldn't be looking at the "he said, he said" aspects of it because "arguments are almost never about what they are about. They're usually the result of unresolved tensions that were already existing." To get beyond a quarrel, you have to look at the factors leading up to it.

## Jose at Harvard

During this period in my marriage to Frank, both boys were in college, Jose at Harvard and Carlos at Berkeley. I loved that Jose was at my alma mater. He is fourth generation Harvard, and I cherished the notion that he was walking the same paths that his mother, his grandfather, and his great grandfather had trod.

Jose had a fortunate thing happen his freshman year. He and his seven suite mates liked each other so much that they all requested to room together for the rest of their college career. I'm told that it's almost unheard of for a group of freshmen to like each other so much that they all request to room together for another three years.

One of the group asked the Harvard official who assigned the freshmen their roommates how the official had happened to select such a remarkably compatible group. The answer was the official and his colleagues had done their best to match up young men who, they thought, would enjoy each other.

However, there were eight young men who didn't seem to fit into any category. The officials simply assigned these "leftovers" to each other. Thus the most successful matching of all happened by accident and default. Jose's college friends are still lifelong friends and still get together at least once a year.

One of my strongest memories of Jose's undergraduate years was my sitting in on one of his calculus classes. There were maybe thirty students, and every one of them, except Jose, was Asian. That impressed me, but it also impressed me that the professor rapidly filled the blackboard with a whole bunch of incomprehensible symbols and then suddenly, the whole room exploded in raucous laughter. The professor smiled genially, apparently having delivered himself of a really great joke.

Jose was a biochemistry major. He got his BS from Harvard in 1995, and his Ph.D. in organismal and evolutionary biology in 2000, also from Harvard.

Actually, when he got his BS, he was heavily recruited by a number of institutions. With the Hispanic name Francisco Jose Ayala, and with a Harvard degree, he was much in demand. He chose Washington University in Saint Louis, but shortly after he settled in there, his professor, Dan Hartle, was asked to teach at Harvard and brought Jose with him.

### Jose's Methods for Handling Distraught Female Undergraduate

As a graduate student at Harvard, Jose got a job as a proctor. That meant being a housefather for approximately 100 students. I think he showed exceptional skill in handling these duties.

He also discovered a magic key for handling distraught female undergraduates. When a young woman would come into his study, bawling, he'd say, "Before we get started, I'm hungry. Would you go to the refrigerator and get me some chocolate ice cream, and get a bowl for yourself while you're at it."

The student would come sit down in his study, now equipped with her own bowl of chocolate ice cream. She'd start, amid tears, telling about how awful life was and she just couldn't cope any more. Jose would listen sympathetically, but he'd also say, "Go on, have a bite," indicating the ice cream.

After a few spoonfuls, the student would start saying something like, "This is really good!" A few more, and her mood would have changed. Jose developed the theory that it is impossible for a young woman to eat chocolate ice cream and be depressed at the same time.

By his second year in the job, he was assigned "the teacup cases," that is the kids who were exceptionally brilliant, but in one way or another, fragile. The training and experience he had in dealing with emotional problems has been a fantastic benefit to me. I often go to him for relationship advice and what he says, having insight into both male and female thinking, is often uniquely helpful and useful.

**Carlos at Berkeley**

Carlos' undergraduate years were also full ones. He entered Berkeley in 1988 at age sixteen and finished in 1993. He would have finished sooner, but Berkeley is set up so that getting the required classes can't be done in four years.

Carlos surprised me early on by giving me a huge expensive flowering plant for Mother's Day. It delighted me but still I asked him how he, a college student, could afford such a lavish plant. He answered that he had won the money playing poker.

That information led to some additional information. I knew he had a job as a security guard, a job which he wanted because when he checked people in the dorm each night, it meant that he got to know a huge number of people, and this in turn fostered his successful run for the Berkeley Senate.

What I didn't know, but learned at this point, was that Carlos pretty much put himself through college with his poker winnings. Actually, in retrospect, I think this was a brilliant thing to do. A lot of life is about assessing odds, reading people, taking risks, making bets, and bluffing. I think it was excellent training for a future businessman.

Carlos continued to demonstrate, as an undergraduate, the business acumen that he had as a youngster. When other fraternities were earning small amounts of money to finance their social activities, doing such things as car washes, Carlos invested a few dollars in having funny T-shirts printed and he and his fraternity brothers would sell them at football games and make thousands of dollars with a small investment of money and time.

## Carlos's Job at Perdue Farms, and Why Poker Was Excellent Training

When Carlos finished college in 1993, he didn't take a vacation but instead went straight to work for Perdue Farms in the international division. He started out with a true drudge job, doing data entry. For a Berkeley star to be doing secretarial work seemed to me a horrible waste of talent. Nevertheless, I did share with him the information that I would personally assassinate him if he complained about it.

I should have saved my breath because he's not a complainer by nature and wouldn't have done such a thing, in any case. His solution to the problem was to learn database programming and, in short order, he figured out a way of programming himself right out of the job.

He began by asking the people who were giving him the data the ideal form for them to transmit it to the next layer of people. Then he asked the people above him what the ideal format for them to receive the data would be. Then, having their buy-in (they had helped design the program), he created an automatic recordkeeping system which was faster, virtually error-free, and pleased everyone. In the process, he had automated himself out of that job and into a better one.

When he had been in this new job a rather short time, he got another promotion, this time to the head of the department. It happened this way.

There were two layers of management above him and in the space of weeks, one guy was fired and another transferred. Although there were roughly twelve people in the department, Carlos, at age twenty-three was the only one knowledgeable about all the aspects of the department so by default he became acting export manager. Every person he supervised was older than he was and some were thirty years older.

The first issue he had to confront when in his new position was that one of the largest chicken deals ever was being conducted with some international buyers. The deal was so big that he was told (in my hearing), "Don't muff this deal, Carlos. Having the domestic market absorb this much chicken will depress the domestic market for the whole industry for the next half year!"

Talk about pressure!

The overseas buyers came in their private jet, and suddenly, Carlos, age twenty-three, was in the negotiating room with some mega-successful, astute, and very tough international businessmen. One of them put his hand on Carlos's shoulder and said in a paternal way, "Don't worry, Carlos, we know you're new on the job and we're not going to be tough on you. You'll be able to make year deal. But because of the domestic conditions in our country, we do have to lower the price three cents a pound."

Carlos answered that he appreciated their situation, but he would be looking for an alternative buyer and couldn't give up the three cents a pound. They shook hands, and the buyers left the office, boarded their private jet and flew away. Carlos had blown the negotiations and would personally be responsible for the price of chicken dropping to possibly uneconomic levels for the entire industry in this country. (It may not have actually been quite that bad, but that's sure how it looked to his mother.)

He spent the most sleepless night of his life. He was fully aware of the consequences of what he had just done.

But the next day, the international buyers called and said that they would pay the three cents that they had subtracted the day before. Carlos answered, "I'm sorry, I can't do that. It will cost you an additional three cents per pound to get back in the game." The buyers agreed to this, and it became a $120,000 swing from what it would have been if Carlos hadn't taken a tough stand.

I told Carlos, "I can understand your not letting them get away with cutting the price by three cents, but why did you hold out for the additional three cents?"

"Because," he answered, "if I allowed them to horse with me at the beginning of my career, and not have a penalty for trying, then they'd figure they could roll me whenever they wanted. I had to establish a precedent."

How did a twenty-three year old have the sense to see this? I was in awe of my own son.

Carlos worked for Perdue for several years, and then took time off to save the vineyard that I owned in Woodland, California. The problem that needed resolving was, my partner, Jim Smith (not his real name) was using the vineyard as his own private piggy bank. For example, as Carlos discovered, he was using the vineyard account to service his entire fleet of cars from a shopping center that he owned.

Trying to get out of this was more than I could cope with. Carlos was tough enough to handle it and get us out of it. Phew!

During this time, he was getting his MBA from Wharton on weekends.

Well, this has been a long, long digression from my relationship with Frank. You see, when I warned you earlier that memory is like a dog that lies down where it pleases, I meant it!

## More Memories of Frank

From the beginning, I felt that Frank and I were in general simply endlessly compatible and I just loved being near him. There was so much for me to admire about him. I loved his rock-solid steadiness and I'm not sure what he liked about me, but I felt that we simply relished being together and having adventures together. I never in my life have felt as relaxed and happy and safe as I did when I was near him.

In fact, another favorite memory is that when we had been out at night and had arrived home in his big black Mercedes, we often stayed in the car for half an hour or so, just talking. From my point of view, and I trust his as well, it was just infinitely pleasant to be this close to each other in a confined space. It was as if the car were our favorite room. We even referred to it as another room in our house. I think there were few evenings when we had been out when we didn't sit in the car and talk for half an hour or so. We could have done the same thing in the house, but somehow, talking there became our thing. Sometimes we wouldn't even talk but would just sit beside each other, enjoying the moments.

(As I write this, I'm convinced that I'll never remarry and quite probably never even have another serious man in my life. How could I ever, ever relish being with someone as much as I relished being with Frank?)

One of the things I admired was Frank's approach to politics. Frank assiduously read newspapers with different viewpoints, and regularly listened to and read pundits from the entire political spectrum. I remember early on, there was a politician whom I couldn't bear, and my instinct was to flee the room every time he was on the air. Frank remonstrated with me about this, saying that as a citizen, you simply had to listen to both sides. Since this was so contrary to my nature, I was lost in admiration that anyone could be so fair and so intellectually honest.

Something that influenced Frank's politics: he loved the Founding Fathers. In later years, his vision would no longer accommodate reading, but we listened to audio books about all the Founding Fathers and talked about them endlessly.

His favorite was Alexander Hamilton, and we not only visited Nevis Island, where Hamilton was born, but we spent a long time going through the museum there. Frank discussed Hamilton with the docent there, and she must have been surprised that Frank Perdue would know so many obscure facts about Hamilton's life and philosophy.

His other hero, by the way, was Andrew Carnegie. He admired Carnegie no end, partly as a businessman, and partly for his wisdom in donating libraries. Frank cared enough about Carnegie to take the trouble to visit Dumfermline, Scotland, where Carnegie was born.

By the way, it was Andrew Carnegie who said something that I think describes Frank: "The average person puts only 25 percent of his energy and ability into his work. The world takes off its hat to those who put in more than 50 percent of their capacity, and stands on its head for those few-and-far-between souls who devote 100 percent."

I keep wondering how to describe what Frank had that made it so joyous for me to be near him. Part of it had to be that I looked up to him so much. I admired his rock-solid goodness, his humility, his fairness, his energy, his ability to see what's important and his genius for seeing, in everything, "how to get from here to there."

### Frank and a Rotten, Terrible, No Good TV News Magazine

Let me give an example of his rock-solid goodness. Actually, I need to amend that; it's not "rock-solid goodness," it's "superhuman goodness." What follows in the next few paragraphs is an example, and after you've finished reading it, ponder if there are many people on the planet who would have behaved the way Frank did.

Sometime shortly after we married, one of the major TV "magazine" shows did a story on carpel tunnel syndrome, with Perdue as an example of the problem. When we first heard that they were doing the show, we were delighted. We had the best record in the industry for recognizing the problem, working aggressively to prevent it, and having results that were ten times better than the industry average.

But that's not how the nationally broadcast prime time show played it. Instead, they focused on how painful and awful the condition was, and then showed Perdue associates who suffered from it.

It's true that some Perdue associates had the condition, but it's also true, and the story didn't mention it, that we were doing everything we knew how to cure the problem and prevent its recurrence, including redesigning the workplace, rotating people into different jobs before the repetition caused problems, and educating everyone about the symptoms so the condition could be caught early, at its most easily treatable stage. There was nothing that occupied management more at this time than addressing this real and very serious problem.

On camera, Frank talked about all of this.

What showed on TV included none of this.

Instead, they highlighted something that Frank said and then corrected, but they didn't show the correction. They asked Frank about a twenty-year-old African-American who had lost a finger. Then, the TV screen showed the young man missing a digit, deformed for life, while you hear Frank referring to the young man as "a boy."

It sounded utterly racist to refer to an African-American as "a boy," but to Frank, as someone in his seventies, a twenty-year-old is "a boy." However, Frank was sharp enough to realize, that in this context, "boy" wasn't appropriate and he instantly corrected himself and referred to "the young man."

The editors ignored the correction and had Frank sounding racist in the face of a tragedy. The tone of the entire twenty-minute segment was that Southern racists were indifferent to the pain and agony of the factory workers, and they were presided over by this monster who thought of African-American men as boys.

When the program aired, Frank and I were traveling, and I can remember watching the show in horror. We, who had the best record in the industry for having the fewest incidences of this; we, who had invested more resources than anyone in recognizing, addressing, and preventing the problem; we were the ones singled out for criticism and disgrace.

The unfairness was driving me nuts. Er, literally. When I'm under stress, my response is to eat, and in the hotel room there was a one-pound can of peanuts. I couldn't sleep a wink and during the night, ate my way pretty much through the entire can of nuts. That's 2,640 calories.

However, while I was sitting on the edge of the bed all night long, feeding myself peanuts by the handful, I noticed that Frank was sleeping like a baby.

The next morning when he woke up, I commented on how well he had slept. His response was, "If I had let things like that bother me, I would have been dead long ago." And then he added words that I will never forget: "Besides, if that show keeps one person from carpel tunnel syndrome, it will have been worth it."

A few paragraphs earlier, I invited you to consider if there are many people who have the superhuman goodness to look at that episode the way he just did. Your answer?

I think Frank was the embodiment of a quote I treasure from Mother Teresa: "If you are humble, nothing will touch you, neither praise nor disgrace, because you know what you are."

It wasn't just goodness, however, that made Frank who he was. His work ethic must have been close to unique. As an example, we often traveled overseas, whether to Europe, Asia, or Africa. During the long overnight flights, I would sleep. Frank, on the other hand, didn't. He used the time, hour after hour, to read, write notes to people, study marketing reports or sometimes just make notes to himself about things he wanted to do.

I sleep on planes, but I don't sleep soundly, so every now and then, I'd wake up and glance over in his direction. Sure enough, even though virtually every other passenger on the plane would be asleep, there would be Frank, the sole person I could see who had the overhead light on and was working.

I've mentioned that Frank's hero was Alexander Hamilton, and Frank used to explain his own success with a quote relating to hard work from Hamilton. The quote you're about to read was so important to Frank and so meaningful to him that he kept a calligraphic version of it (a gift from his daughter-in-law Jan Perdue) by his desk and often quoted it. Here's a version with Frank's, comments in italics, that Frank wrote for his children and grandchildren.

"Men give me credit for some genius. All the genius I have lies in this. When I have a subject in hand, I study it profoundly. Day and night, (*not just 8 hours*) it is before me. I explore it in all its bearings (*repeat— "in all its bearings", not just a few*). My mind becomes pervaded with it. Then the effort which I have made is what people are pleased to call the fruit of genius. It is the fruit of labor and thought."

Alexander Hamilton

When he was in his late sixties, he regularly got by on four or five hours of sleep. I remember being impressed that when he had the choice of an extra half hour of sleep or exercising, he'd choose to exercise.

I've been remembering about Frank's work ethic, but now, switching gears, some thoughts about how Frank was at home, as a husband. One outstanding characteristic was, he was remarkably even-tempered. He could be worried if the business wasn't going well (being responsible for 20,000 jobs is not a responsibility I would want for even five minutes) but there was never, that I can recall, a time when his moods weren't an understandable response to whatever was going on, and within that parameter, he was still remarkably even-tempered.

I guess one of the biggest things was, he was trustworthy. Victoria, my sister, once said that total love is total vulnerability, and the flip side of that, I think, is total trust. I knew that my happiness was as important to him as his own, and I knew I could trust him with my feelings. That meant I could love him more than I ever dreamed of loving anyone else.

But I think it was very much a two-way street. His motto was, "Never trust anyone." And being one of the world's wealthiest men, he was certainly the target of a lot of untrustworthy people, especially women.

It's impressive, looking back on it, how much trust played a role in our relationship. This is repeating something I've already described, but within the first five minutes of meeting each other, we were already talking about trust. We had each agreed that we would never remarry because we were each certain that, as a result of our previous marriages, we would never trust anyone. But then, he looked at me and said, "I believe I could trust you," and I looked at him and said the same thing.

Isn't it strange, to look at someone and feel that you could trust him or her? It's a feeling I almost never have, except for relatives. I believe, that outside of Elaine Barnes and family members, that there were very, very few people whom Frank did trust.

He told me, for example, of how his two best friends had both, in different ways, betrayed him. One stole Frank's breed and used it in his own company, something that I consider beyond dastardly. The other friend hired away one of Frank's most important employees, behind Frank's back. I thought those two actions were outrageous and couldn't fathom why Frank stayed friends with people who put their gain above his friendship.

The answer Frank gave to my question about why we regularly continued seeing these two guys was that while he would never have done such a thing to either of them, that he still valued their friendship, and that people are human.

How awful, to have your two best friends both betray you! And how saint-like to overlook it. Actually, he didn't overlook it because he brought it up many times, how even your best friend can betray trust.

I believe in my soul that I never did anything knowingly that would be a betrayal of Frank's trust. I think with each passing year, the depth of his trust increased. When we first married, he was at the height of his fame and power, but within a couple of years, he turned running the company over to his son, and gave, I think, 90 percent of his wealth to his children. I think it meant something to him that this made no difference to me in my feelings toward him. Actually, I liked it better, that he wasn't in charge of the company, because it meant at least slightly more time for me.

A huge part of our relationship was his caring for his family. And this was, of course, something else I greatly admired about him. We talked about many, many things, but I think one topic of conversation dwarfed all the others, and that was the interest he took in each child and grandchild, and eventually great grandchildren.

For example, if we were on a long drive, he'd typically name each one, and then we'd talk about that child and what was going on in his or her life and how he or she was doing. I suspect that they didn't know just how much they were a part of his thinking.

Although maybe they did because he showed his caring in many small ways. He'd write serious and meaningful cards to each child on his or her birthday. He arranged family trips for them each year to such places as Zimbabwe or Italy or Costa Rica. I believe he cherished the family newsletter because it meant a way of weaving the family closer. He put his heart into his ethical will—more on this later on.

I asked him once what his happiest day was, and he answered that it was when his son Jim decided to join the company. Frank told me that if Jim had decided not to, he would have respected this, and that he wouldn't have pressured him because Frank truly wanted Jim to do what Jim wanted to do.

A memory from this time that I cherish was watching Frank with Carlos plucking ducks. I had a rule on hunting; if you killed it, you ate it. When Carlos brought home maybe a dozen ducks one day, that meant plucking them. For those of you who haven't done it, it's such a messy and unpleasant job that I have puzzled over the fact that our ancestors didn't starve.

I started out helping Carlos at the kitchen sink, but the wretched duck corpses stank (I think it was the contents of their stomachs), and they're infested with both fleas and something else that resembles a flea but it doesn't jump, but rather, crawls. Seeing dozens of these small, icky black spots jumping and crawling over my normally clean sink, I was totally creeped out and fled to the other end of the kitchen. Carlos was left to soldier on at this miserable task.

(Ah yes, you see what kind of mother I am!)

Frank walked through the kitchen at just this moment and saw Carlos gamely going about his dismal task alone. It was taking roughly half an hour a bird. Frank came over to the sink and began helping Carlos, the two guys standing side by side, pulling out the feathers while coping with the smell and the bugs and the tedium, talking and bonding as they did so.

After an hour or so, with maybe eight birds left, Frank came up with a better plan. Putting the remaining ducks in a plastic bag, he and Carlos drove to some guy who plucks and cleans ducks professionally.

Carlos was amazed by the experience. He told me he had never known any grownup to be willing to do something so unpleasant just to help out a kid. The fact that the person who did so was as busy and important as Frank left an impression that neither Carlos nor I will ever forget.

I, who knew Frank well, think I understand exactly what did and didn't make him help Carlos pluck the ducks. There was no possible economic motive. Also, I'm sure he didn't want praise, and Carlos already loved him, so it wasn't to curry favor. No, it was simply that Frank was the most unbelievably generous person I'll ever know. The same impulse that made him give away tens of millions of dollars to charities was present when he saw a sixteen-year-old boy struggling with a lonely and icky task.

## Back to Work

My marriage to Frank was joyously happy, but I still felt the need to work and have some identity outside of marriage. The only work that both appealed to me and that I could do while still being available in my role as corporate wife was writing.

Fred Kline had said I could continue to work for him as the Washington bureau chief for Capitol News. I might have done it, except I really wanted to work for an east coast syndicate.

I figured it should be easy to do because I now had an eight-year track record for never missing a deadline and never having anyone complain about accuracy. Fred Kline wrote me a fabulous recommendation letter, and I now had a portfolio of hundreds of articles.

Also, applying for a job in 1990 was easier because, instead of laboriously typing out individual proposal letters on my typewriter, I could mass-produce mail-merged letters. I sent letters out to maybe thirty different syndicators.

I didn't hear back from a single one of them. Several months into this, I complained about it to a friend with whom I had worked on a DC charity, and she said she'd send my proposal to her friend at Scripps Howard, Walter Veasey. He read my material and pretty much hired me on the spot. As with Fred Kline at Capitol News, query letters got me nowhere, but knowing people who knew people helped me get both jobs.

My column went each week to 420 newspapers. Going with Scripps Howard was a fantastic stroke of luck professionally because Scripps Howard became the second largest syndicator after the *New York Times*. Since the *NYT* didn't have a dedicated environmental writer, I by default with my 420 news outlets, became the most widely syndicated environmental writer in the country.

Actually, it had a wider distribution than that because every once in awhile, I'd get copies of stories I had written, and they'd be from other countries, such as India. I had no way of knowing how often this happened because the only ones I heard of were by accident, such as someone traveling in another country would bring me a copy back, or someone writing me from another country, saying they had seen my columns in their country.

I had a particular niche as an environmental writer. I only wrote success stories. I wrote about good people doing good things that other people could copy.

I also tried to focus on scientists and what exciting and important lives they led. Since I'm a little bit in love with science anyway, and since I'm the mother of a scientist, and since I believe that scientific knowledge will play a role in solving many of the problems we face on this planet, I wanted to do whatever I could to encourage scientific literacy. And also, I guess, since I didn't get to be a scientist myself, I wanted to contribute to the field in the way that seemed most available to me, and that's by writing about it.

Another factor is, I hoped that the stories I wrote might encourage students to study science, so they could have a career in this exciting world. I've heard that at least some teachers used my columns in their classrooms for this purpose.

When I said earlier that I only wrote success stories, it's not that I have a rosy view of the environment. On the contrary, it's because I have such a gloomy view of the dangers we face that I wanted to provide some encouragement not only to others, but even to myself.

Because I was never trained as a journalist, I developed on my own an approach to writing, one that helped me get interviews with world famous scientists, often ones who wouldn't speak with other journalists. I'd interview Mr. Famous Scientist by phone, write the article, and then send it to him for corrections. The article wouldn't go out until Mr. Famous Scientist was satisfied that the story was both accurate and gave the correct people credit. Richard Dawkins and E.O. Wilson were two of my favorite interviewees, and Murray Gell-Mann told me that I was one of only four science writers in the world whom he would trust for accuracy.

The neat thing is, I didn't have to be an expert in what I was writing about. All it took was inviting my subjects to correct my errors. I always felt that it was an exercise in humility, doing this, because it would be rare for me to write a story without at least something needing correction. However, this constant correction did help me, I think, learn to listen carefully and perhaps be more accurate than I would have been if I didn't have the error of my ways pointed out to me so continuously.

I wrote the column for more than twenty years. In my entire career, I never missed a deadline, whether in writing, or preparing for a radio or television show.

However, as I write this at age sixty-nine, I'm glad that part of my career is over. I enjoyed my career at the time, but I wouldn't want to go back to the situation of always facing multiple deadlines.

## 1993, Driving Across the Country and Back

But back to my life with Frank. I was talking earlier (much earlier, I guess) about how we relished each other's company. An example of this was the best trip I've ever been on in my life, driving across the country with him in 1993. Having that much uninterrupted time with him meant deep, searing, amazing happiness.

It was the most blissed-out time of my sixty-nine years. We were both so into the same things. As we drove along the highways and byways in his beloved black Mercedes, we listened to books on tape, particularly about the Founding Fathers, but also about Truman. We planned our driving so we'd have at least an hour of brisk walking each day, often in a National Park. We enjoyed seeing the country, we loved trying regional food, and both of us had precisely the same tolerance for how long we should drive each day.

By the way, we often ate an amazingly bad diet. There were several days, for reasons I can no longer recall, when living on popcorn and Diet Pepsi seemed like the perfect thing to do—so of course we did it. We compared ourselves to teenagers without adult supervision.

We started out the trip with reservations for the entire trip at a series of bed and breakfasts, but after the first day, we had Frank's secretary Elaine Barnes (or was it Cindy Downes, the genius who helps keep me afloat?) cancel all the reservations, so we could just wander around without a schedule and do whatever we felt like doing when we felt like doing it.

One of the things we felt like doing was, we usually stayed at Motel 6! I'm the Sheraton heiress and grew up in presidential suites, and he was high up on the Forbes 400 list of wealthiest people, but we both loved the Motel 6. We didn't need reservations, checking in and out at all hours was a breeze, and the employees were unfailingly kind and agreeable.

I'll never forget how much fun Frank had when we'd wash the car ourselves, during the trip. I'm having a great deal of difficulty trying to recall just why washing a car was so fun for both of us, but I can still see his face, luminous with pleasure and delight as we'd eagerly splash each other and then, laughing, get back to work on cleaning the car together. Only to start splashing each other again. Actually, everything we did seemed magical.

One particular memory I have was visiting, I think, Yellowstone National Park. Since we always walked for an hour or two, we pulled the car off one of the lesser-used roads at a trailhead, and started climbing.

It was a July day, but maybe forty or so minutes into the climb, we hit the snow line. Neither of us had the right shoes for snow, but since we weren't sissies, we began climbing through almost knee high snow in our summer shoes, and in my case, sandals. We kept at it for another twenty minutes and were rewarded by the sight of a most gorgeous lake far below us on the other side of the ridge we had been climbing.

It was so satisfying to have this unexpected view, one we never would have had if we had given in to the fact that we were totally wearing all the wrong clothes and that it was an almighty struggle to get through fairly deep snow. And by the way, it was terribly cold, when we weren't moving. He was wearing a short sleeved summer shirt, and I was wearing a gauzy summer dress, and we held each other in a bear hug to keep warm.

We gazed at the frozen lake for below us for a few minutes, and then turned to go. But just then, a ranger came along. He expressed amazement at seeing us there, saying that in all his years, he hadn't seen anyone come up this far. We chatted for a few minutes and then he went on his way.

We started to descend, but a few minutes after reaching the snow line, we noticed that a bison was behind us. I don't know how much a bison weighs but, at a guess, it's 2,000 pounds, and both of us were pretty convinced that we didn't want to irritate this enormous, wild, somewhat-menacing creature.

We figured that we didn't want to excite it by running, but that we'd walk seriously faster to get away from it. However, as we speeded up, it speeded up.

We started nearly running, and it increased its speed. This was a scary situation because we were in an isolated area and clearly on our own. I'm not sure how far behind us it was but it was way, way, way too close for comfort. My guess, seventeen years after the fact, is maybe thirty-five feet. It felt like five.

What I've just described continued for the next thirty minutes, with us just short of running, until we finally reached our beloved black Mercedes and safety. We could hardly wait to jump inside and lock the door. The beast, which had been following us for forty minutes, stopped close to the car door, close enough that I think I could have touched him if I had opened the window. It just looked at us. We stayed in the car for several minutes, wanting to see what the bison would do.

It just stayed there, watching us, although occasionally it would put its head down to graze.

To this day, I wonder what was going on in its head. Did it just happen to be on the same trail that we were on and it wasn't really following us? Or did we in some way interest it?

There was another walking incident that trip that I'll never forget, but in this case it didn't involve adventure. Rather it involved my learning how Frank was like Napoleon Bonaparte. Here's what happened.

We were visiting the Grand Canyon. Both of us would have liked to walk all the way down but we were under a time constraint because we had to reach Berkeley in time for Carlos' graduation. Still, we decided that we could devote a couple of hours to exploring it, so we walked down for maybe fifty minutes, and then turned around and started walking up.

Frank has a characteristic related to walking that I've never observed in another human being. No matter how steep an incline, Frank would walk up at exactly the same pace that he would use to walk down.

Since the trail was steep, keeping up with Frank was arduous. As a way to slow him down, and thus to catch my breath, I asked if I could take his pulse.

Frank's willingness to humor me in my frequent oddball, out-of-the-blue requests remains baffling to me. But anyway, he stopped and let me take his pulse. Mine at this point was somewhere around 110. His was 40. I thought this was amazing, but then figured that maybe we hadn't been climbing long enough for a rise in his pulse to show up.

I waited another ten minutes and then asked to take it again. By this time, he was interested in it. His pulse hadn't changed. For the rest of the way up to the canyon rim, I periodically took his pulse and it never got above 40. I think mine was 120 for most of the climb.

I later learned that Napoleon's pulse was 40 almost whenever his physician took it.

And by the way, this low pulse wasn't a fluke. Several years later, Frank needed open heart surgery for aortic valve replacement, and before the surgery, he had declined sedatives. I was with him as he was on the gurney, being wheeled off to the operating room. The doctor who was accompanying us took Frank's vital signs.

"Your husband shows no signs of stress," he told me as he examined the equipment that was monitoring Frank. "Only an Olympic athlete would have a heart rate as slow as his!"

I turned to Frank and asked him about this, saying, "I'd expect your heart to be racing. Aren't you afraid?"

"No," he answered. "This is just another day at the office."

My God, what courage! What grace! What *sang froid!* What dignity! And it wasn't denial because the night before, we had discussed the possibility of his dying.

## EggScapes(™) Painful Beginnings

The year 1993 was eventful for me for another reason also. Later that year, I was in a minor car accident, or at least it should have been a minor car accident, but I was thrown from the car and ended up doing a twisting somersault that resulted in a ruptured disk.

It was in Florida and I had to give a speech that night, which I made in spite of being in pain. Actually, I'm kind of proud of being able to give the speech because I wonder how many others would have given a speech with a severely ruptured disk. That was the last time I walked for almost nine months and when I finally had the surgery that cured the problem (the disk was removed entirely), Dr. DiGiacinto, said that he had, in his whole career as a spinal surgeon, seen only two other disks as severely ruptured as mine.

After the accident and before the surgery, I had entirely lost the ability to walk, I was housebound.

I had imagined, before this happened, that having nothing to do but read and watch television would be enjoyable. It was enjoyable, for about two weeks, but then I got so bored with reading and with television that it was almost an allergic reaction.

I began casting around for a hobby that would use up time, and came across the idea of decorating eggs. I thought it would be fun, given that Frank was known as the Chicken Man, to be the Egg Lady.

This coincided with my watching the public television artist, Bob Ross. At first, I couldn't believe that he could paint such wonderful pictures so rapidly, but having nothing better to do, I sent away for his painting kit and began painting his pictures on chicken eggs.

I used to describe myself as the most inartistic person I knew and to this day, I don't fully understand why people voluntarily go to art museums, particularly modern art. However, when doing the painting and drawing myself, I couldn't get enough of it. When I was fully engaged in carving painting an egg, I could forget that my back was not exactly perfect. In its way, carving and decorating an egg was actually a painkiller.

I spent countless hours, especially with my sketch pad and a set of pencils that Cindy Downes gave me. And every technique that I practiced on the sketch pad eventually made its way onto eggs that I was decorating.

I still decorate eggs, and it's been a wonderfully satisfying hobby.

During the months when I was housebound, my condition got worse and worse. I went from having to use a wheelchair to being unable even to sit in one. Toward the end, I was completely bedbound and my life revolved around waiting for the next pain medication. The medication would wear off minutes after I took it and then I was faced with unending pain that was far worse than childbirth.

The local doctor who was handling my case recommended against surgery. He told me that whatever I was experiencing now, surgery would be almost infinitely worse. However, there came a point in the middle of one night where certain necessary physiological functions began shutting down and Frank knew that something had to be done immediately.

By-passing the local doctor, whom Frank had never liked, Frank arranged for Cindy and Greg Downes to drive me, starting at 3:00 in the morning, to New York Hospital. We didn't even have an appointment, but Frank knew people, and by the time we arrived at the hospital four and a half hours later, Frank had a surgeon lined up to take care of me. My condition was bad enough that they put me ahead of all the other surgeries that morning and Dr. DiGiacinto took me as an emergency case.

As I've mentioned, surgery cured the problem entirely. But I have several memories of the surgery.

One is, Dr DiGiacinto, said, "Modern medicine has failed you. A homeless person on the street would have received better care than you did."

At the time, I figured that the local doctor who had been treating me, Dr. E, had just made a mistake. For many years afterward, I told myself that medicine is not a perfect science and that in my case, a good doctor had simply gotten it wrong. I defended him over this. However, at the time of Frank's death, I had occasion to revisit this impression. But that's later on in my story.

Another memory I have of this period is that after the surgery, the mere thought of ingesting a single calorie was for me the most repulsive notion in the known universe. Frank, however, didn't view it that way and with almost animal cunning, got me to eat.

He'd spoon-fed me and had some irresistibly cunning way of tempting me to allow the spoon into my mouth. Like, could I tell if I opened my mouth, if the spoon was in my mouth if my eyes were closed. Once the spoon was in my mouth, he'd turn it over in some funny way so I actually had the food in my mouth and either had to eat it (and please him) or spit it out (and disappoint him). I clearly remember being astonished that he was, on top of all his other skills, an absolutely brilliant nurse. Who could even imagine Frank Perdue, captain of industry, gently and cunningly spoon-feeding his sick wife?

I think in general, if I don't want to do something, there are rather few people who could make me do it, short of physical or economic violence. Frank got me to do something I was dead set against, and he did it through psychological skill. It was a kind of instinctive animal cunning of a benevolent kind.

I think all this took place in 1993. After the surgery, I was again able to walk, which amazed me. To this day, I don't take being bipedal for granted. I also gradually built up the ability to lift things and do back bends. Today, I actually like carrying heavy suitcases or climbing stairs, or bending over backward during a tango; I like these things because I can do these things that I once assumed I would never be able to do again. As I write this in 2010, seventeen years later, I'm still grateful that I'm not in a wheelchair and that I'm pain free.

### 1995, Frank Is Diagnosed with Pancreatic Cancer

This was an example of Frank's facing death with surpassing grace. (And he always did. What a hero! What courage!) As I'll describe further on, in a section specifically about Frank's medical conditions, Frank didn't actually have the disease, but for the first several weeks of the ordeal, we believed that he did have it. The doctors at Peninsula Regional Medical Center had diagnosed pancreatic cancer, but they sent us to the world's greatest specialist in pancreatic cancer to confirm their diagnosis.

This doctor, from Johns Hopkins, showed us a film of Frank's pancreas, and there was what looked like a one-inch blob on one end of his pancreas. The doctor told us that this was cancerous, and they would have to do a Whipple surgery on it.

Frank and I both understood that this was a death sentence. For those who survive this particular surgery, almost none make it past five years and (at least at that time), most would be gone within a couple of years. During those two years, there would likely be constant pain and a dismal quality of life. The outlook was truly bleak. We walked out of the doctor's office and into the corridor on whatever floor it was at Hopkins, with me feeling stunned, half paralyzed, and as if we were on a ship with the floor pitching to one side and then the other.

I was in enough shock and distress over this diagnosis that I could hardly function. However, I was just functional enough to observe how Frank responded.

There wasn't a millisecond of "Oh poor me!" or "Why me?" In the next couple of hours, he took some very specific actions relating to his expected demise, including telling Elaine the diagnosis, and canceling his order for a new Mercedes. Then he went to a pay phone at Hopkins and began returning phone calls.

The phone calls were, in a couple of cases, providing references for people. He was clear-thinking and on top of his game. I felt sure that anyone on the receiving end of his phone calls would never guess that, minutes before, this man had been told that he had cancer and was going to die.

I know that must sound like denial, but it was no such thing. We drove back to Salisbury that afternoon and discussed things that we would need to do in light of what we had just learned. During this time, we also admitted to each other many things that just don't come up during ordinary times. He told me that the happiest years of his life had been with me, and I told him that my life began when we married. He said he felt the same way. We agreed that we had been unbelievably lucky to have found each other.

As I'll describe later, Frank didn't have to have the operation and for absolutely unknown reasons, the tumor shrank and half a year later there was no trace of it. It's an extraordinarily rare phenomenon, and there was even an article about it in the March 2009 Forbes Magazine, that some people spontaneously recover from what was thought to be terminal cancers. In any case, I learned to admire Frank's courage and grace and realism more than ever.

That brings me to something else about Frank. I felt that Frank had such a strong, consistent, solid personality that it was possible to know him right to the core. That coupled with a mutual openness made me feel as if I knew him as thoroughly as another human being can be known. This was in contrast to my first husband. During my entire seventeen years with Francisco, I never felt I knew him. I always felt that Francisco was like an actor and the real him (if there was such a thing) (*Naughty Mitzi—you should take that back! Immediately!*) (Okay, I didn't mean it.) (*Liar!*) was hidden behind masks. Knowing Frank was like brailling Michelangelo's *David*. As you explore him, you find something oversize, unchanging, with a clear form and shape, one that's absolutely solid, unbending, real, knowable, and profoundly beautiful. In contrast, for me, trying to know Francisco was like trying to braille a sagging balloon. Francisco may have been a fine person, but he was not someone I ever felt I knew well.

## Was Anyone Ever More Giving?

Thinking back over Frank's and my joint life, there truly was so much to admire, and so much of it was things that no one else would know. For instance, he made a practice of always attending the safety celebrations that the different plants had, when they had achieved various milestones, such as a million man-hours with no accidents.

I'm the only one who knows what this occasionally cost him. Frank had back problems that would occasionally flare up violently. Since he was a tough man, he'd wear a back brace under his clothes to conceal his condition. In some cases, the celebrations would be at plants an hour or more from us and, if it was the night shift, he'd have to get up at 2:00 .a.m. and drive until 3:00 a.m. to get to the plant.

I'd watch him, tired and in pain, strap on his brace, and then drive off in the wee hours of the morning. I didn't need to ask why he did it. I knew that if there was life in his body and he could do it, he would: he understood that it meant something to the people who had achieved something important that he'd be there, sharing it with them and underlining the importance of their achievement. He wasn't going to disappoint them.

Frank was a profoundly generous person. I remember once we were on a family vacation somewhere and learned that there had been floods in, I think, North Carolina. Frank knew that seventy associates (employees) had had their homes flooded.

Frank dropped everything, went to the phone, and got Elaine to arrange that every one of the affected associates would get a personal check for $1,000 from Frank's own money. But it didn't stop there.

Frank also arranged for each one of the associates to be given $100 in cash, again from Frank's own money, because Frank figured that the weekend was coming up, they wouldn't be able to cash the $1,000 checks, and they'd need cash immediately to get them through the weekend. He figured out which Perdue truckers were driving to the area anyway, and had them carry the cash to the workers in time for them to have it before the weekend. The cash and checks reached the associates the day after we heard about the floods.

Frank didn't have to do this. And he didn't want applause for it. It was simply something he wanted to do and he did it. I don't believe he ever told anyone about it.

Oh, there's one other part to this story. Some accounting expert told Frank that if he could hold off on the $1,000 gifts for a week or so, there could be a way of making the gift tax deductible and it would only cost Frank $35,000 instead of $70,000. Frank's answer, and I heard him make it, was, "They need the money now, not a week from now."

## A Tsunami of Greed, Fecklessness, and Irresponsibility

Somewhere during this period an event happened that might have turned out differently if Frank hadn't been in my court. I was on the board of one of the Blue Cross Blue Shield insurance companies. (To protect the guilty, I'm not going to say which one.) After being a member for a year or so, I became deeply suspicious of management, and eventually uncovered the fact that even though management was assuring us that we were doing brilliantly, we were actually ranked number sixty-four—out of the sixty-four Blues. In fact our accreditation was about to be yanked.

I learned this first from the treasurer, a woman who told me, woman-to-woman, that she had been directed to give misinformation to the board. She told me that at the end of our board meetings, that she and her colleagues had looked at each other in slacked jaw amazement over the fact "that the board had bought it."

I'm not a confrontational person in general, but this went beyond the mere vertiginous incompetence that I had suspected. It had gone past duplicity and seemed now to be in the realm of fraud.

At the next board meeting, I asked the CEO if it was true that we ranked sixty-fourth out of sixty-four.

He said that yes, this was true. The other board members were shocked.

I told him, in front of my fellow board members, that if he had leveled with us, we would have stood by him and fought with him to set things right. However, when he withheld critical information from us, with the result that we didn't know there was a problem, he had prevented us, as a board, from helping with the situation.

And then I asked him, "Tell me why I should trust you."

This line of questioning was causing a sensation in the boardroom because all the other directors were the CEO's personal friends and had been appointed by him. This was not the collegial board everyone was used to.

Shortly after this, there was a board retreat for two days and, naturally, the focus was on the position of our local Blue Cross Blue Shield. But interestingly, the CEO had as one of the first items of business increasing the fees we directors received, from $600 a month to $1,200 a month.

It was to be approved by voice vote, and as we went around the room, each person voted "Yes." Until they came to me.

I voted "No!"

This was unprecedented. The board was normally collegial. They stopped the meeting and we went into executive session while they all asked me why I had voted against the increase.

I told them that we had been asleep at the switch, that under these circumstances, I couldn't possibly vote for an increase in salary. We broke for lunch and then went back into session.

The director's fees were again the subject of a motion but this time it was proposed that we keep the same compensation. Again, we went around the room with each person giving their expected "Yes." Until they came to me.

I voted "No!"

This also caused a sensation, and again we went into executive session. I told them that I would support the motion if they would change one word in it. The word 600 was to be changed to 300. That is, we would be getting paid $300 instead of $600.

My change was accepted and we unanimously voted to have our compensation halved. However, immediately after that, a reporter called from the Baltimore Sun, saying he had inside information that even though the Maryland Blue Cross Blue Shield was in danger of having its accreditation yanked, the board had responded by doubling its compensation.

We were able to respond that his inside information was wrong, that we recognized the gravity of the situation, and had halved our salaries. I've wondered since if my fellow board members gave me any credit for saving them personally from a public relations disaster. It would have been headlines if we had doubled our salaries, and they'd have had to endure the shame—as would their wives and children as well.

I don't know, but I did have what Sherlock Holmes would term "a clue." When my term on the board was up, I was not invited to continue.

That experience has led me to a permanent skepticism about board governance in any organization where the CEO can appoint his board. Oh, and P.S., after I left the board, this particular Blue Cross Blue Shield was part of some kind of merger where the next CEO personally made off with $60 million in compensation. *That's sixty million dollars.*

I think initially I struck a small blow for decency in all of this. However, I accomplished nothing because, in the end, it was all lost in the absolute tsunami of greed, fecklessness, and irresponsibility that followed.

It makes me remember my father's statement that "Anyone in a position of unaudited trust will always steal because they always feel that they are underpaid and overworked." That, and "Man's capacity for self-justification is infinite."

I told Frank about all of the Blue Cross Blue Shield events, and he was endlessly supportive of me. I was bitterly unpopular with my fellow BCBS board members, and I probably didn't leave them feeling all warm and fuzzy about having had a woman board member. Still the chance to shine in Frank's eyes more than made up for it.

## The Millennium

On New Year's of 1999, I had something happen that by all logic should be unimportant, but it meant an unreasonable amount to me. The happening had its roots in my childhood. I remember as a child in Lincoln, Massachusetts, hearing my father speculate that I would be around to see in the new millennium. From that moment on, it became almost a life's goal to in fact be there for it. But accreted onto that was a desire to be kissing the man I loved at this important moment. I can't explain why this was so important to me, but for most of my life, that moment was anticipated, hoped for, and slightly feared, in case I didn't get my wish.

Ah, but I did! We were in Hawaii on a family trip with all the children and grandchildren. They had been dancing on the embankments around the hotel's patio, enjoying themselves with a gusto that I think few other families can manage. When the clock struck midnight, Frank folded me in his arms and we kissed and kissed and kissed. I'm writing this in 2010, and the memory still pleases me.

## Frank's Ethical Will

I've often talked in the autobiography about what a good man Frank was and, as yet a further example of this, I want to include something that he did around this time that I consider epochal. Frank wrote an ethical will for his family. He was going to leave them material things, but he wanted to leave them values as well.

What you're about to read is something we spent many days on. We'd talk, I'd write down the things he said, he'd read them, revise them, add more or I'd make a suggestion. Here's the end result. I'm told that it's used in business schools throughout the land for their students.

## Frank Perdue's Ethical Will

Dear Children, Grandchildren and Family Members (present or future):

I want little more than your long-term happiness. To be happy you need character and self-respect and these come from following your highest values. To be happy, consider the following:

1. Be honest always.
2. Be a person whom others are justified in trusting.
3. If you say you will do something, do it.
4. You don't have to be the best, but you should be the best you can be.
5. Treat all people with courtesy and respect, no exceptions.
6. Remember that the way to be happy is to think of what you can do for others. The way to be miserable is to think about what people should be doing for you.
7. Be part of something bigger than your own self. That something can be family, pursuit of knowledge, the environment, or whatever you choose.
8. Remember that hard work is satisfying and fulfilling.
9. Nurture the ability to laugh and have fun.

10. Have respect for those who have gone before; learn from their
weaknesses and build on their strengths.

Isn't that just brilliant? There's not one word in it that he didn't pore
over and approve.

## Excerpts from My Diary

I have so many memories of Frank and what a good man he was.
But instead of going by memory, I'm going to include here some excerpts
from my diary from around this time, since "the faintest ink is better than
the strongest memory."

*Diary entry from January 9, 2000:* In future years, if I ever wonder
what life with Frank was like, here's a typical interchange. Frank has
just said that he won't go to Lowell Stoltzfus' party, thereby
disappointing the person who had invited him.

I tell him, "Frank, since the beginning of all recorded history—no
since the dawn of time!—there's never been such a horrible, rotten, nasty
stinkweed, ever! *And now, by the way, you have to kiss me because I get
insecure after I've insulted you!"*

So he takes me in his arms and kisses me enthusiastically, in
between laughing his head off. We're always laughing and being absurd.

*Diary entry July 1, 2000:* So much of our interaction is affectionate
joking. We have our own language and could probably talk for ten
minutes without anyone else understanding us. Wubu, wub a wub wub.
(I love you, love my husband.) I'll never have another relationship, other
than with blood relatives, that is as totally fulfilling and close.

I don't think if I were widowed that I would ever remarry because
I think I could never be happy with a lesser man, and it would be
impossible to find his equal. I married a Great Man, and I know it more
after twelve years than I did after one year. He's not a perfect man, but
he's better than any I'll ever meet. Some people find him stubborn and
difficult, but he's a thoroughly good man, and his stubbornness doesn't
bother me because I accept that this is part of what made him prevail in
the business world. He has no personality traits that I find incompatible
with my personality.

## Diary Entries Relating to Dr. Mitzi

Diary Entry February 11, 2001: Something else: in case I forget in the future, here are the ways I think I've saved Frank's life:

- When he had neck surgery, on two consecutive days, nurses came in to give him blood thinner by needle. I knew he was already getting it from the intravenous bag and I asked them to check if he needed a double dose. In both cases they got irritated and said it was written on the chart. I asked them to check with the doctor, and he said the chart was in error and he shouldn't get the additional blood thinner by needle. Vinnie Oliviero says that a double dose of blood thinner could cause internal bleeding in the brain and death.

- When he had open heart surgery, in the middle of the fifth night, I sensed that Frank wasn't doing well and called for a nurse. She said that I shouldn't expect him to be doing well— he had just had open heart surgery. I said, "No, this is serious," and asked her to get her supervisor. The supervisor told me the same thing, so I said get the doctor on duty. He was starting to tell me the same thing and then said, "No, wait a minute…" and then began seeing the distress that I had been seeing all along and telephoned Frank's surgeon at 3:00 a.m. The surgeon said, "Get the lung team!" and four members of it [the team] from all over Baltimore had to rush to the hospital to save Frank's life. The most common cause of death after heart surgery is post sternotomy syndrome, and if the lung team hadn't been there to work on him in the nick of time, he would have died. As it was, we were in the hospital for a total of twenty-one days, during most of which he was unable to take a deep breath. During this time, I didn't leave his side for longer than it took to go to the bathroom.

- When he had a pancreatic problem and suddenly lost twenty pounds, and after being in the hospital for a week of tests, he was scheduled for surgery to remove a cancerous pancreas on a Friday. The Thursday just before, I got the passionately strong feeling that *he was getting better.* There was a look of vitality that I hadn't seen for weeks, he was eating, and his sense of humor was back.

I telephoned the company doctor and said, "You're going to think I'm crazy, but I don't think he's ill." The doctor told me that he'd trust a wife's intuition over all the medical tests at Johns Hopkins and that I should cancel the surgery that was scheduled for the following day. It took more guts than I think I am normally capable of, but I went around to all the doctors, the anesthesia people, the operating room people and told them to cancel the surgery.

They all said it was scheduled and that you couldn't just cancel it. I said do it anyway. It was awful because they all acted with me as if they were all thinking that I had bad motives for this, and I can see that from their point of view it didn't look good for a younger woman to be trying to prevent surgery for her older, wealthy husband. If I had been wrong about his not needing it, I would have had a black mark against my name that could never be erased.

Anyway, the surgery was postponed, and we went home. In the next two weeks, he started gaining weight and getting his energy back. When the doctors examined him again, they said, "The tumor hasn't grown, and it just might have shrunk. We'll postpone the surgery again." The next time we went back, the "tumor" was almost gone, and the final time they checked, six months later, it had vanished. The company doctor said that if they had operated, once they cut the pancreas, they can't go back.

There's a P.S. to that story. A year later, Dr. Schlott invited Frank and me to be present at a lecture he was giving to younger doctors. He told the forty or fifty doctors in the room about the case of a man who had every clinical sign of pancreatic cancer, including CAT scans and MRIs and X-rays that revealed a tumor, plus blood tests. However, his wife had prevented the scheduled surgery because her intuition said that he wasn't ill. It turned out that her knowledge of the man was more accurate than all the tests of the Johns Hopkins doctors. He said it was important for doctors "to listen to the wives."

That whole pancreatic cancer episode was one of the high points of my life. I don't think I'll ever do anything as scary or as important again. [Note from Mitzi, written in 2010: He had another ten good years of life, so it was incontestably the right thing to do.]

- Last year, I had my head against his chest, as I do at night, and his heart sounded different to me. At the same time, he was complaining of not feeling right during the day. In the next few days, he was examined by Dr. Schlott, Dr. Fortuin, and Dr. Merrill. All of them listened to his heart and all of them heard nothing abnormal. I told my friend Dr. Bill Bell by email that I thought something was seriously wrong, and what else could we do? He suggested a twenty-four-hour heart monitor. I told Dr. Merrill, who said that to accommodate me, he'd put it on Frank when we got back from vacation at Nags Head in a week.

I said no, I didn't want to wait that long—we'd skip the vacation and start the monitor the next day that it was possible, which was the following Monday. Frank wore it that Monday, and Tuesday the results were faxed to Dr. Fortuin.

Fortuin called me at 11:00 a.m. and asked how fast we could get to Hopkins. I said we could be there in less than three hours, since I'd need time to pick up Frank at the office. Fortuin said that he'd cancel his 2:00 p.m. appointment and would see us then. It turned out that Frank's heart was skipping beats, as much as four and a half seconds at a time at night, even though it was perfect during the day. We had a pacemaker installed. Dr. Merrill said that there is no question that this saved Frank's life because 4.5 seconds is the outer, outer limit that the heart's electrical system can recover from and a fraction of a second longer, and Frank would simply have died in his sleep.

- When we were driving north on US 13, maybe half an hour from Salisbury, Frank was driving and suddenly swerved into oncoming traffic. To this day, I don't know what happened. It was more than just not paying attention, it was an actual swerve right toward an oncoming car. I grabbed the wheel and pulled us back into our lane. I think we were seconds from a head-on collision. [As I write this now (February 11, 2001), I wonder if it was a mini-stroke or a blackout. At the time, it was totally incomprehensible that this would happen, since, as I say, this was far more than just not paying attention. After it was over, he knew something had happened because he said, "I'm sorry," but I don't think he had any better understanding than I did of what exactly had happened.]

- When Frank broke his neck on April 1, 2000, there was a period of around twelve hours when it was imperative that he not move, but they couldn't put him in a permanent brace because of the danger of his head swelling. I stayed with him, awake every second of the night, cajoling him into not moving. He wanted to get up, or at least sit up, and I would talk him out of it...which was extraordinarily difficult because he had enough morphine so that he wasn't totally lucid to begin with, and then there's the normal Franconian stubbornness added to it. Dr. Merrill says that 1/16th of an inch of displacement, and Frank could have cut the nerves that make breathing possible. That may have been the scariest night of my life.

That's pretty much the end of the stories of how I think I helped Frank have a longer, healthier life. He was in declining health after his neck injury. His personality was entirely intact, but I was pretty sure he had Parkinson's for several years before it was actually diagnosed. Still, we had four pretty good years.

## Frank's 2000 Brush with Eternity and the Great Thing that Followed

On April 1, 2000, Frank had his closest brush with death. It happened when he was driving on US 13 in Salisbury and rear-ended a car when he was going thirty miles an hour.

He sustained three injuries, each of which are normally life-ending. He broke his neck with the separation of the vertebra being almost twice as large as the injury sustained by Christopher Reeves. He also broke off the odontoid process, which, I'm told, people never survive. It's almost the definition of death. He also was on high doses of Coumedin, and could easily have bled to death from his injuries.

He was saved by something as close to a miracle as I've ever heard of. A young man who wanted a career in the fire service had just completed the Emergency Medical Technician training course and was driving along US 13 when he saw the accident happen up ahead of him.

Actually, that he happened to be there at all was itself a miracle. He was driving to a friend's wedding and had planned on leaving half an hour later, but decided to come early, in case his friend needed support. If he had left a minute earlier, or a minute later, he wouldn't have been at the scene of the accident when needed.

As it was, he jumped out of his car, ran up to Frank, and sensing the possibility that Frank might have a neck injury, held Frank's head in both hands to stabilize it until the regular fire department rescue guys got there.

If Frank's head had moved by a hair's breadth, he would have died. As I've said, people do not normally survive breaking their odontoid process, nor do they survive a break in the vertebra as severe as Frank's.

The fire service guys did everything right and he made it to the hospital without his vertebra severing any of his spinal cord or having his head fall off his spine—a danger since it didn't have a functioning odontoid process. Further, in spite of life-threatening injuries and being on massive doses of Coumedin, he didn't bleed excessively. It was all miracle upon miracle.

When the accident happened, I was in Washington, having just given a talk on voter fraud. Cindy Downes called me where I was giving the talk and told me in a calm, matter-of-fact voice that Frank had been in a car accident. She didn't present it to me as being more serious than, perhaps, a broken finger, but the prospect of Frank's not being well had an impact on me that was like lightning bolts.

I hung up the phone in the kitchen of the hall where the talk was (this was the year 2000 and I didn't have what is today the ever-present cell phone), and didn't even stop to say good-bye to the hosts of the event. As I walked (er, rushed) past the table where I had been sitting, I told someone at the table to tell the hosts that there was a family situation and I had to return home.

Driving back was surreal. I had no idea in the world that Frank's injury was even serious, let alone life-threatening. Even so, time seemed to dilate so that I was driving and driving and driving and not getting closer to him. It was as if every cell in my body craved to be close to him even though I had been told that the injury was minor. I didn't want to speed because I thought the worst torture for me at that moment would be to be stopped and have to wait for a ticket.

Cindy told me later that she had been totally aware of what she was

*Frank and I greet the New Millennium.*

doing by keeping me in the dark about how serious Frank's injuries were. She knew that I'd be unglued enough thinking it was only something minor.

This is interrupting the story of Frank's near-fatal accident, but what I just described with Cindy is typical of her. I sometimes think she knows me better than I know myself. Every year on the anniversary of our beginning to work together (and we're now close to our third decade), I write a page or so for her about what we lived through the preceding year. Typically I'd write that she was like a psychiatrist, priest, lawyer, *consiglieri,* fashion expert, household manager, family counselor, and just about every good thing.

Back to Frank's accident. I've written earlier about our getting through this, but Frank had to wear a metal brace for many months afterward. The injury was severe enough that we were told he would need neck surgery to try to close the almost inch-wide gap that had been torn in one of his cervical vertebrae. We were also told that this was double Christopher Reeve's injury and that it couldn't repair itself.

And yet, by some miracle, it did repair itself and we avoided the additional surgery. However, the trauma did have lasting effects. His health was never quite the same afterward.

## 9/11

By 2001, Frank's health was getting shakier. He was eighty-one, and it was harder and harder for him to get around by himself. This increased in the following four years, and for me it was one of life's greatest privileges to be there for him.

September 11 of 2001 will always be etched on my mind. I remember at the time of 9/11 we had spent the evening before having dinner with our wonderful friends the Hus in Chinatown, right near the World Trade Center. That morning, Frank had to go to a trade show on Long Island and I stayed in the Salisbury Hotel to work on my art correspondence school lessons.

Shortly after the first plane crashed into the World Trade Center, Frank's driver and good friend, Kirk Daugherty called to say he might have difficulty picking us up that night because there was some kind of problem with a plane and the World Trade Center. I turned on the TV in time to watch live reporting of the second crash. The announcers were speculating that the odds of there being two accidents were too great, and that this was something more ominous.

In moments, we learned that it had been an actual attack, but still nobody guessed that the towers might come down. We still thought that it was only light planes that had crashed into the twin towers.

But then we learned that the Pentagon had been attacked and that there was still another plane heading toward the Capitol or possibly the White House. All planes were grounded.

I had just recently written an article for my weekly Scripps Howard column on bio-terrorism and figured that people nasty enough to try to kill 20,000 people (which is what the initial estimates were) would have no scruples about employing biological warfare as well. I knew that at least twenty-three countries had bio-weapons capabilities, and it seemed like a real possibility that there might be biological agents dispersed in the city.

I turned off the air-conditioner, stuffed wet towels under the doors, filled the tub with water in case I'd be trapped in my hotel room for a long time, and watched TV. I remember vividly that I didn't feel any kind of fear: just a hyper alert sensation that I was going to do everything I could to survive.

However, at just about this time, I got a phone call from Jose and told him my fears about bio-weapons. He pointed out that since none of the first responders were wearing bubble suits, and since I knew from the article I had just written and from talking with Jose that New York and Washington were the two most highly monitored cities on the planet, he helped me figure out that no bubble suits meant no bio-weapons danger to New York at that moment.

In the midst of all this, I got a wonderful phone call from Jim Perdue. I'll always be grateful to him for this phone call because I figured that with all he had to do, figuring out how a major food company responds to a terrorist attack, including logistics and how to feed New

York, that I would be pretty much the least of his concerns. That he called and worried about me was something I'll never forget and always be grateful for.

Since by now, I was no longer worrying about bio-weapons, I walked to the nearest hospital, Roosevelt Hospital, to donate blood. The scene at the hospital was total chaos. I bet 1,000 or more people were crowding around, wanting to donate blood or help in some way. Interestingly, about three people, myself among them, figured out a way jointly to create some order. We simply went inside the hospital, got lab coats (stole lab coats) and hand wrote signs on regular typewriter paper saying "Official." We pinned the signs to our chests, and started acting as if we were authorities.

Even though we were total strangers to each other, we, in a coordinated way, started herding the people into one long line. Then we asked who was O negative (universal donor) and escorted them to the head of the line. We also knew from talking with doctors inside that there were buses leaving from the hospital to the World Trade Center carrying people with medical expertise. So my fellow "officials" and I asked people with medical backgrounds to leave the line and we'd escort them to the holding area for the buses that were going downtown.

I learned later, from newspaper articles, that every hospital had a similar experience, that people who didn't know each other simply stepped in and got people in lines and in one way or another, order was created. I had the feeling that day that I had witnessed some of the worst of humanity, the mass murderers who deliberately killed as many people as they could, and some of the best of humanity, the people who came together to help.

Frank and I were separated at this time because he was in Long Island, I was in New York, and the tunnels and bridges were all closed. My longing to be with him was staggering.

There were estimates that it might be days before the bridges and tunnels would be open, but that night, I got a call from Ray Hall, the head of Perdue Farms transportation. He said that even though the mass media said the bridges and tunnels were closed, they were nevertheless open for transportation of food, and the Perdue chicken trucks were being allowed to cross the bridges. He said they had arranged for me to get out and rejoin Frank, possibly using a Perdue truck.

Then, around 8:00 a.m. the next morning, I got a call from Ray, asking if I could be ready in a matter of minutes because they could get me to the Long Island Railroad, which was running for maybe, they thought, an hour. At 8:10 a.m. on 9/12, I was picked up and driven to Penn Station in roughly seven minutes. There was not a single vehicle on the road. It was surreal. On a normal day at that time, I would have allowed close to forty-five minutes for the same trip.

I got my ticket and left at somewhere around 8:40 a.m. for Long Island. We met there, and I couldn't believe how comforting it was to be back with Frank. At this point we were able to join Kirk Daugherty and drive back to Salisbury. To get back from Long Island, we were at one point downwind of the still-burning towers and I could smell the smoke from them.

It was a disconcerting smell, partly metallic and partly a smell that I associate with badly burnt toast. Curiously, several times in the course of the following years, I would wake up in the middle of the night smelling what I was certain was incredible volumes of smoke. I'd go to the kitchen, convinced that I had left the toaster oven on and the smoke was billowing through the entire house.

As a nuts-and-bolts kind of person who makes a practice of doubting everything, I had wondered about flashbacks, but now, having experienced them, I'm a complete believer. Each time, it's certain that there was no burning toast in the house, but each time my senses told me unmistakably that there was a vast quantity of incinerating toast happening. My mind told me that there was no such thing. My nose over-rode everything and told me that yes, there were big, black clouds of smoke filling the house.

## A Cruise from Hong Kong to Australia

A few weeks after 9/11, I got a phone call from Jim Perdue suggesting that it would be a really, really good idea if Frank and I went for a trip. Frank and Jim had a deep love for each other, but for Frank, no matter how good his intentions, it was difficult for him to pull back and let Jim run Perdue Farms. I understood this because I knew Frank had had more than six decades of running the company and it was against Frank's nature to stand aside and not say something to someone when he thought something needed saying.

With all the good will in the world, it was still a fact that Frank couldn't be on site and not want to run things. The very good thing is, Frank knew this and was prepared to accommodate this reality. He agreed with Jim and me that travel was the easiest solution to this problem.

I had wanted to travel in the Mediterranean, but the cruise ships in those first few days didn't want tourists with American passports. The next thing available that would get us away within three days was a three weeks' Silver Seas Cruise from Hong Kong to Australia.

Fear of terrorism was so high at this point that tourism had dropped to nearly nothing. Cruise ships were viewed as likely targets for terrorism. The ship had so few passengers that we knew a few more trips like this and the line would become insolvent. I think the occupancy was a catastrophic 15 percent. For us, the silver lining to this was, the entire crew was grateful to any tourists who had ignored the fear of terrorism. They treated us like heroes.

One of my favorite memories from this trip was a storm as we sailed along the south coast of Australia. Even though we were on the eighth deck, mammoth waves were crashing onto our veranda. The boat pitched up and down, like a bucking horse, and sometimes it seemed to be thrown completely out of the water, only to smash down hard against the ocean trough with a great shattering thud. It happened again and again.

No food was served that day because even the crew was sick. Members of the crew told me that few had ever seen waves like this in their lives. The Silver Seas ship, which was large enough to hold hundreds of passengers and crew, was bobbing around in the heavy seas like a cork.

Frank, at age eighty-one, wasn't bothered by it in the least. We'd walk down the totally deserted corridors of the ship, being slammed first against this bulkhead and then against the other, and neither of us could have remained upright if there weren't rails to grab. Neither of us felt the least seasick. Instead, we relished the whole thing as if we were on an exciting ride at an amusement park.

By the way, this was an example of something I often observed in Frank. He was the living example of G.K. Chesterton's adage, "An inconvenience is an adventure wrongly considered."

Which brings me to a comment about age. There were twenty-one years age difference between us, but as far as energy and not being daunted by inconveniences but, instead, simply relishing life, he could have been a kid. Until the very end, our age difference was virtually never a factor in our relationship and we simply loved sharing life's adventures.

## I'm No Longer Employed

While Frank and I were on this cruise, I got a life-changing email. Scripps Howard, my employer for eleven years, was facing severe financial problems and was forced to let go all the columnists who weren't on staff, working in the building. My boss, Walter Veasey, said this was the hardest thing in his life, telling good people that Scripps Howard couldn't afford to pay them any longer.

This was a shock to me because Walter had told me previously that out of 400 columnists, mine was in the top ten for being picked up. He also said that while he didn't have time to read all 400 columnists each week, he always read and enjoyed my columns. I had assumed that my job was secure.

He told me that he could keep publishing my column, but that I wouldn't be getting a check for it. I had always thought that I loved writing so much that I would pay people to allow me to do it. I agreed to this.

I wrote three more columns and then suddenly, for the first and only time in my life, I developed writer's block. I couldn't write. I'd sit in front of my laptop, and couldn't find anything to say. Somehow, the validation of getting a paycheck was much, much more important than I had ever calculated. I felt devalued and unmotivated and finally realized that writing as if Scripps Howard was a charity case just wasn't working for me.

Part of my identity for twenty-one years had been as a syndicated columnist, so not being a syndicated columnist was a blow. Actually, I was still writing a column for the *Salisbury Daily Times,* so I was still a columnist, but it was one newspaper as opposed to 420.

By the way, the column I wrote for the *Daily Times* was about local charities. Once a week, I'd visit a local charity and then write a 600 word story spotlighting the charity. It was a way of giving them a public pat on the back, and a way of letting the public know about the charity's services and their needs.

It was also a fabulous way for me to learn more about my community. I visited drug rehabilitation facilities, homeless shelters, a program to bring deadbeat dads to court, Alcoholics Anonymous, Blind Industries, animal shelters, and a whole host of organizations that were meeting acute community needs. Without the column as an excuse, I think it would have been unlikely for the wife of Frank Perdue to get to be educated about 250 local charities. That was the number of columns I wrote over the years.

## One Door Slams Shuts, Another Bursts Open

However, not writing a syndicated column was a wrenching and unpleasant thing. I decided I had a choice: I could wallow in my horrified incredulity or, instead, I could try to think what I had learned from my twenty-one years of interviewing smart people.

Some things stood out. They're well-known today, but they weren't so well-known back in 2001. I had interviewed medical researchers in fields as disparate as heart disease, diabetes, cancer, arthritis, and Alzheimer's, and in each case, the protective factors were the same: exercise lots, don't smoke, maintain normal weight, and eat a diet high in fresh fruits and vegetables and limit junk foods.

Scientists in their laboratories knew what we should be doing, but how do you translate knowledge into action?

That made me think of something else I had written about: teen pregnancy prevention. As with less-than-perfect lifestyles, preventing teen pregnancy was asking people to go against strong instincts where the short-term rewards are intense and the long-term problems far in the distance.

The public school program in Salisbury had only sporadic success. The issue was presented in terms of good choices and bad choices, and a lot of young women were regularly deciding to make the bad choice. They were egged on in this by the fact that the surrounding culture didn't support the "good choices." Once they left the classroom, they were surrounded by cultural messages supporting sexual freedom.

The Salisbury Christian School took a different approach. As the principal told me, they told the kids from first grade on that doing what it took to have babies was an adult thing and they weren't to do it until they were married and ready to care for babies.

The result has been zero teen pregnancy at the school. Since this was such a contrast with the results from the public schools, I asked the principal what the Christian school was doing right. "The students get a firm and consistent message everywhere they go," the principal told me. "Unlike what happens in the public schools, the messages about sex that they get at school are reinforced at home, in church, and where they recreate."

Hmmm. Could the Salisbury Christian School's approach of having a consistent message everywhere help in the case of lifestyle change? Since prevention is so much cheaper and more humane than treating disease, I wondered if there might be a way to get members of a community to improve their lifestyles by using the same "consistent message" approach that the Salisbury Christian School did.

What if we could get the local radio, television, newspapers, and billboard owners to give local residents a consistent barrage of coordinated messages on healthy lifestyles?

What if we could get the local health-related charities (heart, cancer, diabetes, etc.) to coordinate their messages?

What if we could get people's places of work to encourage healthy lifestyles through contests, recognition, and general support of a culture of wellness?

What if the educational institutions worked together to encourage wellness?

## Healthy U of Delmarva Is Born

To explore this possibility, with Frank's backing, I created four $1,000 prizes that would go to the business, educational institution, government office, or nonprofit that did the most to encourage healthy lifestyles. The local media outlets gave extraordinary coverage to the prize, including 200 public service announcements a week, half a page each week in the local newspapers, and two major billboards in high-density travel areas. And so Healthy U of Delmarva was born.

The Healthy U prizes unleashed unimagined creativity. At one point we had ninety-six organizations competing for the prizes and nearly a hundred different ideas that they put into practice for encouraging healthy lifestyles. This isn't the place for the entire list but here are a couple that I particularly remember:

- At the minor league baseball stadium, food technologists came up with baseball stadium fare that's low fat and lower salt. The Delmarva Shorebirds offered meal packages with black bean burgers and water and fruit, or chicken hot dogs that are lower in fat but taste like regular hot dogs.

- Many organizations decided to celebrate people's birthdays with "fruit cakes" instead of regular sugar cakes. They'd even competed for how elaborate the cakes would be.

Within two years, Healthy U had 1,114 volunteers and 6,003 participants. To recruit volunteers, I'd addressed service clubs, and every single Sunday, Frank and I would attend religious services—in the black, Korean, and Haitian churches, and in others—and I'd get myself invited to address the congregations for five to ten minutes as part of the service. I think in most churches, having a speaker like this during the service was not a normal thing, but it happened.

My pitch was to ask members of the congregation to raise their hands if they had or knew someone who had heart disease. Then I'd ask them to keep their hands up, and next, if a person didn't have his or her hand up, if they themselves had cancer or were close to someone who had the disease to raise their hand. I repeated this for diabetes.

By now, invariably, every single hand would be raised. I'd ask them to put their hands down, and then I'd launch into my stem-winder speech about how all these diseases could be prevented or their onset delayed or if someone already had one or more of these diseases, that healthy lifestyles could slow the progress of the disease.

Since health is such an important concern for most people, I knew I'd have their attention. Plus, I'd given the talk enough times to have the timing and the stories polished. At the end, I'd distribute volunteer cards that included asking them what skills they could contribute. In a remarkably short time I had volunteers who could help with legal matters, accounting, statistics, plus a scientific panel of doctors and researchers. Basically, I had a roster of volunteers that included just about every skill that could be needed.

One guy (a favorite) put down that he was a poet. I thought every good organization needs a "poet laureate," so I named him the Healthy U Poet Laureate. When we had recognition events, he'd write brief poems celebrating them, and I think it went over wonderfully with the audience.

I also had jugglers, tumblers, a clown, and an array of people who would make our events special. The Community Players scripted and performed fabulous yearly award ceremonies for the HUEY Awards. We used the Civic Center, and as part of the ceremony, the winners were brought in volunteered limos, walked down a red carpet, and actor-paparazzi mixed with local media people to make them feel special.

I guess I haven't yet addressed the nitty gritty of how we hoped to make lifestyle changes. The basis of Healthy U was to use education, incentives, teamwork, competition, and recognition to help influence behavior.

Success was measured with a measuring tape and scales. Healthy U volunteers weighed and took the waist and hip measurements of 6,003 people at the beginning of 2003.

Part of the reason the weight loss is so important is that people are unlikely to have achieved it without exercise. Healthy U emphasized exercise and a diet that is high in fruits, vegetables, and minimally refined grains, and these healthy habits are consistent with longer, healthier lives.

However, there are other criteria for success besides pounds and inches. As the State's Attorney, Davis Ruark said, "Even if no one loses a pound or sheds an inch, Healthy U is a success because it has brought the community together in a way never seen before. The program is uniting the community in pursuit of a common goal, improved health. Regardless of nationality, race, religion, age, ability or disability, the participants own this project and take pride in the task."

Actually, my personal criteria for the success of it was the stories people told me. For example, one woman told me that she had lost 120 pounds and had kept them off for two years, once the school where she worked began supporting healthy lifestyles. She had never succeeded in losing weight before, but now had her life back. She had previously been on three pain medications for knee pain and now, weighing so much less, no longer needed them.

Other women told me that for the first time in their adult lives, they were enjoying fashion and makeup because, with their new bodies, they had the self-confidence to enjoy being a woman. A guy who took up running and lost 40 pounds said he would never give up his lifestyle changes because his energy is so good and his mood so great now that he's following a healthy lifestyle.

This is jumping five years ahead of the story, but Healthy U continues to this day, although I no longer have a day-to-day involvement with it. There were several factors that made this happen.

First, in the following year, as Frank's Parkinson's worsened, I had less and less time or interest in putting in the ferocious amount of time and effort that it took to make the organization hum.

Second, I discovered to my utter horror, that the executive director had been consistently fudging the records. For example, when she gave reports to the board, and in press releases, she stated that the average participant had lost more than 8 pounds in the course of a year. I knew of many people (I even have photographs of them) who lost between 40 and 140 pounds so this information had some plausibility to it.

However, one day, out of what I thought at the time was an over-abundance of caution, I decided to look at the data in the computer myself. The results were horrifying.

I have at least some knowledge of database queries and, in fact, I wrote the program in VBA that Healthy U used and uses to track results. Actually, I'm probably a black belt in database programming. When I tried to get the same results by querying the database, I couldn't do it. Not even close. Not for any year.

Sure, there was a vast number of people who had lost very significant amounts of weight. But there was an almost equally vast number of people who had gained weight. On balance, if the input data was correct, the average person probably lost a pound. That's still good because normally you would expect a population of 6,000 people to gain weight rather than more-or-less maintain.

But the problem was, if I couldn't trust some of the data, all the rest was put in doubt. From further dealings, I learned that the director was obsessed with porn and while I have rather little interest in what she did on her own time, I have considerable interest in what she does on compensated time. I learned that she had a habit, on company time, not only of indulging this interest, but would even direct subordinates to buy items at the local substitute love shop "because she was too busy to do it herself."

Or she'd have romantic trysts with a gentleman other than her husband in Baltimore and charge the travel expenses to Healthy U. Or she agreed for Healthy U to acquire expensive printing and copying equipment which was somewhat nicer than what Perdue Farms with 22,000 associates was using, and she got a bonus (I call it a kick-back) from the company she was buying from.

Each of the problems I just described would make me inclined to think Madam X was not the person for the job, but the one that was completely intolerable was the inaccurate data that we had been giving out. I knew she had to go.

The big problem was, the discoveries that I just described, and more, occurred while Frank was in his final decline. I like to think that they wouldn't have gotten so out of hand if I had had more time and energy to be on top of things. Still, I have to face up to the fact that happen they did, and on my watch.

This was at a time when I felt every waking second was involved with trying to be there for my dying husband. The board allowed her to resign, and the eventual disposition of Healthy U was that Salisbury University took it over.

This is actually better than having it run privately. A university can keep better records and is in a better position to produce academic papers which can mean that the healthy-lifestyle concept could spread. I was beyond delighted when Salisbury University took over Healthy U and lifted a burden from my back.

I mentioned earlier that talking about Healthy U would mean jumping ahead of myself, so now, I take a great big hearty jump backward in time to 2001, the year before Healthy U began.

### How I Became Mitzi "the Gun" Perdue

A number of things were going on in this period, but among the memories of this time that I treasure was that I acquired my nickname, "The Gun," as in *Mitzi "the Gun" Perdue*.

Here's how it happened. One day I was driving back from Baltimore to Salisbury and I got a phone call from the Wicomico County Sheriff, Hunter Nelms, telling me that he had just learned that the speaker for the next day's graduation ceremony for the Citizen's Police Academy had taken off for Florida and had pretty much left everyone hanging. Would I give a talk to the graduating class?

I was busy, and this would be majorly inconvenient for me. Still, I calculated that it would be really hard for the sheriff to get another speaker with less than twenty-four hours' notice, and it wouldn't be right to have the twenty-four or so graduates not be shown the respect of having a speaker at their ceremony.

I agreed, and by the next evening, created what felt to me like as good a speech as I'm capable of.

I gave the talk and was inordinately proud of its reception. Before I get to that, though, a word on my approach to all graduation speeches. I write the speech and then, after getting a list of the graduates, print the speech, and using mail merge, have a personalized copy of the speech, bound in a leatherette cover, given as a souvenir to each graduate at the end of the ceremony.

When I actually give a graduation speech, however, I never ever read it. I have it pretty much memorized and simply look out at the audience, without notes, and give the talk. When it comes to public speaking, I can give a half hour or longer talk without notes, and it's pretty close to verbatim what the graduates will be receiving in their bound copies a few minutes later.

(It's funny, I can't remember names, faces, directions, dance steps, and a lot of other things, but I can pretty much remember an entire speech verbatim just from having written it. I am not unaware that this impresses heck out of at least some of the people in my audiences.)

Anyway, this particular talk seemed to go well but alas the sheriff didn't attend. Since I was proud of the speech, I wanted him to read what I had said. After all, I had given the speech to help him out, and I kind of felt that he owed me to read it. I sent him a copy.

A week or so later, I saw him at a social event and asked if he had read the talk. He hadn't gotten around to it, but said he would shortly.

A week after that, I again ran into him at another social event. Striking a pose and doing my best to look fetching, I purred, "Sheriff, did you have a chance to read my talk?"

Again, he hadn't gotten around to it. Something needed to be done! How could I motivate the sheriff to read my talk?

Using desktop publishing, I created a wonderfully professional-looking letterhead that proclaimed **MITZI PERDUE FOR WICOMICO COUNTY SHERIFF.** There followed what was designed to look like a form-letter which enthusiastically invited the recipients to donate funds to Mitzi Perdue's campaign for sheriff. The letter simply assumed that all the recipients would want the pride of being a part of helping Wicomico County elect it's first female sheriff.

I signed the supposed form letter, Mitzi "the Gun" Perdue.

Then in a handwritten P.S. addressed to Sheriff Hunter Nelms, I said I would drop my campaign to run for sheriff, if he'd read my speech!

I mailed the sheriff my fake solicitation letter, and the next day got a phone call from Hunter, telling me he had read the speech, and liked it enough that he'd like me to give the same speech for this year's graduates for the Criminal Justice Academy. I did give the speech, and the next year they invited me to give the same speech again. There's a copy of it in Appendix I.

Because of that, I became friends with a number of people in law enforcement, and am extremely proud of my association with them. Some of them still call me "Gun."

I love it when they do, I guess in part because other than Mr. Rogers, I don't know of anyone who less deserves that title than me.

### 2002, Carlos and Gea's Wedding

It was around this time, that Carlos was finishing his MBA at Wharton, and had gotten engaged to the beautiful Gea Vanden Hengel. I've often heard that mothers feel that their sons' wives cannot possibly be good enough for them but with Gea (and later, with Jose' wife, Erica), I was left with a feeling of astonishment that my own personal son could bring home a woman so gorgeous, inside and out.

We had a number of things that we bonded over, including an absolute love for the *Godfather* movies, an enjoyment of the same kind of books, an interest in homemaking, and thinking that Carlos is wonderful. I liked her sense of humor, her interest in physical fitness, and that she manifested a ton of adorable personality.

Carlos and Gea had a great wedding. Cruise prices immediately after 9/11 were at an all time low, and Carlos discovered that he could pay for his entire class at Wharton to have a four-day Caribbean cruise for the same price that dinner (for the same number of people) would have cost at the Plaza in New York.

Hmmm. Which is better? Four days on a cruise, all expenses paid, dancing, drinking, partying, and having a bridal shower and a wedding, or four hours at the Plaza? Too tough to call?

His whole life, Carlos has simply excelled brilliantly at using whatever resources he has.

My favorite memories of his wedding (it was April 16, 2002) include the fact that it was then that I had the first moment of really feeling like a grown-up. All my life before then, I felt that I could act my age, but the operative word is "act." I could fool just about anyone but, in fact, I felt I was really a teenager inside.

However, at Carlos' wedding, having a daughter-in-law and a future daughter-in-law following after me like a mother duck with her ducklings, I suddenly felt in my bones that if I have these two younger women in my life, then, against all odds and all expectations, I truly was in fact, by definition, a grown-up.

How interesting. What a different way of looking at the world. I'm now the woman that younger women look up to. And it's no longer just a role or a rehearsal, it's—the real thing. *I'm no longer just faking it.*

Another memory from their wedding is, after the wedding, Jan vanden Hengel, Gea's brother, gave the world's best toast. He had Gea and Carlos act out what their first date was like. Carlos had pretended to be blind, complete with a cane, and some goofy-looking protruding false teeth, and Gea had led him around New York, helping him get into all sorts of trouble. They had just met, but they had so precisely the same sense of humor that they simply fell into this funny routine.

## 2003, Jose and Erica's Wedding

A year later, June 21, 2003, Jose and Erica Simon got married at our family home in Dublin, New Hampshire. It was the most beautiful wedding I've ever seen. Erica wore an insanely beautiful Vera Wang dress, and since she's tall and slender, she looked like royalty. My two favorite moments of their wedding was, first, I got to be best man.

*What?*

Yes, I really did. Jose said I was the person he most wanted to have stand up for him, so during the part of the ceremony where the mother of the groom is escorted down the aisle and sits in the front seat, I simply continued on, walked up the steps to the ballroom's stage and stood at the head of the line of ushers.

And further, Erica wanted her brothers to stand up for her so several of the bridesmaids were actually bridesmales! It was such new-millennium wedding!

My other favorite memory was that the lights went out, so the first dance was done by candle light and by the glow of wonderful neon ice cubes. Their dance was an utterly perfect waltz they had learned at Arthur Murray.

That marriage, alas, didn't last. I loved Erica, but seven years after their marriage, it ended. I hate divorce, but I also feel, echoing my mother's saying, "When the house is burning down, you have to get out."

## Frank's Illness

Around the time of the two weddings, Frank was diagnosed with Parkinson's. Awhile ago, I was talking about the role trust played in our life, and I think at the end of his life, he got to know in the strongest way possible that he could trust me. It had to do with his progressive decline caused by Parkinson's disease.

I believe he had it several years before it was diagnosed. I even asked a couple of doctors during this time if he had it, and they said no.

I didn't believe them. I could see the symptoms that became more evident as the disease progressed, including weakness, inability to have the perfect motor coordination it takes, for example, to turn on the shower, slight trembling in the hands, abnormal gait and so on. One thing I particularly noticed was when he walked, one hand would swing normally, but the other, at least sometimes, didn't swing. This was very evident by 2002 at the time of Carlos' wedding.

Because of his illness, somewhere around 2000, I stopped taking any overnight trips that would keep me away from him. That meant virtually full time in Salisbury, without visiting my kids or my sister or friends or attending events, like reunions. I didn't begrudge it because being needed was satisfying to my soul. Taking care of him was a privilege, not a burden.

But since I was home so continuously, it meant a lot of time for such things as decorating eggs, practicing my hobby of computer database programming, and surfing the Internet.

It was during this time that I made what feels like an important discovery in human nature. I've mentioned earlier that Frank and I virtually never quarreled, and the reason was that there was no point: he was always fair and I always felt listened to and understood. What's to fight about?

But there was an occasion, and it happened around this period, when we could have had an enormous quarrel. We were in his closet (it was a large one) figuring out what clothes he'd wear for a party that night.

Suddenly, out of the blue, he started being critical and it was in a way that I had never before heard or even imagined.

His voice sounded angry as he began a litany of my faults. "You were born rich and never got over it! You're spoiled. You're selfish. You're always thinking of yourself. You think the world revolves around you! "

I felt as if I had been ambushed. It was insulting, unexpected, and so unlike him. Every instinct made me want to respond with something harsh in return and then to storm out of the room boiling with anger.

I said "every instinct," but actually, there was one instinct that was the exception, and I listened to it. Instead of responding with anger, I put my arms around him and asked, "Was it a rough day today?"

It turned out that it had been. We ended up talking for half an hour, each of us sitting cross-legged on the floor of his closet, facing each other, as he told how it felt when people no longer had to listen to him and how, with Jim running things, he

*This is a Healthy U birthday cake. Many organizations decided to forego sugary birthday cakes and celebrate with beautiful and healthy "fruit cakes" instead.*

was giving up the authority he once had. He knew that it was right for Jim to have the authority, and having Jim in charge was what he most wanted, but it was making him feel, now in his eighties, like a faint shadow of his former self.

I could see he was hurting and I knew him well enough to understand a lot of what he was going through. I kissed and caressed him, telling him that I loved him more than ever, and he meant more to me than ever. At the end of a half hour of honest talk about the fears and disappointments that came with growing older, I think we both felt as close to each other as we ever had.

Funny, we were carrying out in real life what we had each promised each other when we first met so many years earlier: that we'd rejoice when things went well and support each other when they didn"t.

In the years since that time of sitting cross-legged on the floor, I've often wondered how many quarrels come about because one member of a couple is hurting, and lashes out in anger, when it's really a cry for comfort and support. Even Frank, who had a preternatural understanding of human motivation (he didn't build a 22,000 person company without deep understanding of the human condition and what makes people tick), even he, with a mind as incisive as a perfectly balanced rapidly rotating circular saw, initially hadn't realized what was going on. It's like Dr. Yussef says, "Quarrels are rarely about what they're about," and what's really important is to understand what's behind them.

## Donna Potter, My Internet BF

This period was the beginning of a deep and lasting a friendship with a woman I met online because of e-Bay, the Internet auction site. Donna Potter and I got to know each other because, initially, both of us often competed against each other for monogrammed linens. We had the same last initial and, it turns out, the same ideas on what is beautiful and what has quality. I became conscious that I had an ongoing competitor.

One day, I outbid her on something she really wanted, and she sent me an email asking if she could buy it from me. I said sure, received her money, and unintentionally sent her the wrong set of twelve napkins. Not only were they the wrong ones, they were inferior.

I was mortified when I learned what happened because it had to look as if I were chiseling. I quickly sent the correct ones, and she was so nice about my mistake that I decided she must be a class act.

We started corresponding and, at the beginning, the correspondence was about which linens one of us particularly wanted, and then we'd avoid bidding against each other on that lot. I noticed that she was bend-over-backward fair in the taking turns business. I was starting to get the picture of someone unusually nice and even likable.

Gradually, in the course of our correspondence, we'd mention things that were going on in the world, and I discovered that we held exactly the same political views. If something seemed good and right, I looked at it the same way, and if something seemed horrible and a Threat to the Republic, we also saw eye to eye on that also.

How nice, sitting at my desk, housebound in Salisbury, to have someone to talk with!

The conversations branched onto things like fashion and what our daily lives were like, what her husband does and what mine did. She seemed so classy and proper, however, that I hid one aspect of my personality from her; I love adult humor.

Surprisingly, she had the exact same attitude toward me. I don't know what made us break through that barrier, but when we started sharing some of the Internet's funnier and naughtier jokes, both of us confessed that we had been really hesitant to do this, since we each expected the other to be the pinnacle of propriety.

As the years of correspondence wore on, I began telling her some of my feelings for Frank, the feelings of grief I had of watching him decline and the feelings of helplessness for being unable to stop the decline. This is jumping ahead of the story, but when Frank did pass on, she was possibly the most comforting person of all. Her comforting emails during that period were continuous.

In the years since Frank's passing, our friendship continues. In fact, there's an aspect of it, a small one, that I wouldn't believe if it weren't me who experiences it. Donna has amazing taste and she's more gifted at recommending clothes for me from the Internet than I am at finding them in the best shops in New York.

A large percentage of the clothes in my closet, and frequently the ones I wear the most, are ones that Donna has emailed me about from catalogues, usually with a comment that I might want to look at this dress or that suit or this bathing suit.

Tell me, does it make sense that a woman in Florida whom I have never met and who has never seen me does a better job in picking the most becoming and useful clothes in my closet than I can? But it's true.

We still communicate, as I write this in 2010, and I still confide in her about just about everything. We still talk politics and share naughty jokes and it's generally an immensely satisfying and rewarding friendship. All because of e-Bay.

## Frank's Illness, Continued

Even in his eighties, Frank relished life and participated in it with a zest that would do a twenty year old proud. Around this time we learned that the Perseid meteor shower would be particularly bright that year, and that if we got up at 1:00 a.m., drove an hour to the Assateague Island National Seashore, which is far away from the light pollution of cities and towns, that we would see the meteor showers at their best.

We did exactly that, and even though the night was miserably cold, we lay on our backs, cuddling for warmth in one sleeping bag, relishing the beautiful cosmic fireworks. At its peak, there were maybe seventy or so shooting stars per hour, and we'd gleefully point them out to each other, as in "There's one!" Or "Oh, look at that one!"

I feel as if there's a moral to this story. As we lay on the beach that night, what was going on had nothing to do with the fame and the fortune that had come our way or being the people the world perceived us to be; I wasn't being the Sheraton heiress and he wasn't being the Chicken King. Instead, it was just the two of us, two people who loved each other, on a beach, appreciating each other, loving each other, and happily sharing life's adventures. These moments were as precious to me as anything I've ever known. And now we're getting to the moral of the story part.

Remembering that night reminds me of an old saying that I cherish which goes like this:

"He who loses wealth loses nothing.

He who loses health loses something.

He who loses character loses everything there is."

Frank was about character. Of course he was a character, in the sense that he was an original—quirky, funny, and unique. But he also *had* character, in that he had integrity, honor, moral strength, backbone, willpower, gutsiness, and most of all, he was a genuinely good man. As Hamlet said of his father the King, "He was a man; take him for all in all, I shall not look upon his like again."

Frank may have been getting on in years, but he was so dear to me that evening on the Assateague beach—come to think of it, he was dearer to me than he was when he was twenty years younger and at the top of his game. It was all about character. He had so much of it, and I "shall not look upon his like again." I guess at this stage of my own life, character—good character—is the most important thing there is. I've seen rich people, famous people, Nobel Prize winners, who lacked it, and they were miserable. On the other hand, I know and love individuals on disability on a fixed income whom I admire beyond measure because of their character.

Even the way Frank handled his illness demonstrated character. As he declined, he inevitably became more dependent. A lesser man might have been continuously angry or resentful at his deterioration and might have taken it out on me. But except for the time I described a few pages earlier, when we were in his closet, Frank accepted my care with grace, telling me that I was as important to him as sight would be to another man.

This wasn't about status or fame or money or any of the things that had attracted countless women to him. This was two people who loved each other, and who were working to endure the inevitable, with as much grace and dignity and love as we could.

As his condition deteriorated, he was unable to get out of a chair by himself. We devised a way in which I would put out my bent arm for him to grab hold of and then, by leaning backward, almost like a fulcrum, I could easily pull him out of his chair and into a standing position.

**Sample Diary Entry: December 28, 2004, Three Months before His Passing**

We laugh together so much. We have a whole repertoire of things that make us laugh, including the little rituals for my getting him up in the morning. I ask him, innocently, "Would you like me to sing you a little song?" and he pretends that my singing would be sheer torture and please don't do that, he'll get up! We can (and do) drag this little joke on for five minutes, and I never do sing the song but we both laugh over "the threat."

My husband is the finest human being I'll ever meet. He's brave, kind, giving, humble, fun, funny, pleasant, feels good to the touch, and comfortable to be with and makes me feel appreciated.

## I Lose the Love of My Life

In Frank's Parkinson's, his decline had been gradual. Up until two months before his death, he had been doing really pretty well. Although getting out of a chair was difficult, he could still function pretty well otherwise. Five months before his death, he had been well enough to go on a fairly strenuous ten-day Library of Congress trip to Holland, France, and England. The trip involved lots of walking and parties every night. We went and had a ball and missed nothing. Less than three months before his death, we had gone on a family trip to the Caribbean.

Taking care of Frank at the end was possibly the most fulfilling time of my life (not, by the way, a fulfillment I would choose) because I could completely be there for the man I loved, enveloping him with love. I couldn't stop his disease, but actually, through the entire course of it, I felt that I was needed and loved and that it was an amazing exchange of total love, and (this is repetitious, I know) at the distance of five years, I am happy knowing that the man whose motto was "trust no one," ended up trusting me, and I could prove to him moment by moment that he was right to trust.

It taught me something about love. When I was younger, I had thought you loved someone because you admired them, trusted them, felt physically attracted to them; but with Frank, in his final illness, I realized that I loved him just as much when all the external things were no longer a part of the picture. There was some essence of him that I loved just as deeply at the end as I did at the beginning.

Frank's death, in the end, was a peaceful one. He died in bed with his daughter Beverly Jennings on one side and me on the other, with both of us telling him that we loved him.

There's a part of his death that I wonder about. The Hospice nurse, who had witnessed many deaths, told me the morning of his death that he had less than an hour left. But we knew and I told him that Beverly was driving from Virginia, five hours away to be with him.

He was in a coma, so I couldn't even know that he heard me when I told him that Bev was coming. But he seemed to hold on until Beverly arrived and only then let go. After she arrived, his breathing got slower and slower and then finally, he breathed his last.

If a person has to go, that's got to be the way, in the arms of people who adore you.

## Widowhood

For at least several months after Frank's death, I didn't believe it had happened. I felt that I was in a play or a dream and what seemed to be happening wasn't really happening, and I was somehow expecting that I'd wake up or the play would be over, and we'd get back to our life together. I had this strange mantra that kept coming to me and it was something along the lines of, "This was the day that would never come, so by definition, something that would never come couldn't have come, so this can't be real."

I think it took a full two years before I experienced anything like happiness again. Actually, it was pretty close to a lost two years, between a trifecta of grief, pain, and fear.

The grief is obvious, and I'll get to the fear in a moment, but the pain part involved shoulder pain severe enough so that I couldn't function without strong pain pills  I used to compare it to someone aiming a blowtorch at my shoulders. Once, when I was on my way to visit my son Jose in Dallas, after I got to the Detroit airport, the pain was so incapacitating that I had to abort the trip halfway there and return home. I was within a gnat's eyelash of simply jettisoning my wheely-bag suitcase because I was unable to handle even the minimal extra stress of dragging the bag behind me.

I didn't jettison the bag, but instead managed to keep it with me by forcing myself to walk a couple of steps and then I'd stop and regroup, and then begin again. Getting to the area where I could change my ticket and then getting to the revised gate seemed like trying to scale Mount Everest.

Clearly I had to do something about this incapacitating pain. That year, I went to eight different doctors and endured half a year of completely unsuccessful physical therapy. Interestingly, each doctor had a different diagnosis, and none of them helped. That is, none of them helped until one doctor, the last, asked me what I was able to do for it that made it better.

I answered that there were only two things that worked: the medication Skellaxin, and also alcohol.

He asked me if I realized that Skellaxin wasn't a pain pill; it was a tranquilizer and was virtually the same thing as Prozac. He also said that alcohol acted like Prozac. He said my problem wasn't a torn rotator cuff, it wasn't bursitis, it wasn't a malformed bone that was sawing against my nerves, it wasn't something that could be cured by surgery or physical therapy; no, it was stress, and I needed to address the stress issue if I was to get better.

The stress issue was entirely related to my accidentally being a potential witness in a trial involving a murder. I didn't end up having to be a witness, but the local State's Attorney and the local sheriff each said my situation, as a witness, was serious enough that I needed to take security precautions. The Sheriff advised me, as a security measure, to trim all the bushes near my house, spend $10,000 upgrading the alarm system, and create a safe room in case the security was breeched. He gave me a professional size can of pepper spray and spent an hour teaching me how to use it. He also suggested that I buy a gun and he took me to the shooting range to learn to use it.

*Bathing suit picked out from a catalogue by my Internet friend, Donna Potter. I've never met Donna in person.*

Between grief, pain, and fear, I wasn't in a good place. In October of 2006, my beloved and wise cousin, Astrid Forbes, told me that I needed to do something about my situation and I shouldn't waste any time doing it. She suggested that I move to New York.

# Chapter Seven:

# *2006–2009,*
# *New York City*

Isublet an apartment in New York three days later. People at the time were telling me that you can't run from your problems but, actually, the change made all the difference. Within a couple of months, my entire shoulder problem vanished, and for that matter, so did disabling migraines and I was able to sleep through the night without waking after every little creak in the  house.

It was a great move to make because even though I basically knew only one person, Norma Dana from the Library of Congress, I quickly found a large group of new friends.

Actually, it's not an accident that I met a large number of people. I calculated that I could do something to meet a charitable need and at the same time, as a new person in town, get to meet a lot of people.

Here's what the charitable need is. Charities need to cultivate and recognize their donors and volunteers or they risk supporter burnout. All too often, a supporter helps for several years, but without an active effort for supporter recognition, the supporter may over time, just slip away. The relationships need to be nurtured, but given that the charities need to devote their resources to their primary mission, resources for supporter recognition are scarce.

What I have offered to more than 100 charities so far is to give recognition events at my apartment. I provide the place, the food, the beverages, and the flowers, and they provide the guest list, do the inviting, and they figure out the program, including the speaker.

Between April of 2008 and August of 2010, I entertained 2,307 people. That meant a continuous flow of new people going through my apartment. I'd get to greet every one of them, and it virtually never happened that by the end of the evening, I wouldn't have two or three people asking me out for lunch or dinner or theater or whatever.

A great thing about New York is that at any moment, there are at least three wonderful things one could be doing, and there's no excuse for staying home and moping. There's theater, opera, lectures, dinner parties, charity events, movies, or just hanging out with friends.

Since being widowed, it's also been an opportunity to find out what I really enjoy and don't enjoy, as opposed to blending in to accommodate what others want. To be totally accurate on this point, I deeply enjoyed blending in to accommodate what the men in my life liked, so this wasn't a sacrifice; it was a fulfillment. Nevertheless, widowhood has been a time of learning what I enjoy on my own, not influenced by others.

I have a metric for gauging how much I enjoy something: how fast the time flies or drags when I'm engaged in it. Time flies by fastest when I'm with family members, whether from my birth family or my marital family, or with very good friends. After that, entertaining, studying computer things like Visual Basic or InDesign or PhotoShop. Then, ballroom dancing, followed by reading, especially about science, political theory, or business. I also love sewing, writing family newsletters, and making family albums. I hugely enjoy fashion, design, and just about anything creative.

**How Many Blended Families Can Match This?**

I mentioned a moment ago that being with family tops my list of sources of pleasure. It's an unending source of happiness and pride for me that my sons and Frank's family blended together so well. There's true affection, and I would be surprised if a week goes by when one of my kids hasn't been in contact with a Perdue family member. Jose (the Rev. Dr. Francisco Jose Ayala, Jr.) has even performed the wedding ceremonies for two Perdue family grandchildren. And a really joyful thing at this time was that Jim Perdue appointed his step-brother, my Carlos, to be vice president for international for Perdue Farms.

How many blended families from a Fortune 500-size company get along so well, and respect and trust each other so much that the biological son of the founder appoints his step-brother to be a vice president?

## Frank's Language, a Shock

Oh, there was something else that, if not joyful, was pleasantly poignant. Ray Smith, former chairman of Verizon, has been a chum at the Madison Council of the Library of Congress for almost two decades. He told me one day, over drinks, a startling fact about Frank.

In between sips of pinot grigio at Le Cirque, he had been telling me a funny story about Frank's negotiating some deal with a competing chicken company. "And then Frank said, "the f___ing SOBs came back with..."

"Wait," I interrupted, putting my glass down and staring at Ray, "Did Frank actually use the word f___ing?"

"Absolutely," Ray assured me and then added, smiling, "He was a man's man, and when we talked, that's the kind of language we used."

I shook my head in wonder. "I don't think Frank ever even once used this kind of language with me. I didn't even know he knew that kind of language!"

Ray sat back in his chair, put his hands to his face and said, "I shouldn't have told you!"

"I'm glad you did," I answered. "I'm touched and pleased that Frank treated me with so much respect."

## Girl Friends

It's funny, I haven't found any male companion that I could feel romantic about, although I have many male friends, particularly Robert Cancro, Maury Kanbar, Fred Negem, Michael Ross, Jeffrey Laurence, Bruce Cohen, and Mark Herschberg. On the other hand, there are any number of women whose company I enjoy. Emily Cheng is closest to a sister, and after that, Barbara Bellin-Brenner (my Official Fairy God-Sister and a woman of style, artistic genius, and humor), Margaret Daniels (a younger friend who is adorable, fun and a joy to spend time with), Lauren Lawrence (brilliant, beautiful, an awesome writer and someone with enormous insight into the human condition), Rita Cosby (an inspiration for her love of veterans), Harty DuPont (possibly the nicest woman on the planet), Joycelyn Engle (whose strength and creativity are an inspiration), Elizabeth Kabler (who devotes her life to helping other yet is still a funny, fun, wise and insightful friend), Margie Shields (a dear friend with whom I can talk about anything), Kathy Springhorn (whose sheer goodness is matched by her phenomenal generosity of spirit), Alicia Volk (a woman of incredible taste, understanding, beauty and benevolence) and Barbara Winston (a woman of courage, caring, and commitment to what is best for our country and our world), plus my beloved Phuong Tranvan (a woman of insight, commitment, wisdom, courage and general over-all wonderfulness.)

Other close friends include Deborah Terhune, (whose work in Growing Up Africa shows what one woman can accomplish) Georgia Shreve) playwright, composer, musician, philosopher, director, choreographer and performer, plus Lorraine Cancro and Maria Snyder, my honorary cousins, who feel as close, as real cousins.

## Summing Up

My father ended his autobiography, *The World of Mr. Sheraton*, with a summary of what he had learned in his life. For him, as he looked back over the years, he remembered many errors, such as not buying the Empire State Building when it was offered to him at a fraction of its potential value. But he also felt that his errors were often the foundation for successes because "It is from such lapses that we gain the wisdom on which we can build in the future," and "Mistakes are usually the most effective teacher."

Copying him, I'm trying to think what I've learned, looking back over my years. What seems really important in life?

One thought that guides my life comes from Plato, who said that there are three things that men think will make them happy, but in the long run, they seldom do. These are fame, power, and money. The reason these don't make people happy is that it takes a bigger and bigger dose to make people happy. Or you can lose them. Interestingly, both my father and my husband Frank had plenty of fame, power, and money, and yet neither of them tied their happiness to any of these three factors. I believe both men had in common that they deeply enjoyed their lives but it may have been in spite of their fame, power, and wealth rather than because of them.

Well, if fame, power, and money don't make men happy, what does? Plato said that truth, beauty, and goodness do provide lasting happiness. You don't need bigger and bigger doses of these; each one by itself can make you happy. I think Frank and Ernie (my father) were both profoundly good people, and they were uncompromisingly honest. Beauty wasn't a strong suit for either of them, as in, I don't see either of them as being overly eager to see the next art exhibit. Yet both of them cared deeply about having a beautiful home and both of them could be moved by a beautiful sunset. Truth, goodness, and to a lesser extent, beauty, sums up these men.

And where do I fit in, for all of this? I hope I'm cast in the same mold, although I'm aware that the mold is a smaller mold. If I lost everything and had to live in a cabin in the mountains, I think I could still find happiness. I dearly enjoy whatever limited amounts of power, money, or fame came my way, but none of it ever provided me with 5 percent of the pleasure and joy that my kids, my husband, and my Perdue and Henderson families have given me. As for truth, beauty, and goodness, I consider truth to be incandescently beautiful and goodness is the goal of my life. I can't say that I achieve goodness, but I can say that it is the goal.

Another factor that I contemplate when I look back on my life and the lives of Ernie and Frank is success. I have a definition of success that I came up with maybe twenty years ago when I had to give a talk to seventh graders at the Worcester Country Day School in Maryland. The school had asked me to talk on success, so I spent a day in the Wicomico County Library, reading everything I could find on success. Amazingly, from Aristotle to Martin Luther King to my own mother, the people who wrote about success (or in the case of Mother, talked about it), all seemed in one way or another to talk about success in relation to serving others. I particularly liked Aristotle's, "The only way to find true success in life is to find yourself in service to the community." Mother's was, "Put back in the bucket."

After reading everything I could on the subject, I came up with my own definition, which is kind of an amalgam of all the others that I had read: "Success is measured not by what you can get, but by what you can give."

By that measure, Ernie and Frank were extraordinarily successful.

They each provided employment for more than 20,000 people. People said of Frank that if he hadn't made Perdue Farms the international success that it became, the Eastern Shore of Maryland, without those jobs, would have been destitute. In addition, both men provided services and goods that made people's lives better.

And then on top of that, they were each breathtakingly philanthropic. Ernie once told me that the greatest pleasure he ever got from his money was in giving it away. One of the decisions that made Frank happiest was when he decided to start giving away his fortune while he was alive and could witness the good that came from his philanthropies. Some of the happiest times I ever saw him were the occasions when Perdue scholars would come up to him, years after they had graduated, and they'd tell him about the success in their careers and the successes in their lives that their scholarships had made possible.

Again, where do I fit in, in all of this? Actually, I don't know. I can hope that my articles on the environment were useful, or that the donor cultivation or donor recognition events that I've done for charities have helped, or that Healthy U made a difference in some people's lives. I can't know, but I can be certain that I tried.

And what about the future? People sometimes ask if I'd remarry, or even have a long-time companion. I'm pretty sure the answer is no. I just can't imagine ever again loving someone so much or admiring someone as much, or trusting someone so much.

Still, because of Frank, I've lived because I have loved. When I think of my children, Frank, my Perdue and Henderson families, my friends, my education, my career, I can't possibly ask for more out of life.

I never bargained on having a life this good.

# Appendix I:

# *Criminal Justice Academy*

## ADDRESS TO THE 47th GRADUATING CLASS OF THE CRIMINAL JUSTICE ACADEMY

Director Beatty, Sheriff Nelms, Distinguished Guests, Faculty, Friends and Relatives of the Graduating Class, and most of all: Members of the Graduating Class.

We're here to celebrate and honor an important occasion. I got a clue as to how much the graduates have been waiting for this day when I sat in one of the classes at the academy last month. It was John Tritapoe's class and in the middle of explaining how to calibrate a PBT, John innocently asked the class, "By the way, how long until you graduate?"

Sitting in the back of the classroom, I could hear voices from all directions giving answers like: "Two weeks, three days, four hours, and twenty-eight minutes!" Am I right that you've been looking forward to this day? Have the classes been long? And hard?

Actually, I know that the experience has been hard. Jim Beatty told me that this class is unique because you've had the sad experience of attending the funerals of four police officers killed in the line of duty. You've seen firsthand that your chosen profession is one that can ask you to put your life on the line.

I asked Jim if this had caused anyone to quit the program. He answered that something like this makes a person really think, and it brings home to people that death is a reality in this line of work. Even so, not a single person washed out because of it. I don't know how the community can ever thank you enough for your willingness to put your life on the line as you protect and serve.

Personally, I have unbounded respect, not only for the work you do and the profession you've chosen, but also for the fact that your work makes democracy possible. (At this point, I'm going to guess that you may want to argue with the idea that law enforcement makes democracy possible. But bear with me, because we've now come to what I'm really going to be talking about as we celebrate your graduation.)

The biggest reason I have for admiring you and being grateful to you goes beyond admiring the personal courage and hard work that law enforcement demands. My biggest reason has to do with the rule of law.

A couple of years ago, the *Wall Street Journal* ran a millennium series on the most important developments in the last 1,000 years. The first article said that expansion of the rule of law was the most important thing that happened in a thousand years. The author of the article, Paul Johnson, said, "The acceptance and enforcement of the rule of law in any society is far more important than democracy itself."

I don't know about you, but the minute I read that statement, I started arguing with it. Democracy, I argued in my mind, is everything. It makes us a free country. It's our identity. How could the rule of law be more important than democracy? I totally disagreed with him, at that moment. But as I read on, I changed my mind and now believe it.

I suspect that you will also when you hear the rest. The fact is, if the laws aren't enforced, democracy is only a cruel and empty promise.

Let me give you an example. Remember Kosovo? Kosovo was and is a democracy. It may surprise you to know this ravaged country actually has a wonderful—even admirable—democratic constitution. The people can and do vote, and the constitution says that: life is inviolable; the death penalty is illegal; no one can be deprived of their property without due process; further, a man's home cannot be entered without a search warrant. They have the same kinds of constitutional protections that we do in this country.

On paper, Kosovo's democracy looks wonderful. But without the rule of law to uphold it, look at what happened in that country. Ethnic cleansing meant at least 400,000 refugees. Towns were burned, women raped, men had their throats slit. Who can calculate the suffering when the rule of law fails to support democracy? Without the rule of law, the Kosovo democracy was a cruel joke.

The former Soviet Union was in a similar situation. The former Soviet Union actually had an admirable constitution, and as for democracy, the election turnouts in this "democracy" were always better than 90 percent. But the rule of law didn't exist. Historians estimate that the dictator Stalin sent more than thirty million of his fellow citizens to their deaths. People could vote—in fact they had to vote—but they were afraid to speak. What went wrong? The Soviet "democracy" completely lacked the rule of law. The laws sounded good, but without law enforcement, they meant nothing.

We've been talking about terrible examples involving murder and refugees, but the lack of the rule of law can also cause misery on a smaller, more easily understood scale. I lived in Spain for a couple of years before the current government established the rule of law. Back in 1976, the dictator Franco was still in power, and the amount of aggravation that people endured before there was equality before the law is almost hard to imagine.

Let me give you one small example that I witnessed. One of my social friends was a pediatrician, and I remember one day she came over to my apartment completely distraught. Her eyes were red, and every few minutes she would start crying. We've all seen people cry, but I've never seen anyone cry the way she did. She was so—what's a good word to describe it?—undone by whatever was going on that the tears didn't just slide down her cheeks; they seemed to spurt from her eyes.

I remember putting my arm around her and trying to find out what was wrong. It turned out that she had irritated someone in the government, and a favorite way they had for punishing professional people who got out of line was to have their phone service "accidentally" disrupted.

For her, as a pediatrician, this was a special kind of agony because she knew that some of her little patients could be desperately ill, and they wouldn't be able to reach her. It was a tragedy because she wasn't able to provide her tiny patients with the medical care they needed.

Not having a working phone system was destroying her practice and she was in misery because, first, she couldn't do what was her life's purpose, which was healing the sick and, second, without patients, she had no income and couldn't pay the rent.

Almost the worst of it for her was, there was just about nothing she could do about it. She couldn't sue someone: the courts were corrupt and wouldn't hear the case. She couldn't take to the streets and demonstrate: that would land her in jail. She couldn't write a letter to the editor: the state controlled all the newspapers. There was absolutely nothing she could do except grovel to the regime and swear that she'd never get in its way again.

We've been looking at Kosovo, the former Soviet Union, and Franco's Spain, and in all these cases, power was exercised arbitrarily and without the rule of law. In these cases, and in virtually all cases where there is no rule of law, the people suffer. The fact is, democracy doesn't exist unless it's supported by the rule of law, and of course the rule of law doesn't exist unless the laws are enforced.

And now, once more, back to you and the graduation we're celebrating here today.

By having chosen law enforcement as a career, you are helping democracy survive. Democracy is something we cherish because it does more for human happiness and freedom than any political system ever devised. But it is completely worthless if it's just on paper and doesn't have the rule of law to back it up. By becoming police officers, you're helping to uphold the rule of law that makes successful democracy possible.

On behalf of your community, and on behalf of your country, *thank you—and congratulations!*

# Appendix II:

# *Of Course, This Book Contains a Chicken Recipe*

People often ask me for recipes, so I'll share with you a favorite. It's the one I serve most often at dinner parties because I can make most of it the day before. By the way, I always do the cooking for my parties, so I joke with my guests that they're having a meal "catered by Mrs. Frank Perdue."

## Ingredients

4 PERDUE® Fresh Thin Sliced Boneless Chicken Breasts

1/2 cup minced fresh basil leaves

2 tablespoons olive oil or butter

2 tablespoons Progresso Italian-style dried bread crumbs
   for stuffing, and maybe a cup more for coating

Beaten egg

Additional fresh basil leaves (to garnish)

Butter or olive oil (I use butter) for sauteing

## Instructions

Saute basil leaves in butter or olive oil until basil leaves are soft and wilted. Add bread crumbs. Divide mixture into four and then spoon a quarter of the mixture onto each breast and wrap the chicken around the mixture. Then dip the rolled up chicken breast in beaten egg, and roll in additional bread crumbs. If you put the chicken breast seam side down, it should hold its shape.

At this point you can hold the chicken breasts in the refrigerator for a day or you can immediately saute them in a frying pan until the chicken is no longer translucent. Garnish with fresh basil leaves.

I'd typically serve this with brown rice, along with a mixture of Brussels sprouts and peas, with some chopped red pepper added for color. Dessert would be orange sections, sprinkled with shredded coconut, and for those who like it, a drizzle of honey mixed with an equal part of orange liqueur.

# About the Author

Mitzi Perdue holds degrees from Harvard University and George Washington University, is a past president of the 35,000 member American Agri-Women and was one of the U.S. Delegates to the United Nations Conference on Women in Nairobi. She is currently a member of the Steering Committee of the Madison Council of the Library of Congress, a Trustee of the National Health Museum, and Founder of Healthy U of Delmarva, a 9000-member organization which encourages healthy lifestyles through awards for outstanding workplace wellness programs. Most recently, she's authored an iPhone App, B Healthy U, designed to help people track the interactions of lifestyle factors that influence their energy, sleep, hunger, mood, and ability to handle stress. In addition to being a programmer and software developer, Mitzi is also an artist and designer of handcrafted miniature scenes in eggs such as those showcased at this website.

Mitzi is the author of *The I Want to EggScape™ Book, A Quick Guide To Successful Media Appearances* a biography of her husband, Frank Perdue, and six cookbooks, including *The Farmers' Cookbook* series and the *Perdue Chicken Cookbook*. She is also the author of more than 1600 newspaper and magazine articles on food, agriculture, the environment, philanthropy and politics. She was a syndicated columnist for 22 years, and her weekly environmental columns were distributed first by *California's Capitol News* and later, by Scripps Howard News Service, to roughly 420 newspapers. Mitzi also produced and hosted more than 400 half hour interview shows, *Mitzi's Country Magazine* on KXTV, the CBS affiliate in Sacramento, California. In addition, she hosted and produced more than 300 editions of *Mitzi's Country Comments*, which was syndicated to 76 stations. Her radio series, *Tips from the Farmer to You*, was broadcast weekly for two years on the Coast to Coast Radio Network.

Mitzi Perdue is the mother of two sons, Jose and Carlos Ayala and widow of the late Frank Perdue, President and CEO of Perdue Farms. Their love affair, friendship and marriage took them around the world and taught Mitzi life's lessons which she shares with readers as "Frank Perdue's Ethical Beliefs."